THE OREGON DESERT

INDIAN PICTOGRAPHS IN LAKE COUNTY
Such Indian picture writings are usually not very old because the desert wind and sand
tend to obliterate them in about two hundred years as a rule.

JOHN DAY
Canyon City

SNAKE RIVER

VALE

MALHEUR NATIONAL FOREST

River

BURNS

HARNEY VALLEY

Malheur Lake

Harney Lake

MALHEUR

Blitzen River

WILDLIFE

Owyhee

JORDON VALLEY

REFUGE

Frenchglen

STEENS MOUNTAIN

Roaring Springs Ranch

ALVORD DESERT

THE OREGON DESERT

SCALE
0   10
MILES

Desert dimensions —
Approximately 180 x 250 miles

Map by Cathrine D. Young

Fields

Trout Creek

O N

Denio

McDermitt

N E V A D A

THE
OREGON DESERT

By

E. R. JACKMAN

and

R. A. LONG

ILLUSTRATED WITH PHOTOGRAPHS

THE CAXTON PRINTERS, LTD.
CALDWELL, IDAHO
1967

First printing May, 1964
Second printing June, 1964
Third printing August, 1964
Fourth printing January, 1965
Fifth printing July, 1965
Sixth printing July, 1966
Seventh printing October, 1967

Library of Congress Catalog Card No. 64-15389

Printed, lithographed, and bound in the United States of America by
The CAXTON PRINTERS, Ltd.
Caldwell, Idaho
107552

CONTENTS

ILLUSTRATIONS

THE OREGON DESERT

THE UNSHORN FIELDS

E. R. Jackman

Since man first chipped words on slabs of stone, he has tried to describe the desert. He has said it is cruel, brutal, ruthless, ugly, horrible, appalling, and fraught with terror.

He has fled from it, fearing the thirst and death that stalked its interminable reaches. At the word "desert," imagination pictures the dying man, forcing his failing steps toward the false promise of the mirage, calling thickly with his swollen tongue, "Water! Water!" And, of course, it is a lack of water that makes a desert.

The Oregon desert is the "high desert" and is not so hot as Iran, not so wind-combed as the Sahara, and its nights are usually cold. It may be snow-covered in winter.

We Oregonians didn't know it was much of an asset. We shooed strangers away from it, showing them our mountains and trees, as the real-estate man keeps the prospective house buyer away from the side with termites.

When the wheels of the covered wagons rolled to Oregon in 1843, the immigrants sought a land of trees and water. That's what every homesteader longed for—a place "with wood and water." Members of the famous lost wagon train of 1845 that mistakenly wandered into the edge of the desert, and picked up some nuggets, unaware of their nature, suffered badly from thirst, and their experience warned others away.

The fur trappers stuck to the river valleys. They had no way to carry water and even if they had horses, that didn't help much, for a horse in use can't carry enough water for himself. They were afraid of two hundred waterless miles; they were after beaver pelts, and beavers are water animals.

Explorers, such as Frémont, carefully charted their courses through timber with numerous creeks. In 1860, the miners came and they toiled along the creeks. The gold was in the mountains with the water to wash it out.

History evaded our desert. Oregon was a land of trees, water, and greenery. "It's cool in Oregon" and "It's green in Oregon" are the slogans of our chambers of commerce. Harry Leon Wilson, in a magazine article, called the state "the green land."

Things are changing lately. Maybe it's the johnnies with the geiger counters who imagined to a man that uranium *had* to be way out in the ginsengs near nowhere. Maybe it's the movie heroes encrusted with alkali. Maybe it's the influx of crowds of dudes to Arizona to escape from the crowds of dudes in Florida. Anyhow, America is suddenly desert conscious.

In Oregon a quarter of our state is desert, and we'd better be getting proud of it. Reub Long says that if we don't the dudes will take us just like we took the Indians. Nevada, Utah, and Idaho have deserts, too, though story writers have mostly looked elsewhere.

Most of our desert is in the counties of Deschutes, Crook, Lake, Harney, and Malheur. There are twenty-four thousand square miles of it, the size of West Virginia. Reub says you don't measure desert distance by miles, but by looks. It is ten good looks across.

This part of Oregon, the southeast quarter, is roughly 200 miles by 130 miles, and it isn't much like most ideas of the webfoot state. The water that falls here never reaches the sea. It sinks, or wanders into alkali lakes with no outlets. The desert is a wide, high plateau broken by huge faults, or cracks in the earth's crust, with one side tilted into spectacular rocky cliffs, half a mile straight up. It is

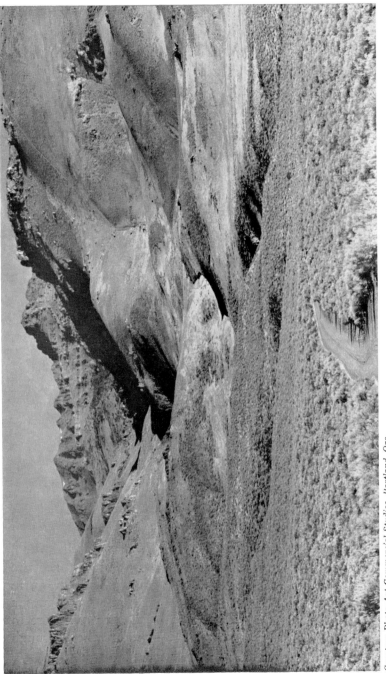

Courtesy Photo-Art Commercial Studios, Portland, Ore.

ESCARPMENTS, OR FAULTS, SUCH AS THIS, SOME OVER THREE THOUSAND FEET HIGH, ARE A FEATURE OF THE OREGON DESERT

rough, petrified grandeur. It is dry, cold, hot, sandy, and full of geology. An awful lot of wind passes through, though residents explain they don't have any right there.

All of this sounds disparaging. A poor place to spend the vacation; the bigness is almost like a noise. There aren't any sermons in running brooks. No brooks. No cathedral aisles among the tall trees. No trees, except the scraggly junipers. But out in that country the hysterical radio commentator, frantically searching for molehills to make mountains of, doesn't seem important. Talk runs along more constructive lines—feed for cattle, the price of weaners, water, salt, windmills, and wells, and when you begin to think you are hearing something important, you are being spoofed with expert guile.

The talk is almost always good—tolerant, humorous, unhurried. The humor is likely to be of the old fashion—the kind that made America famous because of the manner of telling, not the snappy wisecrack.

Dr. Chilcote, botanist, went with me to Fort Rock, where we met Reub Long, who took us to the summit of a high hill where we could see the desert for miles. Dr. Chilcote was botanizing the desert flora and had to know the country. Reub showed the roads, the landmarks, and the ranches, far apart. The visitor pointed at a ranch barely in view, and asked who lived there. Reub told him. Dr. Chilcote said, "And what kind of man is he?" Reub considered this carefully and answered: "A long time ago, when they were killing people over to the east at Wagontire, Sid Rogers spent the summer there. When he got back in the fall, I asked him what he'd learned. Sid was a man with a deep, booming voice and a kindly manner. So he said (and here Reub assumed the kind voice of a grandfather talking in a rich rumble to a favorite child), 'Reub, when I was a little boy, my papa told me how to git along, out here in the desert. *Always* ride a *good* horse—and breathe—through your nose.' "

Roy Morehouse, recently deceased, was another Fort

Rocker. He told of the difficulty in getting hired help during the war. Why should a good active man work on the desert when he could get triple the wages in the shipyards? "One evening, as we were sitting down to supper, a man came along who wanted a job. He seemed strong, and I was tickled to death. He sat down to eat with us, and after the rest had eaten all they wanted, the new man ate everything that was left—all the potatoes and bread and everything. So I said to myself, 'Now that man, to have an appetite like that, has either *done* a lot of work, or he's getting ready to *do* a lot!' I watched him at breakfast and it was the same thing over again, which convinced me I was right—he'd either done lots of hard work or was getting ready." Roy paused and said reflectively, "You know, I kept him on the payroll for three years and never did find out."

Fort Rock brings Indians to mind. The desert is a rich mine for hunters of Indian artifacts. On Reub's place is a cave, and a little digging in the floor brought out some well-made sandals—not leather moccasins—real woven sandals, such as the ancient Greeks wore, with a cap over the toe. Their radioactivity was measured and their age was put at over nine thousand years. Man with some measure of civilization lived on our desert long before he moved to New York or Chicago.

Who owns the Oregon desert? Mostly Uncle Sam. Lake County is 66 per cent federally owned, and adjacent Harney County, 70 per cent. This Federal ownership is a mixed blessing. It was offered free for seventy years with no takers. Homesteaders moved onto the land with water, and left the desert to the government's devices.

The government looked out the window, the wind blew, the sun baked, and the land was a prey to wild horses, itinerant sheepherders, fire, and grasshoppers. They nearly ruined it—so far as any cash value was concerned. Many of the homesteaders left before they proved up, but plenty of those who did get title to their land sold it for five cents

to fifty cents an acre. Today the land is suddenly worth
more, because it is space, and space now has value in America.
People are moving onto it because there is room, the air is
pure, and nature is close by.

Are there any towns? Yes, such towns as Blitzen, Wagontire, Plush, Fort Rock, Brothers, Riley, and Denio. There
are stories in most of these names. The few citizens of
Plush wanted a name for their thriving metropolis. They
suggested various names to the Post Office Department. They
liked the sound of Fairview and Pleasant City. But the
private whom the Postmaster General had put in charge
of names wouldn't accept either one. It seemed that somewhere else in Oregon, the citizens, in a blinding inspirational flash, had thought of Fairview first. One night, in
the still nameless town, there was a big poker game. All of
the tinhorns had been crowded out and the money had
finally settled into the hands of an Indian and a cowboy.
Then came the big hand. The cowboy bet all his money
and the Indian called by putting up his horse and saddle.
He said, "What you got?" The cowboy said, "I've got a
flush." The Indian said, "Me plush, too." A big laugh went
up and the town was named "Plush."

For trees the Oregon desert offers only the juniper—the
tree that can take it. Did you ever stop to think of the
miracle in a seed? A little thing that looks like dozens of
other kinds of seeds? But each ragweed seed develops a
plant that *always* is exactly like other ragweeds—same shape,
same leaves. Why don't they ever make some error and
grow into an oak? The juniper, of all the plants, has no
shape of its own. If you will think of any kind of a tree
you want to, you can find a juniper shaped like the tree of
your choice.

These junipers make fine posts and the homesteaders
would have had even tougher going without them. These
tough, gnarled old trees, snarling at the weather, were here
before Columbus came. Old-timers swear that the posts
have been known to wear out three sets of post holes. They

FIELDS, OREGON, IS RIGHT OUTDOORS
The earliest settlers had to use distance for fences

last for a lifetime in the desert sand. Junipers are beautiful in form and color. And despite constant cutting for posts, firewood, furniture, and doodads for tourists, they are increasing. Their wood is rich, varied shades of red and white, impossible as lumber because nearly every tree is full of crevices, making gaping holes in the boards. It works up wonderfully for bowls, plates, paperweights; it can be horrible in unnatural designs of donkeys with holes in their backs for planting a cactus.

The desert vegetation is all gray. Some is gray-blue, some gray-green, but all of the typical plants are gray. And so are the lizards, rattlesnakes, coyotes, deer, and most of the birds. Gray is such an uneventful color. The desert skies at dawn and dusk are often color gone crazy. Wild streaks and splashes of all vivid colors. Life on the desert is rough and tough, but it isn't gray. But the plants are gray: sagebrush, rabbit brush, grass, saltbush, and most of the weeds.

The flowers are gorgeous, though: primroses, buttercups, Indian paintbrush, larkspur, phlox, and the beautiful coral mallow. Their vivid colors flash as suddenly into view as a startled antelope.

Writers tend to describe the desert in polysyllabic words. Chet Craddock, of Burns, says that a four-syllable word to a trained writer is as natural as a hair in the biscuit. They say the desert is unchangeable, immutable, inscrutable, unnatural, indefinable, uninhabitable. These words are poor, as I see a desert. It is dry, hot, cold, gray, hard, vast, and fierce. Let's call it raw.

The perils of the desert are etched deeply by the symbolic skull, white in the pitiless sun. The deadly rattlesnake is nowhere welcomed as a friend, or the buzzard or the coyote. The quick winter blizzard, materializing in a matter of minutes from a sunny winter sky, has probably claimed more victims on the Oregon desert than the canteen, surreptitiously emptied by the hero's skulking rival.

Our desert isn't bad in summer. Maybe it's the Oregon

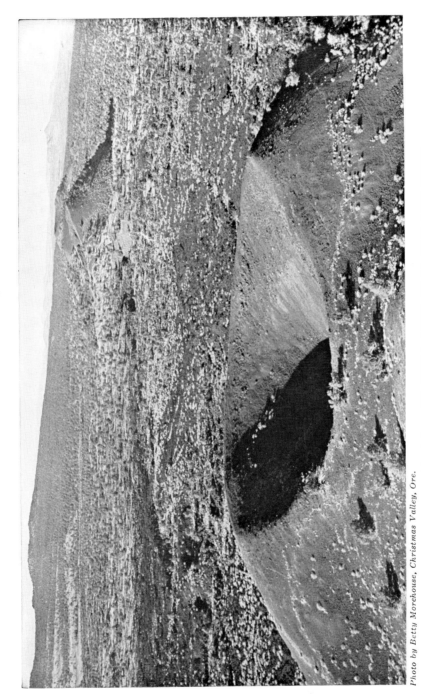

Photo by Betty Morehouse, Christmas Valley, Ore.

VOLCANIC CRATERS, BIG AND LITTLE, OCCUR IN OR NEAR LAVA FLOWS

There are four in line in this view, one nearly hidden. The picture was taken from the air east of Fort Rock.

eggs, but it takes a full three minutes longer for 'em to fry on a sun-heated rock than is reported from California.

One thing on the desert, winter and summer, waits for its victims—the stillness. Minds attuned to city clatter revolt in utter stillness. It bears down in a vast conspiracy of quiet. Lost persons instinctively listen in an agony of effort, straining at the absence of sound. They hurry toward some fancied sound, then listen again in rising panic. Such persons would better stay on the pavement. Even confirmed desert lovers form the habit of talking to themselves. When they begin answering back, it's time to get away for a spell.

It is hard for two men to live together for long under desert conditions. In the mountains, they call it "cabin fever," but in the desert the fever comes faster, and they are likely to quarrel over insignificant things. Heat and solitude, wind and sand, breed unbearable annoyance.

But out here the world is more like it was at first. First things come first, such as thirst, hunger, and cold. Nature may be tough, but she's honest. It's man against the elements. Man feels, at times, a frustration about the marvelous things he has wrought. Our houses are filled with gadgets that whir, grind, spin, tick, or flash. We don't understand them, and they harry and annoy us. We like man as an individual, but we dislike a mob. We don't care much about nervous breakdowns and ulcers. Our desert won't assay one ulcer to the township. It would be ironic if the best life should turn out to be farthest away from our civilized efforts.

The desert does something to each individual who lives there long. Part of it was once homesteaded. Most of the settlers came with money, enough to get started, and some stayed a long time. Eventually nearly all failed and left. Reub points out that the desert gave something to each; a big open country where you have to rely upon yourself makes differences in character and outlook. The changes, though, depend upon ability to appreciate the wideness.

If a man is big enough to expand with his surroundings,

he becomes broader, more tolerant. A narrow, mean man draws inside, loses breadth, merely as self-protection. So on the desert you find the widest and the narrowest; the expanding with the contracting; growing personalities and withering nobodies; great generosity and degrading meanness.

The desert has attraction for most, even if they fear it. Poets have felt it, as they have felt the drama of the sea. Both stretch out limitless, untouched by man. In the stillness you can sometimes hear the clear "faint sound of beauty's horn." You can't hear it in a traffic jam. Other lands have been changed; fields have been leveled and plowed; alien grasses grow green in the fields. But the desert shrubs were there ten thousand years before Columbus came; the sandals found in Reub Long's cave were woven from the tough fibers of sagebrush.

God made the desert. Man, as yet, hasn't unmade it. Meditation, the profoundest way to worship, is easier there, undisturbed by the noisy symbols of civilization. The oldest of all religions, the Vedantist, has, as its written creed, the Veda. One passage says, "Brahman is not split by time and space and is free of all change." The Koran, speaking of Mohammed, says, "The little winds run lightly about the earth at his bidding." These things take on meaning on the desert. Many of our poets have talked of the desert:

Longfellow said, "the sea-like, pathless, limitless waste of the desert."

Bryant mentioned ". . . there the unshorn fields, boundless and beautiful."

John Clifford said, "The anvil wears the hammer out," and this is perfect for men who toil on the desert.

And Lowell spoke of "the desert's awful frame."

In this same spirit of meditation, Reub Long said, "Many men, in trying to change the desert, only change themselves—often for the better."

We pride ourselves upon our capacity for invention. The results ease our lives, release us from dawn-to-dusk labor, but crowd us into cities.

LEAVING, BUR:
The scenery is like this over much of Nevada, U:

After that sequence of events: invention, factories, crowds, mass production, distribution, centralization of efforts in great cities, we don't like what happens. In gathering into the cities for mass production, a sort of industrial inbreeding, we have some advantages. Geneticists say that inbreeding can concentrate the good genes, but it concentrates the poor genes, too. So in the cities we have concentrated unemployment, crime, juvenile delinquency, hysteria, mob thinking.

Perhaps these "unshorn fields" of the desert, this one area where time and space are unimportant, will prove to be a particularly important part of Oregon where we can go to get a better perspective.

The desert spring is something very special. Most beautiful things are short-lived. Suppose a sunset lasted forever —we would scarcely notice it. The glory of the dawn passes as we watch. Utmost perfection in a rose exists for a day. So it is with spring in a harsh and forbidding setting. The air is not yet filled with the summer dust; it is sweet, clean, and bracing; distant hills are magically close at hand so that every person owns two telescopic lenses; desert flowers tentatively offer their gentle and beguiling paradise to passing insects; all of nature is tasting life to the full.

I once read a little verse about spring, ostensibly written by an Englishman. I do not know the author, so I cannot give credit, and I read it so long ago I cannot guarantee exactness. But, as I remember, it went:

> Ah, spring!
> You perfectly priceless old thing.
> You're so fearfully bright, so frightfully right,
> And one feels as one feels when one gets rawther tight.
> We shall soon have the jolly old bee on the wing—
> Er—ah—Spring!

That is a sort of parody upon the poetry of spring, but somehow it does manage to hint at the magic of a desert spring, so fearfully bright, so frightfully right. Every living thing there will soon find its existence threatened, but for the time being it is a joy to be alive, so let us all eat, drink the elixir of life, dance to the music of the spheres, and be happy.

BOY ON A HORSE ON THE DESERT

R. A. LONG

THE RANCH I HAVE AND THE THINGS I'VE DONE WERE DUE
to horses. I had work horses for hire by contractors for
freighting, haying, or construction jobs; I owned riding and
pack horses for running dude outfits in the mountains; I
raised riding horses to sell; I supplied bucking horses for
rodeos; I broke horses for hire or just for fun; I caught
wild horses and drove them in bands to the railroad; I bought
and sold horses, hoping to make a profit; I kept horses for
people short of pasture. A couple of times I rented horses
and horse gear to movies. I am a horse-made man. There
aren't too many persons in Oregon so horse diversified.

I find that you can't learn to write a book by riding a
horse any more than you can learn to ride a horse by reading a book. I can't seem to round up my wild thoughts
and get them all running in the same direction. So, like
showing a bunch of wild mustangs to a prospective buyer,
I'll have to run these random horse ideas across in front of
the reader one at a time.

When I was twelve, my horse and I were out doing a man's
work. I was helping Tom Cronin and Denny O'Connor
lamb a band of sheep at Benjamin Lake. I had an exceptionally good saddle horse, half thoroughbred. I went out
one morning to bring in the sheep-camp horses; the others
were there, mine was gone. He was hobbled and I trailed
him for three or four miles until a snowstorm blotted out
the track. The next day I couldn't pick up his trail. We

hunted everywhere and I went home, thirty miles, to see if he was there. He wasn't. I was desperately upset, as a boy might be now who had just wrecked the new family car.

A month later, while trailing the ewes and lambs to summer range, we crossed the road used by the homesteaders to freight their supplies in from Prineville. Looking up the road, I saw a freight team coming, my saddle horse in the lead. There is nothing so degrading to a good saddle horse as a collar.

I went up to the team, stopped them, and with never a word to the driver I unbuckled the hames, belly band, bridle, and collar, dropped the harness in the road, got on my horse and rode him away, leaving the driver sitting on the wagon seat, astonishment on his face, his teeth in his mouth. If I had let the driver go, then preferred charges against him, it would have meant innumerable trips to Lakeview, a court trial, a lifelong enemy. The man would have been held up to public scorn. This way no one knew about it and i got my horse back with no expense.

We had two horses called Stub and Frank. They worked together all their lives. Finally Dad turned them out to grass, too old to work. Stub finally died five miles from water. Frank stayed by his dead friend for days. When he could stand the thirst no longer, he went to water, came back. After that he went to water every day but came right back, and two months later he died within one hundred feet of the carcass of Stub.

Dad's homestead was at Christmas Lake, and when I was small we went to Prineville once a year to get supplies, nearly two hundred miles. One fall Dad didn't go, but Sid Minkler, who worked for us, took four horses and a wagon, and I got to go along.

We'd pull into a water hole, let the horses drink, fill up the barrel for camp use, move on a mile or two where there was good feed for the horses, and camp. Feed was scanty close to water. On this trip we saw two buck deer fight, and I remember great numbers of sage hens around the

Walker cabin, twenty-five miles north of home. Near the Stone cabin, on land now owned by Chub Frazee and known as Little Jack's place, we found a big bear track. No one seemed to know who built the Stone cabin, but there were holes in it for rifles.

But the big thing of the trip—I bought my first new saddle. I bought it with my own money, saved a little at a time by selling coyote hides or doing little things for freighters or men driving stock. The saddle cost $13.50. I was seven years old.

REUB LONG AND HIS SISTER ANNA LONG, ABOUT 1902
In front of the cabin at Christmas Lake where they were raised. Reub, aged four; Anna, aged two.

I was five years ahead of my age all the time, and by fifteen was a grown man. When I was twelve my mother worried constantly about me, and my father said, "He's all right. He can take care of himself." When I was twenty my mother figured I could go anywhere or do anything, but Father worried terribly when I was out of his sight.

The summer I was twelve, Denny O'Connor bought one of the nicest little horses you ever saw, a little buckskin with black stripes around his legs and a dark stripe down his back. He had a pigpen brand on the right shoulder. Somehow Denny lost him. A horse outfit found him, took him up, and kept him. Their headquarters were 150 miles away. Denny came to our place at Christmas Lake just as we were cutting hay. He told my dad he'd work in my place and give me ten dollars if I'd go to Maury Mountain and get his buckskin.

Dad told me to take a big part-thoroughbred we had, and go to Lew Bennett's place on Camp Creek and Lew would help me. The first night out I went to Last Chance and stayed with a part Indian named Frank Abbott. Frank lived by a winter lake, where he had corrals and dependable water from a seep hole in the creek bed. It was a natural

THE SAME TWO AT THE SAME PLACE FORTY-SEVEN YEARS LATER, IN 1949
The old cabin still stands, 1963. The logs were hauled from the Lost Forest, twenty miles to the northeast.

stopping place for all travelers from Christmas Lake to the
Bear Creek-Hampton Buttes country. I rode only twenty-
five miles that day.

The next day I made Lew Bennett's, thirty-five miles.
He was haying and couldn't stop, but told me how to get
to Maury Mountain. He said, "If I was you, I'd just go
there and get him, rather than go into Prineville and get
a replevin."

The next day I found the little buckskin, caught him,
and about four o'clock left for home straight across country to the east of Pringle Flat. After some miles, the little
horse got so tired he wouldn't lead any longer, so I rode
him and led my own horse. I went right over the hogback
between Last Chance and Frederick Butte. I got home just
as the sun was coming up—a ride of seventy miles from
Maury Mountain.

It was a black night, and the way led partly through
juniper country I didn't know. I don't remember that I
was scared until I started downhill toward home. Then I

OLD CABIN WHERE R. A. LONG WAS RAISED
It appeared like this in 1963. Built about 1880, it is now over eighty years old

could see horrible big shapes in the dark and could hear noises I never heard before or since. For all I knew, some-one was after me for taking the horse.

Another time I made nearly the same trip to Bear Creek to the ranch of a big man named Warren Libby. The country was open—no fence all the way, sixty miles. Two of our heifers had wandered off and got with his cattle. Dad sent me after them.

There was a place called Held, then with a school, and the teacher boarded at Libby's. The teacher had two daughters. So, altogether, the place was cluttered up with strange females. When Mr. Libby asked me to eat with the family, I was too bashful to say anything. I'd been out all day without food and I sat and ate and ate.

Finally, I could eat no more, and for the first time refused some food when the dish was passed around. Mr. Libby said, with a severe air, "Now, go ahead and take some and don't do like you did last time and say you left here

R. A. LONG, ABOUT 1910

He was doing a man's work at age twelve. Several of the others are dead. Names, *left to right:* R. A. Long, Harry Roberts, Charlie Jefferies, Frank Pratt, Bert Wardwell and Sam Farra.

without enough to eat!" The teacher and the two girls laughed.

I took this as a way of saying I'd done too well at the table. I know I blushed, and it bothered me terribly. Things like that can trouble a boy for years.

Another embarrassment came at mealtime, too. I went into the Brattain place, near Paisley, to stay all night. I had never seen a revolving table and never heard of one. I helped myself to the gravy, but just then someone spun the table, leaving me with the big gravy spoon. Not knowing what had happened, or what had become of the dish, I sat there embarrassed and bewildered. All the cowboys laughed.

Now I enjoy it when someone laughs at me, but it is misery for a youngster. He doesn't know it isn't important, and usually no one tells him. He has to live with his embarrassment.

When I was a boy, Prineville was the big town. Bend and Redmond hadn't come into the picture. When we wanted supplies, it was either Lakeview, to the south, one hundred miles, or Prineville, one hundred miles north. Of course, the really big marketplace, the one with a railroad and a river, and a big hotel, and sin and all sorts of exciting things, was The Dalles, but a boy my age could hardly hope to go there.

The winters had snow then. A man only went to Prineville, in the winter, after lots of preparation. He had to figure on two horses, so he could alternate them breaking trail through the snow. He rode one and let one follow, which they did, often without a halter. Sometimes a man couldn't make it, and had to turn back. If a sudden blizzard came up, things got serious pretty fast. It wasn't like a timbered country where you had material for a shelter and a fire. Here was mostly open country, or juniper-sagebrush. The sage was usually the only fuel. There was no shelter.

The first really big tragedy I can remember was caused by the weather. We got along by not buying rather than by selling, so we children didn't know much about toys except by looking in the big mail-order catalogs. But one year the folks thought it rough on us kids to grow up without any toys, so they sent to Prineville for a few playthings.

Byron Cady was going to bring them out to us, and the excitement while we waited for him was almost unbearable. He showed up a day overdue, when we learned of the tragedy. Cold and snow came to him on the way, and he had been forced to use our toys for kindling to start a fire that kept him from freezing.

We ordered lots of stuff from Sears, Roebuck. Mother had ordered a doll—from the description she thought she'd get a big doll. It didn't come. About a year later, a cowboy coming our way picked up a weatherworn package. It had been out there most of one year, lost by some other cowboy. But it was two halves of a doll, with a painted cloth middle to be stuffed. Mother was frightfully disappointed, but we played with the rag doll more than anything else we ever had. We made some spurs for the doll out of some cut nails. It was hard to make them stand out from the doll's heels as they should. We rode broomsticks for horses all around through the sagebrush, taking the doll with her spurs everywhere we went.

Of all the men out on the desert, I think I held Dad Worthington in the highest regard. In a tough and rough country, he maintained a kind of Southern gentleman air —a courtesy that seemed instinctive. Someone described a gentleman as a man who never unintentionally hurts anyone's feelings. Dad Worthington was surely a gentleman.

If a man came to borrow a saddle horse, he'd rope one out of the cavvy and present it to the stranger as a nobleman might bestow one of the royal jewels. He'd say, "Suh! This is a fine hoss. Mrs. Wo'thington could ride this hoss." There wasn't any Mrs. Worthington and never had been.

He was the range boss for the big ZX Ranch when I was young. We haven't had many big cattle outfits in Oregon, such as you read about. You can count them on

the fingers of one hand, but the ZX was one. It would have
been natural for every little boy on the desert to look up
to the ZX boss as the most important man on his horizon.
It would have been just as natural for such a man, with
maybe twenty thousand cows to look after, to ignore a
ragged little guy with no apparent prospects.

The year I owned my first riata, given to me by my
grown brother, Dad Worthington let me ride with the cowboys as they took ten thousand cattle off the range. You've
got to realize what both those things meant to a ten-year-
old. Every boy in those days fooled around with a rope,
but he had to be content with an ordinary hemp rope,
whereas a riata was of braided rawhide. It took days to
make one. A good one still costs a dollar a foot, whereas
a hemp rope costs thirteen cents a foot. So right from the
start, a riata owner was a sure-'nough cowhand. To get
to ride with the tough, experienced men who rode for the
ZX was a glory of its own.

When we got to the slough, running into Silver Lake
from Paulina Marsh, there was a bridge, but you can't put
ten thousand cattle onto a narrow bridge, so there were
cattle swimming on both sides, and the bridge was full,
too. There was a solid mass of cows, all horned. The horns
were bobbing, cowboys yelling, calves bawling, horses dashing—a wild picture you can't see now. The calves, born
on the desert, had never seen water in quantity, so they
were running everywhere, lost and afraid. The cowboys began to rope them and start them across by dragging them
into the water.

To show that I knew what to do, I roped a calf expertly
enough. But the calf made a dash into the water and jerked
the riata out of my hand before I could get my dallies. I
couldn't fight through the swimming cattle, and I thought
my riata would be a casualty of the roundup—that it would
disappear under the water and into the mud, proving that
I wasn't fit to own such a thing, or big enough to handle it.

Dad Worthington, with all he had to do, saw my trouble,

rode into the herd on the far side of the slough, found the
calf, still with the riata on him, roped him, took my riata
off, and returned it to me with no word of scorn or reproof.
He didn't laugh at me or mention it to the men. He let
me keep my self-respect—and that is important to a ten-
year-old boy. Right then I appraised him in a dispassion-
ate way and concluded he was the greatest man in the
world. I still think so, showing what a precocious boy I was.

Some things built up my self-respect. My dad sold some
two-year-old steers. They were on the range near Sand
Springs at the edge of Lost Forest. It was in haying time,
so he sent me, a small boy, to gather up the cattle with
the buyer, Tom Hutton.

We camped there for a week, found thirty-one steers of
Dad's, and I was mighty proud when I started home with a
check for $620 fastened in my shirt pocket with a big safety
pin my mother gave me for the purpose. This was about
1906. I was eight years old. So far as I knew, that was
the most money in the world and it was entrusted to me!

We couldn't grow much of a garden at Christmas Lake.
Aridity and frost most all summer combined with wind
and alkali to limit gardening. But we had to live, so when
I was eleven I conceived a plan that turned out real well.

Over at Summer Lake the elevation is lower, and there
are numerous springs that aren't hot, but they modify the
temperatures. Probably that big lake, twenty miles long,
busily evaporating all summer, helps, too. Summer Lake had
gardening ingredients we didn't have: water for irrigating;
deep, black loose soil without alkali; and no frost.

I saw Ralph Foster and he let me put in a garden on his
place on the west side. I rode over there, forty miles, then
worked on the garden, hoeing and irrigating it all day, and
rode home the third day. I felt important that fall when
we hauled home two big buckboard loads of vegetables.

Mother served meals to travelers, so those vegetables helped
our own food supply and brought in a good many dollars
we wouldn't have had. I don't believe we knew anything

about vitamins and the advantages of green leafy things. But we did know that straight beans could get monotonous after a couple of weeks, and an onion and a carrot didn't hurt a bit. Besides, Mother sort of sensed that such things reduced demands on the medicine chest.

When I was going to grade school, an old man who had worked for us became partly paralyzed. One Halloween, some neighbor kids, Elmer Anderson and two brothers, Delmer and Nelson Powers, and I, took four horses of Dad's and a wagon and went out and sawed a wagonload of juniper wood. On Halloween night we quietly unloaded it in old man Orr's yard. He was amazed to find he owned a big pile of firewood.

The homesteaders were all around us from every state in the Union, and they tried to behave like Westerners.

One came into our camp riding a mule. He had a new outfit: saddle and long hard-twist rope. He was pleased as punch at being a cowboy. Two other mules of his had strayed away and we had picked them up with a bunch of horses. We had sent word to him, so here he was to take them home. We watched, amazed, as he tied one end of his new sixty-foot rope to each mule. While he was still on the ground, holding the middle of the rope, the mules ran in opposite directions, catching him in the bight. He went up into the air and we had to catch his mules for him.

Then he got into his saddle, took a turn around his saddle horn with the middle of the rope, a mule on each end. This would normally be a recipe for suicide, but somehow the Lord was with him and the mules didn't play ring-around-the- rosy.

The mule he was riding had been trained to pull and was good at it. When he started, one mule decided to go along home but the other liked his taste of freedom, and put on his brakes. This caused the rope to slide around the horn with a lot of speed and the smoke just flew from his saddle horn until the other mule was pulled right up against it. At that point his ridden mule got down and

WHICH ONE SHALL I CATCH?
Reub Long surveys a group of his horses

Photo by Joe Van Wormer, Bend, Ore.

pulled like a wheeler on a freight wagon. The new saddle stood up on end and something had to give. It was the balky mule. He suddenly decided to come, but the other mule set his brakes. At that, the rope pulled clear out to the other end, the saddle horn again pouring smoke.

As far as we could see him, he pursued this odd zigzag course, first one mule hanging back, then the other, with him riding proudly, secure in his knowledge that he was master of a difficult situation.

I am telling this to show the kind of education I got. Part of it was negative, because in this case I learned how not to lead two mules.

For formal education, for some time, we rode to Silver Lake from my brother's place, eleven miles, making a twenty-two-mile ride for the day. In bad weather or when the marsh was starting to freeze, we had to go around, making it fifteen miles one way. It made kind of a long day for us then—eight hours in school, around four hours on the road, and meals and chores to work in before and after. But we didn't know that a later generation would consider even a mile too much of a hardship, so we enjoyed the ride. One thing sure—we didn't need any school gymnasium!

I started to school at Silver Lake, but the desert filled with homesteaders, many with children, and they demanded additional schools. One was started at Frank Anderson's homestead, because he qualified as a teacher and wanted the extra money. He taught in one of his two rooms and lived in the other. This was only two and a fourth miles, as the jackrabbit runs, from home. My sister Anna and I went there.

The next school was in the Willis Powers homestead house, three and a half miles away. We walked in good weather, rode when the weather was bad. The teacher was Mr. Peyton, another homesteader.

Anna had a buckskin horse that any cowboy would have been proud of and she could ride with the best. She once rode that horse from the Hays Ranch at Silver Lake to the

Anderson place at Christmas Lake, twenty-two miles, in two
hours. This was over Hays Mountain and rough going.
We didn't race our horses because Dad wouldn't hear of it.
The homesteaders were of all sorts, hardly any of them local
people. These boys and girls from such places as St. Louis
or Scranton, Pennsylvania, didn't know how to ride and
most of them had no horses at all, or else only castoffs not
much good for anything. Anna and I, with our good horses
and knowledge of riding, maybe lorded it over the others
a little. It seems now maybe we did.

A family named Phelps moved in and the children came
to school riding burros. During recess or noon they would
let the rest of us ride the burros. Since then I have been
humiliated by professional humiliators, but I never felt it
so keenly as the day the burro bucked me off right before
the whole school—just after I'd been bragging more than
a little about how I could ride.

After grade school, I was a man and didn't have much
business in school, but I attended high school in Silver Lake
off and on. I started late in the fall and quit early in the
spring. I just went when work was slack. I never did finish.

Education, though, isn't confined to schools. Shortly after
my high-school days, for example, my horse fell and I auto-
matically threw my arm out to break my fall. My arm
broke, and that saved my life, because it taught me how
to take innumerable falls afterward—you turn in the air,
get your arms folded and your head behind your shoulder,
light on your shoulder and land rolling. My schooling was
therefore limited but my education long and thorough.
Horses kept running through it, teaching me something
every day.

THOSE WITH THE LEAST STAYED THE LONGEST

R. A. LONG

OUR FAMILY MOVED TO CHRISTMAS LAKE FROM LAKEVIEW, one hundred miles south. There were Father; Mother; a ten-year-old brother, Everett; a sister, Anna, six months old; and I, two years old. We arrived on the desert in 1900, so as to start even with the century and make it easy to remember.

Dad wasn't a newcomer to Lake County. He was one of the first to range cattle there. He and a partner lived at Jacksonville and Dad decided to herd cattle on the open land around Wagontire. They bought cattle on time, trailed them across the mountains, ranged them on free grass, then sold them. It worked well until 1878, the year the Bannock Indians started to drive out the whites. They found Dad's cattle and killed all of them. Dad went back to Jacksonville and worked for eight years as a hired hand on the Beall ranch to pay for the cattle. This was close to the Hanley ranch and my mother worked there for the Hanleys for some years. Bill Hanley, of Harney County, was from this family and Mother knew him well.

Until my house burned in 1962, I had an old rifle the government issued to Dad for his part as a volunteer in the Bannock war.

When he was free of debt, he returned to Lakeview and got a job in Warner Valley with the Seven T Ranch, named for their brand, 7T, later owned by Doc Daly. Father then came to Lakeview and freighted from Madeline Plains, in

ANNA, MRS. MARY LONG (REUB'S MOTHER), AND REUB AT THE OLD
LON LONG HOMESTEAD
Anna is now Mrs. Leston Linebaugh and she still lives at Silver Lake

California, to Lakeview. Still later he and Henry Leehman ran a livery barn at Lakeview. By 1900, he had noticed that the men who got ahead owned land, so we moved to Christmas Lake where he bought a meadow watered by springs. When homesteaders began to crowd him, he home-steaded. Our old cabin still stands as this is written, 1962. We had a notable big old barn of hand-hewn timbers, with pegs to hold it together, and the few nails used were the old square-cut kind.

The only way to get to town was on horseback or by buckboard. The nearest doctor was at Lakeview, and it was eighteen miles to the nearest neighbor. I grew up with coyotes and jackrabbits. Some people said I was so wild I only came in for water after dark.

We moved straight to Christmas Lake from Lakeview, up the east side of Summer Lake, past the Thousand Springs Ranch, owned by Bonham, up the Juniper Canyon route. There is no road there now, but people went that way then, rough and rock-decorated as it was. In the lead of our family caravan was a six-horse team with two wagons, driven by Dad; Mother with two horses on a buckboard with baby Anna and me; then a hired man and Everett driving cattle and loose horses.

The fences were down, and the first part of that summer was spent in building fence, but when haying time came, Dad went to the UR Ranch on Silver Lake and worked, taking his pay in hay to carry our stock through the winter. He hauled the hay, loose of course, to our place, eighteen miles, and barely had enough to last through.

By spring the cattle were thin. In March things greened up in the warm spring sun. Dad took all the cattle to the foothills along Pike's Gulch and turned them out. The grass was short, the cattle poor, and he lost over half of his small herd, mostly from larkspur poisoning. This plant has a marvelous, rich, dark royal-purple color, but it never looked pretty to Father after that.

Mother ran an informal inn, because we settled on one

"UNCLE" GEORGE DUNCAN AND EVERETT LONG
George Duncan *(left)*, first postmaster at Silver Lake, was the first person to recognize the value of the tons of fossilized bones on the bed of Fossil Lake. He interested scientists, who came and carted away wagonloads of them. Everett Long *(right)*, now deceased, was Reub's elder brother. The dog's name was Bugle. Pictured is the doorway of the cabin where Reub grew up. At the right of the door is the coffee mill. Every homesteader ground his own coffee in those days.

of Oregon's crossroads. In the early days, The Dalles was headquarters for the United States Army in eastern Oregon. Southward, the next headquarters was at San Francisco. It was necessary to have a military route between the two places. This passed through Christmas Lake and later became a road. We'll call that Road Number 1, and it had considerable north and south travel. It came past our place and was the route we traveled when we first settled at Christmas Lake.

In 1862 gold was discovered near Canyon City. Immediately heavy traffic developed from the California and Nevada mines to the John Day "diggin's." The road led diagonally northeast from Yreka, came close to our place, and was known as the Yreka Trail. That is Road Number 2.

Road Number 3 led east and west. It came from Jacksonville via Fort Klamath and went to Fort Boise. Originally it was a military and miners' road, but later it was used by homesteaders, horse buyers, cattle and sheep drivers, and peddlers. It crossed Road Number 1 at our place.

Number 4, in 1900, was used the most heavily of all and, in a slightly different location, it is still used. This road led from The Dalles to Shaniko and Prineville, southward to Silver Lake and on to Lakeview. For many years wool was hauled in big wagons to The Dalles on this road. After Shaniko got a railroad, that was the marketplace. Its greatest usefulness crumbled when a railroad was built to Bend in 1911.

Homesteaders flocked in all over the desert from 1905 to about 1915—a few after that. Little towns began to spring up everywhere. Within a distance of a couple of looks, we had such promising new towns as Fremont, Lake, Sink, Fleetwood, Connley, Arrow, Buffalo, View Point, Cliff, and Loma Vista. My mother was the first postmaster at Lake and my Aunt Anna Long was the first postmaster at Sink. All of these towns are gone now, in some cases with no sign a town had ever been there. One of my stock-watering windmills is all you can see at Fremont. The one

Courtesy Schmink Museum, Lakeview, Ore.

A RABBIT DRIVE IN THE DESERT

On February 5, 1911, this drive netted 1,811 rabbits. Rabbits ruined the hopeful young crops of the homesteaders, but they furnished meat for the settlers and for their dogs, cats, and chickens.

other remnant is a mounting block that aided ladies in divided skirts to get on horses with sidesaddles. The block helped the ladies to climb into or out of buggies without exposing an ankle, and helped them in mounting a horse. The sidesaddles called for divided skirts.

At its peak, Fremont had a creamery, cheese factory, hotel, store, livery stable, dance hall, blacksmith shop, and post office. A few towns had newspapers. Fremont was the first town for all travel from the west and north, and stages stopped there daily. Its population was the first on the desert to learn of important happenings.

Fremonters explained that they had no cemetery because most folks would rather be dead somewhere else than alive there; that the only two graves were those of the doctor and the undertaker, who both starved to death.

Our log cabin, still standing, had three rooms; we cooked and ate in one, slept in the others. The house has a rock fireplace. When cooking, I'd explain to visitors that I got so good by cooking pancakes on the griddle inside, then flipping them expertly up the rock chimney and running outside to catch them, each turned right side up, nary a flake of soot.

Mother was a famous cook, but from the minute she started a meal until it was on the table, she apologized. She had a new kind of flour and didn't know just how to mix it—the wood was a little green, so she couldn't get the oven just right—the baking powder had lost its power, sitting there so long.

Father was different. He had done lots of catch-as-catch-can cooking but never really got the hang of it. When he started a meal, he told how fortunate the prospective eater was; how the thing he was cooking was something they'd been known to come for clear from Alaska, just to learn the recipe; the only bad thing about his cooking was that no eater of it had ever been known to be satisfied at home any more.

He could make biscuits like I've seen nowhere else. They

were the wartiest and the soggiest; when he made them of soda, they were all full of yellow spots.

A family named Wilson lived at Lanning Corner near us. The corner was named for an old bachelor who lived nearby. The Wilson children liked him and always carried their happy tidings to him. Once the whole Wilson family came to our place and Mother fixed up a fine dinner. When they went home, all the little Wilsons came running to Lanning, waving their hands and yelling, "We—had—pie! We—had—pie!"

With the wave of homesteaders, each week showed new shacks sprouting in the sand. There was a lot of visiting, welcoming the newcomers. The folks would get together and compare notes. Each wanted to believe he had made a good location and they *wanted* people to like them. The old-established livestock men, with irrigated land, didn't believe in plowing up the desert and called this army of newcomers "sandlappers." This was partly contemptuous, partly just good-natured, and the drylanders retaliated by calling owners of grass meadows "tule rooters."

Slim stayed on long after the other homesteaders had gone. Every homestead had a big pile of chips, marking where the woodpile had been. These often grew into a respectable mound.

So Slim moved from shack to shack, staying in each one long enough to use up the chip pile. His mother lived with him and he would go away and leave her for days at a time. As I accumulated more land, one after another of the deserted claims, I naturally acquired numerous cabins. Slim moved into one of them.

I went around now and then to be sure that the mother was getting along. I found on one trip that Slim and his mother had nothing to eat but milk and flour. He kept a cow or two and had a can of cream. He had a Model T but no gas. Fort Rock had a creamery then, so I gave him enough gas to go there, where he could sell the cream, buy groceries, and buy gas to get home.

He arrived there, sold his cream, got his money, bought gas for the return trip, then spent all of his money for groceries. He got in his Ford and drove home, forty-five miles, well satisfied with his day's work. That is, he was well satisfied until, arriving, he found he had left the groceries on the counter in Fort Rock. He was out of gas again.

Bill Crees was a stern old German with a big moustache. He had little but was independent and proud, almost beyond understanding. At last he grew feeble. The neighbors decided he needed wood and food. There wasn't much organized welfare then, but two other neighbors, Roy Morehouse and Elmer Wertzbergher, interested the county court, who furnished them a sack of potatoes, a sack of flour, and beans and bacon enough to see him through the winter.

Then a problem arose—how to present this food over the stubborn barrier of his fierce pride. Neighbors elected Roy Morehouse as spokesman, thinking he had the most diplomacy. Roy and Elmer went into Bill's twelve-by-fourteen shack, the bed on one side, the stove on the other. They talked all around the subject, couldn't open up a proper approach, so in desperation Roy blurted out the news, almost belligerently, as though defying him to refuse.

There was dead silence. For minutes, the only sound was the clock ticking. Finally Bill said, "Well, you tell 'em I'd like one thousand pounds of rye seed and my taxes paid."

At Silver Lake were two bachelors. One talked oddly and was sensitive about it, ready to fight if anyone laughed at him. I was present when they had a bitter row and agreed to break up their lifelong partnership. They divided everything—horses, land, machinery, household goods—all except two dogs, Bacon and Beans, and their brand, a 4S on the right shoulder and a wattle on the nose. These caused a deadlock.

Finally the lisping one shouted to his brother Bart, "U

Photo by Merritt Parks, Fort Rock, Ore.

TWO THINGS USUALLY MARKED THE ABANDONMENT OF A HOMESTEAD: EITHER THE WELL FAILED OR THE ROOF FELL IN

Sometimes the two occurred simultaneously

tan have Bacon but u tant have Beanth and u tan have 4-eth but u tant have that wattle on the nothe."

This went on for days and eventually they went back into partnership because neither would agree to take the dog Bacon.

Ted Armstrong talked slowly. The ZX had some cattle at his place over on Wagontire, forty-five miles from our place. Some ZX riders came for them in cold weather and deep snow. They got to our place at night. We fed their horses, filled them up on hot food, and gave them beds. We got them up early, fed them, and they started at daylight through the snow in zero weather. No cowboys took lunches.

They arrived at Armstrong's late at night, cold, weary, and hungry as tigers. All day in the cold breeds appetites unknown to calorie counters. They told their story. Armstrong said, very slowly, "Yeah! You boys put your horses in the barn and feed 'em some hay and come in and go to bed and git up in the morning and we'll have a real nice breakfast. Yeah! A real—good—breakfast—in the morning."

Ralph Foster, of Summer Lake, was afraid of no one. When a bunch of toughs moved in and stole some of his calves, he tracked them to a corral. Three of the thieves were there. Ralph rode silently into the corral, counted out his calves, and drove them home. The thieves prided themselves upon how tough they were and his nonchalant way of completely ignoring them was hard on their reputations as competent bad men.

Later I was putting up fence with him. He had a rifle on his saddle, but right then he was pounding in a staple and I was holding his horse. A bullet came singing by his head, followed by a rifle report from a sand knoll one hundred yards south. Not bothering to get his rifle, he instantly charged toward the knoll, waving his hammer. The would-be assassin got on his horse and fled.

The homesteaders were beaten one by one. Those who

Courtesy Photo-Art Commercial Studios, Portland, Ore.

PINE TREES ENCROACH UPON THE DESERT WHEREVER RAINFALL GETS UP TO TWELVE INCHES
Here a homesteader failed right at the edge of forested land

arrived with the least stayed the longest. The ones who came with money usually came without experience and hired the others. The result was that the well-to-do who came with money and no experience left with experience and no money.

Another thing evened everyone's prospects periodically. We had hard winters then. Everyone accumulated some livestock, but few put up much hay. The desert had land too far from water for summer use. Most persons turned out their stock in the winter. The animals could use snow for water, so could roam at will, find the good feed, and come through smiling.

But about once in ten years would come a winter that killed all the stock. That was called an "equalizer" and everyone started even again.

Some of those who stayed the longest didn't cuddle up to the law closely. Some were handy at reworking irons, others found ways to deliver Lake County horses at Idaho points, and a few were pretty good at arithmetic. They figured that five dollars' worth of sugar, if treated right, would bubble itself into clear, water-colored moonshine worth twenty dollars. Containers cost money. The quart fruit jar was everywhere, so the saying grew up that you could tell a desert drinker by looking at the bridge of his nose. If it had a deep crease it came from trying to get the last drop of moonshine out of a glass fruit jar.

Poor moonshine was a shining tradition on the desert, not the exception. The worst I saw was from a barrel in an attic. The chimney from the big stove, in what this man called his living room, ran up the side of the barrel, which kept it warm and working fast all winter. In the fall he put in a couple sacks of rye, brown sugar, and maybe some prunes, and sat down in his rocking chair and waited. All winter he threw in whatever was around, say potato peelings or weevily cereals.

When the owner thought a fortunate guest should sample this, he climbed the ladder nailed to the wall and went through the trapdoor into the attic. He took a big dipper that hung on the barrel, shoved back whatever was floating, dipped out the bubbling mixture, poured it into a pitcher, then came down and poured the liquid into tin cups. As the evening wore on and the owner found that the ladder steps eluded him, the more hardy of the guests had to go up the ladder for a refill.

The product was all in the name of hospitality and good clean fun—no taint of commercialism. The pure stuff was more efficient than that weakened down by passing through pipes. It would make you quite a bit sicker, too. Several folks around us quit drinking for life every time they visited this homestead.

After I got some land, the price of beef slid off to almost nothing and I decided to get something salable from my cows. I ran in a bunch with some good-looking dairy equipment, and after a few unfortunate trials, I taught them to let me milk them. My hands didn't seem to fit their handles well. Maybe I'd handled a rope too long, but I gathered a lot of milk, and put the cream into a big tall jar with a wooden plunger. This had holes in it to allow the cream to circulate as the operator moved this piston-like arrangement up and down.

I soon achieved butter, but I couldn't get it together. I thought maybe I could pour it into a big cloth, hold it over a tub, and squeeze the cloth. This might have worked, but as I really put my strength into it, the top of the cloth flew apart and I lost that churning.

Just before the next churning Mother came out and said my cream was spoiled and unfit for butter. I fed it to the pigs. It was too rich for them or something, for they died. I always blamed Mother for this because I might have had butter and pigs, whereas I had neither. I was out of the dairy business.

I've done all right on the desert with horses, and fairly well with rye hay for winter feed. But one year, handicapped by some money I'd made corraling wild horses, I decided to farm. I hired some neighbors to plow up three or four hundred acres, clear the land, and seed to rye in the spring. Good years aren't expected here, but that year it rained. Normally we don't count crops by tons, feet in height, or bushels to the acre—if they are alive they are a success.

First thing I knew I had over a half section of the nicest rye I ever saw, about four feet high and thick. I began to stew around and worry; I had no machine to thresh it, no trucks; no storage, and here were hundreds of bushels of

Photo by Merritt Parks, Fort Rock, Ore.

HOMESTEADERS' WIVES NEEDED SOMETHING GREEN IN THE MIDDLE OF THE GRAY DESERT

Nearly all of them planted a matrimony vine. In addition to the spot of green, it furnished shade for the kitchen and was kept growing by dishwater and scrub water.

THIS HOMESTEADER, LIKE MANY IN EASTERN OREGON, DIDN'T MAKE IT

When the land was plowed, it blew away

it threatening me. Mother said, "Reuben, why did you seed it?" And I told her, truthfully, "Mother, I didn't have the slightest idea it would grow."

So, a failure in dairying, and unadapted to farming, I went back to raising horses—at least I knew the problems. Lately I've pretty well switched to cattle, but I stayed on the desert and bought out others solely because they tried to farm or dairy, whereas I took the desert at its word and used it for what it is best adapted to—horses.

I have done business with some hard characters. Numbers ended in the penitentiary, and others escaped it only by dying before the law caught up. More than once I looked into the business end of an angry gun. I have speculated often upon what a narrow line there is between what I am and what I might have been, good or bad. Some insignificant little thing could have changed me into a horse thief or a preacher.

But perhaps I am overemphasizing the bad. The homesteaders, as a group, were wonderful people. They wanted only one thing—to make a home where they could raise their children. There are mighty few bad horses or bad people, and the bad ones were mostly made that way by some cruelty along the way, usually when young.

I survived on the desert where hundreds failed. Someone is always asking how I did it. I explain that every successful person has to be famous for some one thing. If a surgeon, and he develops a new operating technique, he ends up famous; or a musician composes a completely new musical arrangement. In that same way, I did something that, so far as I know, was never done by another soul—I performed a Caesarean on a mamma porcupine.

The homesteaders had no chance. A homestead is supposed to be farmland—but the desert isn't farmland. Rainfall can drop to as low as five inches in a year, which won't raise any known crop. So they were poor, deluded persons. But they were *not* beaten, bitter, or downtrodden. Against all reason they were happy. I have met dozens of them since—in all walks of life, and, to a man, they remember their homestead days as the happiest time of their lives.

A great deal of family visiting went on and socials, baseball games, parties, kept them busy socially. The literary society stimulated debates, speaking, singing, little plays, essays, orations—all sorts of attempts at culture that you can laugh at if you want. It was just that kind of thing that developed such folks as Abraham Lincoln. I read lots of poetry then, and I still remember pages of it. Such things as "Thanatopsis," Robert Service—and some of Shakespeare. Later I made a nuisance of myself repeating it to such emi-

Courtesy Schmink Museum, Lakeview, Ore.

EACH SMALL TOWN ON THE DESERT HAD ITS BASEBALL TEAM FROM 1900 TO 1920, AND RIVALRY WAS OFTEN EXTREME
Standing, from left: Joe Long, Mike Hough, Rufus Cochrane, Gus Schroder, unknown, John McCormack. *Center:* unknown, George Drum. *Seated, front:* Bert Gowdy, ———— McCurley, Billy Sutherland. Probably about 1905.

nent literary critics as you'd find in cow camps and around the sheep. There the dogs seemed to enjoy it, the herders went to sleep, and the sheep left the bed ground.

The old, successful ranchers, as mentioned, viewed the homesteaders with pity and contempt, but in case of real need, they'd usually be around with a quarter of beef and a load or two of hay. They didn't want children, women, or animals to suffer.

Baseball brought them together. In 1910 every little town had its baseball team, and the pride of a citizen in his team was something past understanding. Paisley and Silver Lake had baseball teams and many of the husky young home-steaders were good baseball players. I pitched for Silver Lake for a while when I was sixteen. The ranchers would hire a homesteader if he were a good pitcher or fielder, and pay him top wages just to keep him in the country.

Betting was high at these community baseball games and intercommunity rivalry almost unbelievable. The desert towns didn't have much loose money, so our games were just for fun.

Human nature prevailed on the desert and many young, good-looking homesteaders married into the old stockmen families. So, what with one thing and another, not all home-steading turned out badly.

UNCLE SAM IS RICH ENOUGH TO GIVE US ALL A FARM

E. R. JACKMAN

MUCH OF THE LAND FROM BEND TO BURNS AND FROM Prineville to Lakeview was homesteaded. President Lincoln signed the first real homestead act in 1862. A homesteader had to be twenty-one or head of a family, and either a citizen or one who had made a declaration of intent. In the next twenty-one years, in all of Oregon, there were only 4,617 homesteads that actually passed into private ownership. On the desert, these original homesteads were mostly around the scanty water. A homesteader had to stay for five years, except that he could commute to a cash entry in six months and buy title, for $1.25 an acre, but who would do that? He could get the land free in the end—why spend money for it?

But by 1910, homesteading got into high gear, spurred on by as lively a bunch of rascals as ever roamed the range. A man who decided he was an unhappy medium—too light for heavy work and too heavy for light work—could set up an office in Prineville, Bend, or Lakeview, and advertise that he would locate all the land-hungry right out in a neglected part of paradise. These ads filled Eastern papers and proved irresistible to schoolteachers, bank clerks, and others who believed in fairies. The butcher, the baker, and the candlestick maker all wanted land.

In 1909 the law was amended to allow a man 320 acres of nonirrigable, nonmineral, and nontimbered land. By this time most of the plowable acres had been homesteaded, so this applied mainly to grazing lands. In 1916 the Stock-Raising Homestead Act was passed, enlarging desert homesteads to 640 acres. During the next eighteen years, many of these desert homesteads were filed on, mainly to sell to adjacent landowners, because no one could make a living on a square mile of desert unless he had some peculiar talents.

In 1934, the Taylor Grazing Act came along, withdrawing public lands from homesteading, thus reversing a 150-year-old policy of getting public land into private ownership. As it stands, a man can still file on a desert claim, provided he can prove that his quarter section is more valuable for agriculture than for grazing. The only way he can prove that is to get water enough to irrigate it.

Anyhow, from 1862 to 1934, seventy-two years, the government gave away its land to all comers. There were Federal land offices in every Western state and those in charge were graded by their ability to dispose of land, free.

The Western railroads all got into the act by granting special low fares to families coming West to homestead. In addition, the railroads advertised heavily, each telling of the wonderful free land available along its lines.

The local "locaters" preyed upon the land-hungry. It was a little risky for a schoolteacher from Bangor, Maine, to pick out a piece of land out from Lakeview. She might choose land already claimed by another. She didn't know where section corners were. She knew nothing of climate or soils. So a locater got hold of her, perhaps found she had a two-thousand-dollar nest egg, and charged her half of it to find for her some fertile virgin land. The land was free, so he was charging her for something she had a right to have without payment.

But even with government, railroads, and local vultures all doing their best to give away the government land, there were 170,000,000 acres in the West that no one would take. This is the "public domain," or that portion of it managed by the Bureau of Land Management. It is "the high desert" of Oregon, nearly all of Nevada, a large part of

has filed notice of intention to make Final
Three-year Proof, to establish claim to the land
above described, before P. D. Reeder, U. S.
Commissioner, at Silver Lake, Oregon, on the
15th day of July, 1916.

Claimant names as witnesses:
L. W. Boman, H. W. Ostrom, W. T. Eakin,
all of Arrow, Oregon: F. P. Petit, of Silver
Lake, Oregon.

JAS. F. BURGESS,
July 6   Register.

NOTICE FOR PUBLICATION.
DEPARTMENT OF THE INTERIOR.
NOT COAL LANDS.

U. S. Land Office at Lakeview, Oregon,
May 12, 1916.

NOTICE is hereby given that Layton F.
Tucker, of Fleetwood, Oregon, who, on January 23, 1913 and October 1, 1913, made Homestead Entry and Additional Homestead Entry
Nos. 06347 and 06934, for Lots 9, 10, 11, 12 & 5, Sec.
1, Township 26 S. Range 15 E. Willamette
Meridian, has filed notice of intention to
make Three-year Proof, to establish claim to the
land above described, before J. D. C. Thomas, U.
S. Commissioner at Fort Rock, Oregon, on the
1st day of July, 1916.

Claimant names as witnesses:
G. Clyde Briggs, E. W. Garver, M. Fleet, C.
W. Moore, all of Fleetwood, Oregon.

JAS. F. BURGESS,
June 15   Register.

NOTICE FOR PUBLICATION.
DEPARTMENT OF THE INTERIOR
NOT COAL LANDS.

U. S. Land Office at Lakeview, Oregon,
May 12, 1916.

NOTICE is hereby given that Jennie Overall,
of Stauffer, Oregon, who, on February 28, 1913,
made Homestead Entry No. 06426, for SW¼,
W½SE¼ Sec. 29, NE¼NW¼, NW¼NE¼,
Section 32, Township 24 South Range 22 East

THE LAW REQUIRED THAT SUCH NOTICES AS THESE BE PUBLISHED
BEFORE MAKING FINAL PROOF OF OWNERSHIP OF A HOMESTEAD
Local papers charged ten dollars for each notice and most desert papers carried eight or
ten in each issue from 1910 to 1918. This allowed even small towns to have newspapers.

Utah, and parts of all the other Western states. There are 13,000,000 acres of it in Oregon, about the combined acres in Delaware, Rhode Island, Connecticut, and Maryland.

The homestead era was pathetic, I suppose, looking back on it, but at the time it didn't seem so. It was exciting and there wasn't anyone to tell those folks, licked before they started, that they were ill-fed, ill-housed, and ill-advised. They were all there on the desert with a common cause, and they had lots of fun. They could go anyplace that a horse would take them. Any one of them was welcome at any other cabin anytime, and if there wasn't much to eat, at least it was shared. "Look over the table, stranger, and if you want something you don't see, we ain't got it." The lighter rations were paid for by the pleasure in the children's shout, "Here comes somebody!"

These people would have been genuinely shocked at a word of pity. Most of them were not much of anybody where they came from, but on the desert, for the first time in their lives, they amounted to as much as the next fellow. They were proving up on some land and they were excited about it, and happy.

They came from everywhere and knew nothing of the country. They thought that "rainfall follows the plow." They were of every occupation. The only thing they had in common was ignorance of dryland farming.

I suppose the Eastern schoolteachers were the most notable group. They came with a dreamy, mystical approach, hopelessly impractical.

In 1912 Alice Day Pratt, an old-maid schoolteacher from New York, was living on her homestead thirty miles south of Prineville. She wrote in her journal:

The possession of ancestral acres is bound up with sentiment, yet—virgin soil bestows an inspiration of its own. How the centuries have toiled through fire and frost and wind and wave and springing life and long decay to lay their fields so wide and deep. They alone among the fields of earth have suffered neither neglect nor ignorance nor folly. Reverent as Adam we should come to them.[1]

---

[1] *A Homesteader's Portfolio* (New York: The Macmillan Company, 1922).

But who knows? The desert gave to many more than it took away. Those years on the desert were certainly different from life in Farmington, Maine, or Shade Valley, Pennsylvania. They met a colorful, rambling, good-humored tribe impossible to meet at home. They met Indians and cowboys. They saw one segment of the West in the horseback days. Many of the women married, some to sons of well-to-do stockmen and others to hardworking bachelor drylanders. But I'll bet those who returned to Farmington and Shade Valley often sat looking from the schoolhouse windows after the children had gone home, thinking of the wilder scene in Oregon. Maybe not. Maybe they were embittered, and felt they should sue the desert for breach of promise.

They all picked up things of value on the desert. What they found depended upon their own reserves of mind and spirit. What they saw depended upon their equipment for seeing. A few items: the sudden white flash of the flag of a startled antelope; the pure beauty and joy of the meadowlark's song on a spring morning, an outpouring of happiness far beyond the ability of the most gifted writer; the link with the wild primeval in the long, drawn-out wail of the coyote on a winter night; the clear air and closeness of the stars in the inverted bowl of the sky; the splash of distilled beauty of the Indian paintbrush etched in bold color against a dark lava rock; the doe, daintily picking her way to water with her pretty spotted fawn. Such items can't be bought in a Pittsburgh supermarket.

There were other trinkets around, too, their value dependent upon one's understanding. What is a lifelong friendship worth, formed from shared hardships and privations, and built upon mutual help in sickness and storm? What is the value of the discovery by a young man that he has reserves of resource and strength that he knew nothing about, leading to a sturdy self-respect lacking before? What of the bigness of the land; the wide reach of the vision, the far horizons; the lift of the eye upward half a mile to the top of the rimrock; the ageless desert itself?

I mentioned that the homesteaders had fun. And practical jokes. One of these, successful beyond the wildest dreams, was perpetrated by a couple of high-spirited boys near Fort Rock. There were around one hundred homesteaders who gathered each Sunday all summer long at an ice cave back in the lava beds adjacent to the Fort Rock Valley. The lava beds are tortured, indescribable badlands. Molten lava cools in front, but the flowing mass behind pushes over the huge cooled blocks and then, in turn, cools. The result is chaos, frozen into cliffs; huge amorphous piles; beautiful little hidden gardens of wild flowers; spires without form; sudden slabs as slick as glass; caves and caverns, big and little.

In this particular place, where the homesteaders had found inexhaustible ice, there are, all around, some miniature volcanoes. The surface cooled, but the hot material below generated huge pressures from imprisoned gas. Where this gas found a crevice and shot up with great force, carrying molten lava with it, the lava cooled at the edges, but the gas continued to come, thus forming perfect miniature volcanic cones, about thirty feet high, each with its little crater.

So the two boys happily concocted disaster. They spent the week surreptitiously working like mad, throwing inflammable stuff into the crater of one of the volcanoes. Juniper branches, dry grass, old fence posts—anything that would burn. They poured kerosene over the pile and waited.

The crowd assembled—men, women, and children. They made ice cream, played horseshoes, and swapped the inevitable stories. "Say, I got a new kind o' desert squash just built for this frosty climate. But I plumb fergot to jump back after plantin' it and I like to never got outa there. Finally I outrun it, but Grandpap, he couldn't make 'er. We ain't seen him since." "They say it's too frosty here for watermelons, but I got some that grow so fast the frost can't ketch 'em. They ain't practical, though—them vines jest spread so fast that the friction from the sand grains wears the melons out—they get drug to death."

As the men talked and the women spread the lunch, the boys climbed unobserved, tossed down a lighted match. Suddenly a picnicker turned white, pointed a shaking finger at the black smoke, and dashed for his horse. All hell broke loose. The boys didn't dare tell about it for forty years. Suppose, in a crisis like this, *you* took the horse and dashed away, leaving wife and children with a buggy. She might forgive you, but you'd know what she was thinking when she looked at you with contemplative eyes. They claimed big six-footers wore down to five feet six in no time. A whole book could be written about the things that happened. Some neighbors gained stature, though, and several marriages resulted. A few divorces, too.

So the homesteaders left, their cabins and houses were mostly taken or burned, and nothing is there now but some rusting barbed wire, a few juniper posts, and maybe a broken dish and a busted wagon wheel.

The homesteaders, full of hope, plans, good humor, and determination, had three material assets: flour sacks, whiskey barrels, and five-gallon kerosene cans. Let's take the cans first. They were incredibly versatile. Here are just a few of the uses:

Cut the top off, pound the jagged edges down flat and you have a water bucket to stand on the kitchen table. Or make a nice round stick from an old pitchfork handle, cut it to fit snugly the inside of the top of the can, drive a nail in from each side, and you have a bucket with a handle, for carrying water from the well or windmill. Or tie a long rope to the handle, run it through a pulley, or around a windlass, and lower it into the well to haul up water. Thousands of horses and cattle were watered that way. It was the job of every farm boy to keep the water trough full.

Have one can just special, without a handle, to boil the

babies' diapers in, and to accumulate the unwashed diapers, awaiting the boiling.

Instead of cutting out the end, cut out one side, and pound down the edges, as mentioned. This is important, because a careless man, leaving a sharp, jagged edge on a can, could amputate a finger some day or night when he grabbed the can in a hurry. So, take a can with the side cut out, or, better, four or five cans, set them on some wooden boxes in front of a window, fill with soil with some horse manure at the bottom, and thus provide an indoor window garden for cactus, geraniums, fuchsias, and begonias with ornamental leaves. These were truly important to wives of the homesteaders. Women like something green and growing, especially when the landscape outside is gray and dry. The wives liked to trade this greenery with other women. It helps any woman to have something others want; whether it's a recipe or a Martha Washington geranium.

If real handy with tools, partly cut one side, then with a wooden block and a hammer, pound the side inward slightly, keeping the edge straight all the way across. This made a self-feeder for little chickens and turkeys. Pry up the edge of a coop a little, just enough so the big chickens can't crawl under, and set the feeder inside. With grasshoppers, ants, bugs, and weed seeds, the full-grown poultry didn't need much grain. This was particularly true if the boys trapped coyotes or would shoot rabbits to furnish meat for the chickens.

This is just a starter for the cans. Cut down the corners and get a flat piece of tin. Cut a round hole with a chisel. The homesteaders had no bricks for chimneys so, wherever a stovepipe went through a wall or a roof, the flat side of a can could be nailed up and the pipe could be put through the hole for a fireguard. A city inspector might frown upon this type of fire protection.

A pack outfit consisted of the saddle and the pack. The saddle had two sticks that crossed in front and two that crossed behind. Hung from these crossed sticks, one on each side, was a leather pouch, just the right size to hold a light wooden box that originally held two kerosene cans. **Reub** tells how to make these.

Cover the light box with a piece of rawhide a little scant, cut from a green hide. Stretch the hide over the box and sew with rawhide thongs down the corners, pulling the stitches, thereby stretching it very tight. When this dried, you had a better box than you could get in any other way. Two leather slings were put around the box and riveted to it right through both leather and box. These slings had loops to hook over the forks of the saddle and made a wonderful alforjas, one on each side of the horse.

If the horse bumped his pack into a tree, they could "give" and not crack or break. Once in camp, they made good chairs, cupboards, and tables.

The cans were grain cans, too, usually with a light wooden frame at the top, so the edges wouldn't bend. They made handy measuring devices for rye seed.

Sometimes a man long on cans would flatten out the sides and tack them to the windy side of his house to keep out the dust, snow, or cold wind. These cans aren't so easy to come by now. Electricity has pretty well outlawed kerosene lamps and lanterns. I don't believe a homesteader could make out now.

Whiskey barrels also made it possible to homestead. Many of the homesteaders didn't drink, but they could buy the barrels for fifty cents each and nowhere else could they get such big, sturdy containers. One stood at the house corner on each side where it collected from the roof the scanty rain or melting snow. Even the families with wells used barrels for rainwater, for it was soft, whereas some wells yielded alkali water, unsuitable for washing the long hair of the womenfolk. Many families had to haul water, and a wagonload of barrels filled with water would be about all a team could pull.

They held grain for feed and seed. Mice and pack rats wouldn't usually gnaw through a whiskey barrel, whereas a pine box scarcely made them pause. Most folks had gardens, and a barrel made a fine container for kraut. Another served for putting down salt pork. All families stored food in barrels or stone crocks, because in those days tin cans would poison food stored in them very long. The tin is different now. All frontier folks had a deep fear of ptomaine poisoning. They didn't understand it, so tried to prevent it by avoiding things that had produced ptomaine in some neighborhood family.

But the most useful thing was the ever-present flour sack. I don't see how any homesteader could have lived in any decency without them. They furnished social security from the cradle to the grave in the form of diapers and underwear. They made curtains, towels, and aprons. Sewn together with No. 50 thread, and filled with rye straw, they made mattresses, or "straw ticks."

They entered into conversation all the time. Reub tells of his younger sister Anna, just before her first year of school. The talk was about the cotton plant, and the uses for cotton. To impress its importance upon her, someone said, "Anna, what are your clothes made of?" Anna said promptly, "Goods and flour sacks."

Any young couple could start housekeeping with whiskey barrels, flour sacks, and kerosene cans. Oh, yes! They needed one other thing they could get free—wooden boxes. They made chairs, cupboards, closets, bureaus, trunks, pantries, and safety-deposit boxes for such valuables as the big mail-order catalog. The family without a catalog didn't really live. Sears, Roebuck didn't develop any other name except "Sears and Sawbuck," but Montgomery Ward was "Uncle Monty" or "Monkey Ward."

Reub says that the big thick catalog served the homesteaders as shopping center, means of entertainment, fashion guide, seat for the baby at the table, cutouts for the kids, and when replaced by the new issue next year, it was a standard toilet article.

Most homesteaders went out once a year to buy supplies.

They always came back with an almanac and a calendar. The almanac had all kinds of recipes, remedies, tables of measures and weights. There were the signs of the zodiac and reliable information about one's horoscope.

They had the exact time when the sun came up and every watch was set accordingly. There were long-range forecasts showing rainy periods. Everyone overlooked the times when the almanac was wrong, but commented favorably when it hit a storm right on the nose.

Newspapers were necessary. Most families didn't take a paper, but it was possible to get some free. A daily was useless for news, for most homesteaders got their mail twice a month. When a man would go to Prineville or Lakeview, one of his jobs in town was to get a stack of papers. Town people accumulated them and gave them to homesteader friends. The inside walls of nearly all desert shacks were covered with newspapers stuck on with paste made from flour. In case of a broken leg, it was cozy to lie in bed and read on the ceiling the stirring story of Dewey sailing into Manila Bay.

Bert Peck, of Morrow County, told me that some Eastern relatives sent his family a big boxful of old issues of the Chicago *Inter-Ocean*. Folks came from miles away to read the items on their walls, on the theory that the farther away the news came from, the better it was bound to be.

A few papered with dull, unattractive red building paper, and I've seen one or two use black tar paper. These were generally thought to be a little odd.

By the time a homesteader's child got to be six and could show up in school, he was often boosted to the second grade, because he had to be pretty dull if he hadn't learned to read from the wallpaper.

There were no refrigerators, so food was fresh, salted, dried, or canned. In the wintertime, when meat would freeze on the north side of the house, there might be fresh beef, venison, or pork, but in the summer there was no way to keep it. There was no ice on the desert.

Salted side meat, with gravy made from the meat drippings, was pretty good. Often there was either fresh bread or big, heart-warming sourdough biscuits. Whenever light bread was made, enough of the dough was saved to make a couple of pans of rolls. You take one of these rolls, right from the oven, break it (don't cut it), put a big pat of fresh, homemade butter inside, place the halves back together, and—oh, man!

In the early spring, dandelion, mustard, or pigweed greens, were wilted with hot drippings from the salt pork and boiled eggs were sliced on top. I can't think of anything better after a winter running heavy to boiled beans, the "Harney County strawberries."

Homemade butter was universal. It cost nothing, because the cows gave the cream free. But it brought problems. The butter at some places defied description. At others it was delicious. Occasionally the cows would eat wild onion in the spring. Wild onions are as good as tame for seasoning a salad, but they don't help butter much. The butter turned bad gradually, and the owners might not be aware of it.

Jesse Minson, of Powell Butte, told me of his bachelor homestead days. He kept his butter in a small stone crock on a shelf. He didn't know it was getting distressingly fragrant until a stranger stopped one evening and was naturally asked to eat and spend the night. The stranger helped with the dishes, and, in cleaning up, asked where the butter was kept. Jesse pointed to the crock. The stranger tossed the small pat at the crock with the admonition, "Jump up in there, you little. . . ." That caused some suspicion in Jesse's mind, but the butter tasted all right to him.

The kerosene lamp and old dented lantern were the most used things on the place. In winter a man could put a horse blanket on the hack seat and another over his knees, set a lighted lantern between the blankets, and let the storm rage—his legs were warm. Most lamps were unadorned, but once in a while, if a homesteader worked for the ZX for forty dollars a month, he'd like to come home with some tangible evidence of his concern for the family. He'd ride around by Silver Lake or Paisley, buy candy for the chil-

Photo by Jim Anderson, Oregon Museum of Science and Industry, Portland

FRED WRIGHT, A LONGTIME RESIDENT OF THE FORT ROCK AREA, AT THE OPEN WINDOW OF AN ABANDONED HOMESTEAD SHACK

dren and get his wife a lamp with a big bowl with red roses painted on it. His homecoming then was a time of rejoicing. Chimneys of lamps and lanterns were cleaned with a dry newspaper. It was quicker and better than to wash —besides, you saved water that way. Neighbors judged other women by the brightness of the lamp chimneys.

The worst hardship was the dust. A little breeze would start around Bend to the northwest, would get into the spirit of the thing, whip itself into a frenzy, and by the time it got to Christmas Lake, it would be blowing the quills off the porcupines. Reub tells about one wind that blew a sage hen against a rock cliff and just held her there until she laid eleven eggs. Easter occurred during this time and two were Easter eggs.

Scientists say that man can adapt to any kind of weather except continuous wind. Unremitting, unrelenting wind blows ambition right out of a man, leaving him without hope or plan. In the winter it can kill him, just by blowing away his heat, and in the summer it can kill his soul. The homesteaders' houses, of board and batten, couldn't hold out a determined wind, and many a man came in from his day's work to find his wife crying hysterically as she looked at a dish of mashed potatoes, too covered with dust to reveal its identity. The desert was awful hard on horses and women.

Water wasn't too hard to find on the Fort Rock desert, so most everyone who could raise the price at all had a windmill. But in other parts of the desert the homesteaders claimed it was as far to water straight down as it was to haul it from a source ten miles away. No one has made a permanent home on the desert who had to haul water for household use.

Hauling water is bad enough if you have nothing else to do, but to try to farm at the same time is a tough deal. A man can't get into the livestock business to any extent, for he can't haul it as fast as one hundred head can drink it. The homesteaders really wore the water out. Maybe it took a gallon to wash the dishes. Depending upon what the meal had been and the state of the dishes, the same water then might be used for mopping the floor, feeding the pig or the chickens, and it would end its career by watering the matrimony vine that grew over the kitchen window. The water used for a Saturday night bath was just at the beginning of a long and useful life.

Of course, a lot of things we wash didn't get washed much. Reub says the bachelors either used sand or their elbows on their dishes. The bowls were often selected of a size to just fit the elbow. He tells of the two bachelors who took turns coming to his place, each telling how dirty the other was. There wasn't much to choose between them, but they could see the other's dirt, whereas the slow accumulation in their own houses passed unnoticed.

One of them gave Reub a painfully minute description of the other; how his bedclothes, once with a pattern, now were a greasy gray; how the dishes, now filled in, had corners when new. He wound up with the crowning indictment: "And as for his dishrag, Reub! Why, good God, you could *stab* a man with it!" This was illustrated by a forward lunge with his finger, the motion a swordsman uses to finish his opponent.

I stopped once to talk to a drylander who was mowing some straggly rye hay. His horses were thin, but curried, and he was ragged but clean. His voice had permanently congealed on a high note in his youth, but he seemed to have no control and at times it broke to bass unpredictably. I asked him what he fed his horses when working them like that. He said in his high squeak, "Every day I feed 'em the hay I cut the day before, but at night," and here he tumbled to bass, "I turn 'em out an' by God they just got to rustle for themselves."

In any case, out of the thousands I have known, I never met one who felt sorry for himself. They were as well off as the neighbors and they had things to do on the desert. Roads had to be located, schoolhouses built, the Grange organized. Nearly all amounted to more than they did where they came from. They learned to live with what they had. They shared goods, knowledge, and know-how with neighbors. A woman who knew how to do everything taught the newcomers and was far more important in the community than the president of the Chamber of Commerce.

From society's viewpoint, the worst thing about homesteading was that it was hard on the land. Millions of acres were plowed that should have been left as "unshorn fields."

FROM EOHIPPUS TO PALOMINO

E. R. Jackman

From the time the first daring caveman felt the increased sense of power as a horse carried him, the human race has known that a horse brings dignity to the rider. Reub says that if you think all men are equal, you've never been a pedestrian and met a man on a good horse.

Riders just naturally look down upon the man on foot. The horse led man toward civilization. The early military nations spread by cavalry. Some advanced peoples, as the Mayans of Central America, disappeared because they had only human beings to bring food to the cities, and as soon as the distance grew so that a man could carry only enough for his own consumption, the great cities were doomed. Without the horse, a country could be only a local success.

The Great Khan, a Mongolian who ruled China 165 years before Columbus, had the best cavalry units of all time. He had three armies and must have had a Ph.D. in psychology, because one army used only black horses, the second white horses, and the third were mounted on bays. Great rivalry sprang up between the three armies and they tried mightily to outdo each other in conquering other nations. They were successful and the Khan came closer to ruling the entire civilized world than any other man, before or since. He owed it to his superb cavalry.

Of course, modern Oregon never saw horses until they began to drift this way from New Mexico. They didn't drift of their own accord; the Indians bought or stole them and sent them northward from tribe to tribe. All of our horses trace to Mexico where the Spaniards brought them from Europe.

The Spanish King bestowed huge New World land grants upon noblemen and favored army officers. These folk took root and raised horses on a bonanza scale. Among the first laws proclaimed in Mexico was a stern decree forbidding all native persons to ride horses. Only the superior Spaniards could be mounted. The word "peon" means pedestrian. That law was impossible to enforce and lasted only about twenty years. The big ranches had horses by the thousands. There weren't enough Spanish to handle them and peons couldn't outrun a horse. So the law, as a matter of necessity, was quietly ignored, and some of the best riders the world has ever seen have been Mexicans. Many of the early-day ranchers in Oregon hired Mexicans to train and care for the horses. Tebo, a gifted Mexican, was Pete French's foreman. John Devine, first permanent settler in Harney County, had mostly Mexican riders.

The enthusiastic reception of the horse in Mexico led at once to a whole new vocabulary and even now most of the horse equipment for both riding and packing has Mexican names, or words derived from them.[1] Even the word "mustang" comes from Spain via Mexico.

Eastern Oregon had native horses once—way back before two thousand feet of lava covered the land and before the Cascade Mountains were hatched.

Little pigmy horses ran around over the landscape and left their fossilized skeletons in mud that was later pressed into rock by the weight of lava above and the pressure of gas below. "Said the little Eohippus, 'I am going to be a horse, and on my middle fingernails I'll run my earthly course' " runs a famous poem.[2]

Somehow the little Eohippus never did make it in Oregon.

---

[1] See Appendix A for a limited vocabulary of horse terms derived from Spanish words.
[2] Charlotte Perkins Stetson Gilman, *Similar Cases*.

He crossed to Asia on the land mass that once existed where
Bering Strait is now, and really did form the modern horse.

Bones of a large type of prehistoric horse were found at
Fossil Lake, near Reub's place. The John Day basin has
provided numerous fossil skeletons of small horses.

Scientists love the horse because the different stages of his
existence have been traced back for forty million years and
fossilized or petrified remains illustrate each hesitant step.
He climbed from a little five-toed animal up to the noble
steed of today, dropping toes as he went. Today's hoofs
came from the claws or nails on the five toes, so the poem
of the little Eohippus who planned to run his earthly course
on his middle fingernails is scientifically exact.

As he slowly evolved from a rabbit-sized animal General
Evolution mounted him and rode off in all directions. In
the forests he took one form, another on the plains. Probably one hundred different species have been found—more
in North America than elsewhere, but in all continents
except Australia. He fled across the big eastern bridge to
Siberia and covered the land area of his time.

About a million years ago came the start of five big ice
invasions. They didn't cover all of North America or all
of Europe, but during these recurrent ice ages, each last-
ing 100,000 years with 100,000 years between them, the
horse mysteriously disappeared from North America and
from most of Europe. The ice didn't cover Oregon, but
the horse left. He survived, though, in Asia and forms of
him, such as the zebra and the wild ass, lived on in Africa.

The modern horse developed in the countries around what
we know as Persia and Arabia, and man hasn't improved
him much.[3] Arabian horses were the standard that others
were judged by and it's still hard to beat a good Arabian.
The good riding horses of the world trace to the Arabian,
modified by other breeds for special purposes.

When Spaniards came to South America, hard on the heels

---

[3] Frederic Brewster Loomis, *The Evolution of the Horse* (Boston: Marshall Jones
Company, 1926).

of Columbus, the king ordered them to bring horses and other domestic animals on every trip. They were out for gold and jewels and they didn't care too much for this forced farm order, the first Agricultural Adjustment Act. It created a problem on the little sailing ships. The animals all drank water, and that took up space. When the Ancient Mariner shot the good-luck albatross, and the winds quit, it didn't take long for the water-drinking animals to threaten the lives of the sailors. In such cases, the animals were shoved overboard. Early Spanish records show that around 30 per cent of the horses that left Spain died, or were jettisoned, on the way.[4] The horse latitudes were so named because ships were becalmed there and horses were sacrificed to save water.

These horses, from Andalusia, were mostly Arabian, with some Barbary Coast mixture, hence the name of "Barb" often given to them. Barb was never a breed, just a point of origin, as Middle Westerners for fifty years talked of "Oregon" horses, as opposed to Texas strains. Pure Arabians were solid colors, white, black, bay or chestnut.

At Redmond a few years ago, at the races during the county fair, an Indian's black horse consistently came in behind a white man's white horse. The last evening of the fair, the Indian appeared on the street reeling and wobbling and waving eight hundred dollars in bills. He said he'd bet all of it that his black horse could beat the white man's white horse. Some local boys got together and agreed it was a shame to take his money, but after all, money didn't stay with a drunk Indian and they might as well have it as someone else. The Indian got the sheriff to hold the stakes.

The race was at ten o'clock at the fairgrounds on Sunday morning. When the time came, the Indian arrived on an altogether different black horse, one that ran right away from the white horse. The sheriff paid the Indian, pointing out that the terms of the bet mentioned no particular horse.

---

[4] J. Frank Dobie, *The Mustangs* (Boston: Little, Brown & Company, 1952).

The horses in northern Asia were stockier and spread in time to northern Europe. Our draft breeds originated in England, Scotland, Belgium, and France. But we are interested here in the riding horses of the Spanish.

The Spaniards mostly rode stallions. It was unmanly to ride mares, and gelding was not a general practice. The wandering friars of both the Old World and the New commonly rode mules, as a sign of humility. The mule, "with no pride of ancestry nor hope of posterity," was part of the humble garment of piety.

This is just to furnish background for the advent of the horse into Oregon, somewhere around 1750.[5] Riding horses develop best in arid countries, and are better suited to the desert than any other domestic animal. They even fare better than deer.

We didn't have wild horses in Oregon at first. Dobie says that wild horses reached their peak in Texas in 1848, when there were a million head running loose in that big state. In 1848, although Oregon was settled to a greater extent than any other Western state, it is doubtful if there was even one wild horse here. In Lewis and Clark's time, 1805, most Oregon Indians didn't have horses. The Nez Perce, Shoshones, Cayuse, and Snake Indians had them, indicating that the horse came directly north from New Mexico, not from California. The Nez Perce, alone among North American Indians, paid attention to their horses, gelding unsuitable stallions, and training their horses systematically.

Of all tragedies among the red men, the tragedy of the Nez Perce was the greatest. Broken treaties, senseless orders, complete lack of understanding, characterized all of our dealings with them. Even in the so-called Nez Perce war, they weren't trying to go to war; they were only trying to get out of an intolerable situation by going to Canada.

They developed the spotted roan, now called Appaloosa—so far as I know the only Indian tribe in either of the

---

[5] For a further description of horses in Oregon, see *Gold and Cattle Country*, by Herman Oliver, published by Binfords and Mort, Portland, (1961).

Americas that, by selective breeding, originated a more or less dependable strain, or breed, of horses. When Chief Joseph and his band were finally captured, their horses were taken from them and killed or dispersed. This interesting breed was almost lost, but, luckily, some were left. They are popular now and are increasing.

Other Indians made no contribution to the horse picture. The Cayuse Indians had lots of them, but let them get along as best they could until the term "cayuse" came to mean any fuzzy, unkempt, underfed and overused pony. There was a story around the desert about the horses that got such big "witches tails" that the weight pulled their skins back so they couldn't shut their eyes. Of course, this was fatal—they died from lack of sleep. Reub says that when he was little, children were told that the witch knots came because, at night, witches rode the horses, and they'd better not let the knots get started, because in time only the witches could ride them. The children didn't really swallow this but, just in case, every boy carefully combed the tail of his horse.

Horses didn't appear on the Oregon desert in quantity until it was settled up, and it wasn't really settled until after the last of the Indian wars in 1878. The Paiutes and Bannocks couldn't be trusted in the presence of an un- guarded scalp. They might just lift it out of absentminded- ness, or just to keep in practice so they'd do a workmanlike job if called upon. As a result, there weren't many settlers, because at best they were a long way apart, out of sight and sound of anyone else. This distance was expensive— for one thing everyone had to keep his own tomcat.

But, starting in 1880, population came fast, and came in with horses. America was pioneered by a man on a horse and developed by a man behind a team. There was a stream of incoming people on every road into southeastern Oregon from 1880 to 1915. Usually a family would have at least two wagons. One wagon would be loaded with lumber and stuff for a house. The other would have some horse feed,

seed grain, maybe some chickens, and a plow or something
with which to start farming. There would be a few children, often on horseback, and their job would be to keep
loose horses and cattle coming along. That wasn't so hard
as it sounds, because after a few days on the trail, the loose
stock seemed to form a sort of togetherness.

There were homesteaders who came with nothing, so they
couldn't lose anything. It was a practicable sort of plan.
Nearly everyone had horses—anywhere from one on up to
a regular cavvy, with bell mare and all.

Some found land, developed water, and their descendants
have been the bone and sinew of the country ever since. I
don't know whether the stock business attracts good people,
or whether they get that way through the ownership of
animals. But among stockmen there is a willingness to take
responsibility for one's acts. They don't whine when they
make a bad deal, and try to blame someone else. They don't
run to the government for help in a crisis. They are the
last defense the nation has against the prevalent "gimme"
disease, and against socialism in any form.

Some settlers went into horse raising in a big way, counting their horses into the thousands. All the homesteaders
had horses that ran out on the desert part or all the time.
In hard times and low prices, the horses just stayed out
there, maybe for ten years. The stallions gathered little
harems, all the mares had colts, and the increase was tremendous. The census takers tried to count them, but when
a man couldn't say how many horses he owned, how could
he tell the census taker? So census reports of horses on the
desert were distinctly on the haywire side.

But for what they are worth, the census shows that horse
numbers in Oregon grew to 49,000 in 1867, or twenty-four
years after the first big immigration in 1843. From 1880 to
1890 the number nearly doubled, running up to 220,000.
By 1916 there were 300,000, their peak. They declined to

40,000 in 1958, and are now increasing at the rate of nearly 10,000 a year.[6]

All through the twenties and thirties, you could see horses and people moving off the desert on every road. In the summer of 1920 I was driving south from Baker. Halfway to Huntington I met a mighty sorry-looking outfit. The one wagon had the tires tied on with baling wire, which, of course, would break often. The harness, too, was cobbled up with the same universal farmer's friend. There were two thin milk cows and an extra horse, extra thin. The man and his wife had faces tanned the color of buckskin and of about the same consistency. But the man's eyes were bright, and he had good-humor lines running back from the corners. I stopped to see if they needed help. They didn't, but this conversation followed:

I: Where are you from?

Farmer: Mister, I been on the road now more than ten days and this is the first anyone has asked me that.

I: (hastily) Gosh! I didn't mean to be nosey, I was just trying to be sociable. It sure isn't any of my business.

Farmer: Oh, it ain't that! But everybody else I've met knew I was from Harney County.

So one reason for the decline in horse numbers was because homesteaders were getting out. Other reasons included:

Tractors began to displace horses in the fields, and autos and trucks displaced them on the road.

Horses became almost worthless.

Severe farm depressions in the twenties and clear through the thirties led to the sale of anything saleable, regardless of price.

Demand for horses for fox food arose, clearing out thousands of them.

Canned food for pets grew into big business and horses furnished the cheapest meat.

---

[6] See Appendix B for census figures.

A sudden demand for pony coats gave temporary value and thousands were moved out.

Taylor Grazing Act in 1934 made it illegal to pasture them on government land without grazing rights and payment of fees.

In 1916 we officially had 300,000 in Oregon. It is safe to say that we had another 100,000 unofficially. If we use that figure, it makes 400,000 horses in the state, whereas in 1958 we had only 10 per cent, or 40,000. Many of the new horse faces are Welsh and Shetland ponies, or are special types for riding clubs, such as palominos, quarter horses, pintos, and Appaloosas. It's doubtful if we will ever get back to anything like former numbers.

So the descendants of the little Eohippus are descending upon us again. You hear an increasing amount of horse talk and I am glad of it. According to Arab desert folklore, the horse was created from the desert wind and he was called "The Drinker of the Wind."

An old English saying runs:

> Your head and your heart—Keep up,
> Your hands and your heels—Keep down,
> Your knees press into your horse's side,
> Your elbows into your own.[7]

---

[7] Margaret Cabell Self, ed., *A Treasury of Horse Stories* (New York: A. S. Barnes & Co., Inc., 1945).

MY SADDLE'S MY HOME

R. A. LONG

THERE ARE NUMEROUS SCHOLARLY BOOKS UPON THE WILD horses of the West. They are written by anthropologists, historians, and humanitarians, whereas I am a sagebrush desert rancher. I dreamed once that I went to Heaven. St. Peter looked me over more than casually.

St. Peter: Where you from, cowboy?

I: The Fort Rock desert.

St. Peter: Well—all right, you can come in, but I can tell you right now, you ain't a-goin' to like it, because it ain't a bit like Fort Rock.

I grew up surrounded by thousands of wild horses; I made a living for years by rounding them up; I have broken many of them; I've trained them for others.

My pardner, Jim Schroder, and I had our own brand on horses on the desert, but we didn't have much money—we didn't have *any* money!

All at once the price for these half-wild horses jumped from three dollars to ten dollars apiece. They had been worth maybe three dollars after rounding up, and it cost more than that to catch them. Ten dollars doesn't sound like much dinero now, but if you multiply it by thousands, you increase your capital scandalously. There was little time to lose—we didn't know how long this bonanza would last, and we knew that the west wind, the buzzards, and the coyotes would all be carrying the news to every corner of the desert.

We knew that a man named Currier with the Circle brand wanted to sell an unknown number. They ran right where ours did and we guessed he had five hundred or more. So we hothoofed it to Currier's and found three other buyers there. The others were buying on a delivered basis. You could keep lots of dust off you by buying that way. But Currier didn't care much about absorbing all the tiredness you can get into yourself by breakneck rides among the rimrocks.

So, as he hesitated, we rode up and kindly offered to buy the horses as is and where is. Nothing could have been closer to Currier's own ideas. He instantly offered them to us for $1,500—$500 down, thirty days to gather them, and $1,000 due when rounded up. And right there I got my first inkling of the advantages of doing business on other people's money. They call it finance, but up 'til then, it had been a closed book. We told him his price was high, but just, and we'd take 'em. We'd have to go into Bend, though, and make arrangements for cars to ship them, feed while in the corral, and things like that. Then we'd be back and pay him.

We started to Bend with Oscar Kittredge in his car, ran out of gas at Lava Butte, and pushed it on in—eleven miles. Of course, we could get in and ride down the hills. It was night and we spent the rest of it out in the beautiful moonlight. The next morning we found the man who wanted horses to ship to Butte, Montana. We sold him 200 at $10 each and got $500 down to bind the bargain. At the time it didn't even occur to either of us to try to borrow from a bank. Believing too much credit has ruined many a man, we'd carefully preserved our position of having none.

When we got back to Silver Lake, we were broke. Around our country you can always borrow five dollars, even if you only want it to get drunk on, so I borrowed five, bought gas enough to drive to Currier's place, and paid him the five hundred dollars we received from the Butte man. When the buyer had asked me what the brand would be on the horses we were to deliver, I told him, "A circle upside down on the side next the rimrock." He decided we must be all right, and entrusted the five hundred dollars to us.

We brought these two hundred half-wild horses in right on the dot, received $1,500 more for them and paid Currier $1000. This had worked out all right. We'd sold something we didn't have; we didn't know where it was, but had delivered it on time and had $500 we didn't have before. We gathered 1,500 horses in all, with the Circle brand.

The Curriers had been good horsemen for generations and had raised fine animals. They had the know-how for raising, breaking, and handling saddle horses, and were good

Photo by Joe Van Wormer, Bend, Ore.

"AROUND THE RIM CAME A SNUFFY BAND, AND CLOSE TO THE LEAD WAS AN AL-MAN"

Reub's AL brand has been prominent on the Oregon desert for nearly a hundred years at handling wild horses on the range. They sold out to us only because handling desert horses is a young man's job.

As a sort of parenthesis, in 1957 some riders found two white horses with the Circle brand on them, remnants of the Currier ownership. Soon after we bought that brand, we quit using it, thirty years before these horses were found. These old desert animals had been out in the wind and sand, cold and heat, for a long time. They were strong proof that to live in the desert, a man or a horse must have:

1. Vitality—lots of it.
2. Instinct to find water, feed, and shelter.
3. Enough luck to last a lifetime and ability to not be at the right place at the wrong time.

In the books they call that "survival of the fittest" and the scientists make quite a fuss about it, but in this case it benefited the race nary a bit because both horses were geldings.

I had been raised on a horse right from the start, and so had Jim Schroder. This Currier deal convinced us that we were on the right track and horses could provide our beans and bacon. The two of us lived horses day and night for the next six years, running a horse outfit as partners. Then I bought out Jim. He went to California and became well known as a fine superintendent of a big stock ranch.

Some things I learned about horses were:

Gathering wild horses is an art.

You need a right good horse to operate on.

The formula for such riding is not written on a bottle.

Some men never learn how.

Some horses, especially stallions, are just too smart to catch.

When rounding up the wild ones, you are an object of suspicion to every other man, woman, and child on the desert.

Horses can go without water a long time if they have to.

It takes lots of training to learn how to run wild horses, but it isn't much good except to teach you to run more wild horses.

Your success depends as much upon the other fellow as it does upon yourself.

A careless man gets to be dead soon.

Wild horse runners rarely die of consumption.

If you believe in regular habits, keep off the desert.

I've read a lot of books; what they tell you in the thirteenth chapter of the best book on economics doesn't help much when after wild horses.

You can do everything exactly right and then have the weather beat you.

Sudden, unexpected things were always happening. I was chasing some wild ones with a real good horse. I hadn't ridden him hard. I was a couple of miles from the horses I was chasing, just trotting, waiting for a chance to head them where I wanted them to go, and I was taking it easy. My horse staggered, I jumped off, jerked off the saddle, and he was dead before I could look around. I packed my saddle ten miles to the east end of the Diablo Trail, cached it, and walked in to the Jim Small ranch at the head of Summer Lake, twenty miles.

A man named Bill lived in eastern Lake County. He was hailed into court for stealing a horse. He hired Sam Jetmore to defend him. One who never heard Sam address a jury has never heard a lawyer. He played on a jury the way an old master plays a piano—calm, assured, the sound rising, swelling, ringing, falling to an incredulous whisper. It was almost worth while to commit a crime just to hear Sam get you acquitted. That's what happened to Bill.

When they settled up, Sam said, as friend to friend, "Bill, you are free as air, and they can't ever bring you in here again on this charge, but if you care to tell me, and just between us—*did* you steal that horse?" Bill said, "When I came in here I was fairly certain I was guilty, but after hearing your plea, I have a reasonable doubt."

Mr. Kilgore came to us to sell his Billy Goat brand. He wanted to sell out slick and clean, about one hundred head.

We'd seen fully that many horses wearing the Billy Goat, so we paid six hundred dollars for the brand, shaking hands with ourselves over the fine deal. His horses weren't extra wild and would be easy to gather.

We didn't get around to gathering them until the next year. We combed the desert with a garden rake and finally found twenty head. Kilgore hadn't looked after them and they had been picked up, one by one, and spirited away.

We didn't have trouble with owners. We would not take a bunch off the desert unless all the brands were accounted for. For example, we'd send word to the Lane ranch at Silver Lake or to Holley Swingle at Fleetwood, or to Jim Small at Summer Lake, that we had a big chestnut with a white left hind foot, or a little black mare with a star and ask them their wishes. Should we hold them, ship them, or just turn them out? Sometimes we'd ship them and give the owner the money. Sometimes the owner set great

PART OF A HORSE-RUNNING CREW IN THE DAYS OF WILD HORSES
Left to right: Lyle Wood, R. A. Long, Jim Schroder, and John Lutz, all good hands in any man's camp. This picture was taken about 1925.

store on an animal that seemed worthless. The owner would often come, look at the horse, and then decide. We always let the owners make their own decisions.

From 1928 to 1934, we sold over three thousand head, all gathered from the big open range in an area 150 by 100 miles.[1]

In running horses, there would sometimes be a crew of twenty men. This, though, was usually to round up horses for a group of owners. Maybe some in the crew had lost a good horse, so were interested only in that one animal. Often the man who furnished the camp outfit was the boss, or else a boss was appointed by common consent. There had to be a boss capable of organizing the project as carefully as a football coach works out a play. Each man had a certain job, to be done at exactly the right time.

When gathering horses to sell, we had a crew of five. Almost every day we had unpaid volunteers. Usually they were suspicious horse owners, out to see what we were up to—to check on our vision to see if it was 20/20, or whether maybe it should be doctored with a .30-30.

Brand inspection was pretty perfunctory. Much of it was done in a hotel room and a good drink of whiskey might make it *real* accurate. The inspector would say, "What do you have this time, boys?" Or he'd ride up to a corral at the shipping point and look over the top rail at the horses, veiled in a thick haze of dust.

We didn't use ropes much in the open country. The horses always ran in bands, and if you ever roped one, you would have that one only. When we got them into a good corral, we did lots of roping. We had to castrate stallions, brand colts, and throw some of them down to read brands. We usually team roped, horseback. Some were good ropers, others were especially good at, for example, making out dim brands, or separating unwanted horses.

If we had one hundred horses in a corral, very likely

---

[1] See Appendix C for boundaries of our horse-hunting area.

TAKING WILD DESERT HORSES TO MARKET

Shorty Hawkins (see page 273) in foreground. The horses were owned by Rankin Crow, son of Dave Crow (see page 120). Reub Long spent his early years in the midst of such scenes.

over half were our own horses. Perhaps thirty would belong to other horse owners and would be branded. These owners might or might not want to sell. Maybe ten would be truly wild horses, unbranded and unclaimed. Usually we couldn't get word to at least one owner. He might be in the penitentiary, or in California. We had to sort these horses out and turn them loose. It is rarely the case that a horse wants to leave a herd. It took skillful riding to get him headed for the gate, away from the bunch. The gate tender had to be fast. He had to have the gate wide open to let the racing horse through. But hard on his tail were all the other horses and the gate had to be slammed shut instantly.

On one occasion I'd picked up a good strong Swede who wanted a job. It didn't take long to find all the jobs he couldn't do. But after demonstration, I thought he could handle the gate. The horses were wild and milling. Finally we got one headed for the gate at full speed with ten others behind him, glimpsing freedom. As the big black ran through, I yelled, "Shut the gate, Swede!" He said, reasonably enough, "Vell, Mr. Long! Yust vait until I get my gloves on."

A fellow I was riding with and I jumped a bunch of horses out near Christmas Lake. Bill was riding a colt that wasn't well educated. At Hayes Mountain, I headed them, got them against a bluff, and stopped them. They were milling a little, not sure what to do, but, aided by the rock bluff, I was holding them all right.

Bill came in, late, mad at his colt, and fighting himself and the colt, too. When wild-horse hunters get in close enough to see the horses, they begin to pick out individuals and talk about them. I imagine elephant hunters do the same. In this bunch was a big brown saddle-marked horse that had had his tail pulled, showing that he was probably someone's saddle horse. Bill yelled to me, "I wonder who that big brown horse belongs to." He had to yell at the top of his voice. I could see his mad, hanging out all over

Courtesy Schmink Museum, Lakeview, Ore.

A TYPICAL FOUR-HORSE STAGE, 1890

The hotel was conducted by Mrs. M. McMillan. Nearly all passenger traffic came and went by stage. In more mountainous country, stages usually used six horses.

him, so I yelled back, "What *color* is he?" This, on top of the colt's actions, his failure in the enterprise, and maybe some things I didn't know about, was more than human flesh could stand. He shouted back, "Brown! You God-damned fool! Brown!"

When Jimmie Schroder was holding a herd, and I was bringing in more horses, he said he could tell how wild my bunch was as soon as I came in sight. He didn't look at the running horses—he looked at me. If I had my hat in my hand and my saddle blanket under my arm, he and others holding the herd would better get far back, because I'd need all possible room to get 'em into the bunch. But if I was just riding easy, they didn't need to take any precautions. My bunch was coming along agreeably.

I always rode with a loose saddle so my horse wasn't hindered by a tight cinch. In case of a *real* hard ride with lots of doubling, turning, and speed, the blanket might work loose. There was no time to stop and straighten it, so I just jerked it out and held it under my arm.

On these hard runs, always over bad terrain, with badger holes, lava pockets, and hidden rocks, I found it a good scheme to tuck the McCarty into my belt. Then if a horse fell down, or bucked me off, he wouldn't run off, leaving me to walk in. Blackfoot Indians used the same trick in running buffalo.

Every fall a few horses stayed out in the hills when the snow started. If we left them up there where the snow got deep, they died during the winter. It was thirty miles from Silver Lake to the Sycan River in the high timber. On this year snow was already two feet deep and crusted. When we hit the Sycan Marsh, it was a big white expanse. You couldn't tell about creeks or depressions—a white world where earth and sky blended into an invisible horizon.

In those days I read Robert Service a lot. I sat on my horse and thought of his lines:

Photo by Joe Van Wormer, Bend, Ore.

"A GOOD THROW, BUT MY PARDNER BEAT ME TO IT"

Were you ever out in the Great Alone,
When the moon was awful clear,
And the icy mountains hemmed you in
With a silence you most could hear?

And I thought of the phrase from Service, "Where the silent sky communed with the silent snow."

Our horses wouldn't go into the big swamp, afraid of what might be under the snow. So I walked and led my horse for seven or eight miles, and the other horses followed, seeing me ahead.

We got into the ZX headquarters at midnight. My overshoes were full of snow and the thermometer said zero. Albert Johnson of the ZX took us in and fed us. Jim Schroder, my pardner, and two others were with me.

We rode out the next day to gather up strays. I was running some horses across the swamp where the snow was too bright and white to see anything. My horse broke into a washout six or eight feet deep. I was thrown violently into the snow, which went down my neck, up my sleeves, and under my jacket, making me a part of the cold white landscape. The snow promptly melted; then, as my body heat was used up, my clothes froze stiff. I moved about like the ancient knights in iron suits, that is, when I could move, for when I got in that night I was frozen to the saddle.

The next day I had a high fever and was soon delirious. It seemed to be a case of sudden and advanced pneumonia. "Pewmony" as one of the men called it. Jim Schroder rigged up a sled, tied me on it, wrapped his horse's legs heavily with burlap sacks so the crust wouldn't do so much damage, and he pulled my sled by his saddle horn the thirty miles to Silver Lake.

My mother took care of me—we didn't have a doctor. When the fever broke, I was so weak that she had to lift my head to give me a sip of water.

That story is a tribute to a horse as much as to my pardner

Courtesy Lake County (Ore.) Chamber of Commerce

STARTING TO HAY ON THE ZX RANCH NEAR PAISLEY

These large ranchers hired men and their horses from desert ranches from miles around. Reub Long took hay contracts for many years

and my mother. Thirty miles through deep snow, pulling a load from saddle horn and carrying a man in the saddle —that's something lots of horses couldn't do.

This was Jim's favorite horse Jerry. When Jim was a boy, he worked for Bill Brown. One year the crew gathered an unbranded flaxen-maned two-year-old sorrel colt off of Jerry Mountain, in Crook County. The buckaroos gave the colt to Jim, who named it for the mountain. He grew to be a fine horse. His stamina was a legend, with many stories of the long hard runs he made after wild horses. When Jim and I dissolved partnership, he left Jerry with me. I took care of him until he died of old age. He was as good as they come.

Horses differ in stamina and spirit fully as much as humans do. Some give up as soon as things get tough. In a bad winter, under exactly the same circumstances, one horse will die—another will pull through.

Once, in the early summer, we left a saddle horse in the corral at the Bennie VanDorn ranch. My pardner thought he had told his younger brother to turn him out, so we rode off without a care. We were gone seventeen days. The horse was still alive, and was useful after a bit of re-cuperating. He had neither feed nor water all that time. Few horses would have lived. It's a matter of spirit. In similar cases, I've seen horses get lockjaw in three days; not tetanus, but paralysis of the muscles from lack of water and feed. I never saw this type of lockjaw except in a corral, usually when horses were turned in hot and sweaty. With horses worth less than ten dollars a head, we didn't have much experience with veterinarians, who lived 150 miles away.

I had the two best veterinarians in the world: Father Time and Mother Nature. A fair rule is: never try to doctor a horse if you don't know what's wrong. Mother Nature diagnoses and Father Time can usually cure him.

When horses appeared on the desert in tens of thousands, water became ever more important, because it's a long time between drinks out there. In some winters there are lakes, some of them alkaline. As the horse numbers increased, the feed around the infrequent water holes decreased, so that horses had to go farther and farther to find something to eat.

When traveling with freight teams or on horseback, we would aim to find water before dark, so we could give the horses their fill. We didn't normally carry any feed except grain, so we'd have to drink up, then hit the trail and pull away four or five miles to where feed was good. Then we could turn our horses loose to graze during the night, or hobble them. There isn't enough feed on the desert within the radius of a picket rope, so staking out is no good. A bronc hobble was carried by many riders, and sometimes by freighters. It was a strap with a buckle on one end, a ring in the middle, with a loose end strap on the other. With the loose end twisted around a front leg, run through the ring, then around the other leg, making a figure 8, it was a fast way to hobble a horse. Some riders used it to make their horses stand still while saddling.

Horses will go thirty miles from water and stay three or four days, even in the summer. A cow can't live that way —she can only get about ten miles from water, and that is why horses, for a long time, pretty well dominated the desert.

Early in my horse career, I decided I'd learn all I could about horses. In those days a Professor Barry had full-page ads in such literary magazines as the *Breeder's Gazette*. He recommended himself highly as the world's foremost authority on horses. I read his book carefully. He was an exponent of ingenious rigging and tackle. He led me through chapter after chapter on how to use rigging in breaking the horse, teaching him to lead, to stand while putting on the saddle, and how to accustom him to the saddle. After doing all of this, it said, "then you have your assistant ride him." I always liked that part.

So I led out my rigging-trained colt, tied him to the hitching rack, and brought out an old crooked-legged mule

I used to break colts to work. I hitched them together and tried to drive them. When they started to run, I couldn't remember what the book said. There wasn't any time to read it, so I had to let them run. I decided that I couldn't learn how to break horses by reading a book.

My truck with teachers was limited and I could forget almost as fast as they could teach. But I can praise one of them, an old fellow called Professor Experience. I was only ten when I was out riding near Fossil Lake, which had water in it at the time. Some of the men were bringing horses to the lake as a rendezvous point and it was my job to keep them from drinking so they'd hang around long enough to let the riders come in with some other groups, thereby consolidating several small bunches. But no horses came. It was warm, but not hot, a day strictly on the balmy side. Just staying there, completely inactive, gradually tired me out, so I badly needed sleep. I lay down in the shade of a big sagebrush, but I couldn't sleep because my horse crowded around, pulled on the reins, nosed me, or stepped across my feet.

I decided he was deliberately keeping me awake, so I got up and kicked him in the belly. He pulled away from me and left me to walk back ten miles to Christmas Lake. A young cowboy couldn't forget such things, no matter how hard he tried.

Near Sheep Rock is Pack Saddle Lake. We were camped there catching wild horses. As was often the case, we couldn't find any hotel right around there so we used a small pack string to carry beds, camp gear, and a limited food supply. I'd just bought a new saddle. During the night the fire seemed to suddenly flame up. I remembered there wasn't any wood close to it, so I jumped up to find my new saddle was burning. Also a pack outfit. My saddle had one side burned off. Only the packsaddle tree was left, with the rigging burned off. We cached the saddle tree in the rocks, hence the name Pack Saddle Lake.

Another time we were running wild horses in the Sheep

Photo by Joe Van Wormer, Bend, Ore.

A LAVA OUTCROP AT THE TOP OF A BUTTE, SAGEBRUSH BELOW

Nearly all girls and women on the desert help with the buckaroo jobs. Here, *left to right*, Eleanor (Mrs. R. A.) Long, R. A. Long, Dick Brown,
Bernie Brown, Dean Hollinshead, and Sharal Painter.

Rock country between Abert Lake and Christmas Lake desert. We had delivered a bunch to the buyer at Bend, who was shipping them to a horse-killing plant at Portland. We moved back to Wagontire. The outfit consisted of my pardner and me, four hired riders, and our saddle string, sixty horses.

We stopped at Wagontire to shoe our horses at Frank Dobkin's place. He was on the old Francis Hutton ranch, Linc Hutton's dad. We always carried extra shoes and shaped them on rocks, wagon tires, or anything hard and unyielding. Every man had to be able to shoe horses.

While the men were busy with horses and shoes, I went out to explore the water situation. Pack Saddle Lake was getting low, but it should have water for another week. I came back and told the crew there would be water enough for ourselves and horses. Two days later we put the camp on the pack horses, gathered in the riding bunch, and went to Sheep Rock.

The weather was hot, the other water holes had dried up, and Pack Saddle Lake was the only water for miles. Several hundred horses had gathered in and the lake had turned to mud—all the water had been used.

Here we were, thirty miles from water in unseasonably hot June weather; neither men nor horses had had water since early morning. I asked the men if they thought we should get out of there that night, or camp and try to take some wild horses with us as we went out next day. They said since we were there, we'd better try to catch a few horses in the morning.

We had twelve baby-size cans of condensed milk and I dealt them out—two cans to a man. Each understood that's all the drink he'd get for another whole day.

By the time it was light next morning, we'd had breakfast, were packed, and ready to go. We got about one hundred head of wild horses. We arrived at the Henry Hatch place at 6:00 P.M. that evening with our pack string, our saddle horses, and a herd of one hundred wild ones.

I don't remember that we suffered much. The horses we rode were thirsty and gant. We cut out the saddle horses and brought them to a well where Henry had a hand pump. We pumped steadily until midnight, taking turns, before we got our saddle horses watered. The wild bunch had to wait until next day. We took them on to Christmas Lake.

Henry Hatch had the Viewpoint Ranch. Today, on that ranch, you'll find irrigation pumps pouring out thousands of gallons a minute to water large fields of pasture and hay. The ranch is owned by a group of Californians and is managed by Frank Anderson and Dick Brown.

Horse Expressions I Grew Up With[2]

A way of describing a good rider: "He fit a bronc ride on a rough old pony."

Getting bucked off: "I reached for the saddle horn and got a handful of sand." Another is: "If the ground hadn't 'a' got in the way, I'd 'a' been goin' yet."

A poor rider: "He couldn't ride in a lumber wagon with his coattails nailed down."

"Once you get to chasing wild horses, you'll never be any good for anything else, ever."

Of camp food: "It's good enough, what there is of it, and there's plenty of it, such as it is." (Some old desert hand evidently told this to Will Rogers because he used it once to good effect.) "When it's smoken', it's cooken', an' when it's black it's done."

A man afraid of his horse: "He got up, hid behind the horn, and tried to steal a ride."

To describe a bucking horse: "He's frog walkin' "; or "he broke in two"; or "he come apart."

Of a poor stallion: "He'd better be barren than degenerate."

---

[2] For a list of terms used by professional horse buyers, see Appendix D.

"When a thoroughbred neighs, a hundred jackasses bray." (This is an old Persian saying, perhaps three thousand years old, showing that people and horses haven't changed much.)

Pete Gruber had a horse named Nash, one of the best cow-working horses I've ever seen. Pete was a good hand with a bullwhip. Nash showed uncanny intelligence in working cattle and the folks around claimed "when Nash and Pete get after a cow with a bullwhip, they can put her through a knothole in a board fence."

A man who says he was never bucked off is careless with the truth, or he's never ridden many horses.

Someone afraid to ride his horse in the early morning, would lead him for a time. The expression was, "I'll lead him 'til his hoofs sweat."

For a man in trouble: "He's footin' it alone on the hot sandy desert."

When I left a hired man I'd tell him, "You hold up the neckyoke, 'cause I'm pullin' on the stay chain."

"A big hat does not a cowboy make, nor fancy rig a hand."

GO SLOW AND GET THERE QUICKER

R. A. LONG

A CATTLE HERD ON AN ALL-DAY DRIVE DIVIDES INTO THREE parts: the lead, the herd, and the drag. You know those in the lead, you can't help but notice the drag because you try to keep them moving, but you don't look at the main herd.

It's the same in politics, or the Cattlemen's Association—everything. So if you crave to be noticed, and lack qualities for leading, get into the drag. People become famous that way.

I've learned, too, that three things pull a lot easier than they push—rope, people, and cattle. When driving a big bunch, a rider who knows the country will take a few ahead of the herd. They pull the other cattle along. The lead man always gauges the speed of the leaders, holding them back if necessary, so that he won't go off and leave the herd.

If moving across hilly country with a large herd, as soon as the lead cattle get to the top of a sharp divide, they will walk downhill faster than the rest of the herd can climb on the other side. The lead man, in such cases, has to hold the leaders back, or the herd will be cut up into several smaller herds.

The herd isn't home until the tail end gets there. There is art in getting the cattle to string on a drive; when riding the sides, crowd them closer in when coming back against the herd than when riding with them.

It takes two men to drive 50 head, three men can drive 200, and ten men can drive 10,000 if they are dry cattle and the country is right. With cows and calves, these figures are way off—it takes more men.

Cattle will drive much better into the wind than with it. I haven't any idea why this is true. It doesn't sound reasonable. It isn't true in a case of a blizzard. I am talking of a normal wind.

Whenever there is a hazard—a crossroad, a stream, a well-marked trail going down the wrong canyon—someone has to be there fast, so with a really big bunch a man has to be close to the lead to function at such places and keep the herd from straying.

Too many riders drive only the drag. If you whoop and yell and run at them, the tail end gets wider and wider; the cattle get mad, just like people when someone is pushing them around. If you go slow you get there quicker.

When separating cattle, a poor hand on an ill-mannered horse can be like a heel fly in a rodero. A good man with a good rodero manner, mounted on a good horse, is exceptional. A poor hand on a good horse gets into more trouble than one with a poor horse. (Don't get rodero mixed with rodeo.)

If you rode up to a rodero in the old days and wanted to talk to the boss, you would look for a man with an old slouch hat, worn chaps, much-used saddle, and he'd be on a good horse. The fellow with a fancy outfit was *not* the boss. The only exception to this in early Oregon was John Devine, the first permanent settler in Harney County. He always looked like a Spanish nobleman.

You notice things on the trail. There are little brown birds, smaller than blackbirds, that like to ride on the cows' backs. Maybe they eat flies that bother the cows, but anyhow the cows don't try to switch them off and you get the idea the cows like them. They usually come in pairs and often stay with a herd all day. We called them "cow birds." All the old-time cowboys said they were good luck

CATTLE DRIVE ON REUB LONG'S RANCH
Moving cows and calves to a different pasture west of Fort Rock

—if they stayed with you all day, the cattle would drive well. Similar maybe to the sailors' belief that an albatross brought good luck to a sailing vessel, making the favorable winds to blow.

When I was ten I saw one of the last of the big drives, with over ten thousand head. ZX was the biggest owner, but other cattle were from smaller outfits around Wagontire, Hampton Buttes, Silver Lake, and other places.[1]

I rode up on a high point with Sid Rogers to see this herd. He pointed out the long string, at least twelve miles of cattle, and said I had better take a good look—I might never see this sight again. Riders were there from every ranch for a hundred miles, just as they were in the 1880's. Participation by all the ranchers around was the rule for a few more years, but it was on its way out.

About this same time I remember a roundup with four cook wagons at Benjamin Lake. There were three cow wagons and a horse outfit. The cooks wondered how many men they were feeding, so they counted the dirty plates after breakfast one morning. There were eighty-one.

When the men lined up in the morning, it looked about like the corrals at the Pendleton Roundup. Over five hundred horses were in the caviattas of the four groups. The men and horses combined to produce a colorful, action-filled sight. Some of the things you'd see—all going on at once—included:

Bucking horses.

Loose horses that had jerked away, maybe trailing a riata.

Horses losing their saddles.

Riders reaching for the ground.

Cowboys hobbling mean horses so as to saddle them without getting a hoof in the middle of breakfast.

Riders dashing around to catch horses.

Cooks serving the nighthawks.

But you *wouldn't* see much hilarity. This was all business.

---

[1] In Appendix E are listed some of the other brands present.

Photo by Joe Van Wormer, Bend, Ore.

BRINGING UP THE DRAG ON A DESERT DRIVE

The drag sometimes takes more man power than the rest of the herd put together. A typical sagebrush scene. Reub Long at the left.

As soon as the horses got in from the night feed grounds, some miles away, a good roper, often the boss, would step into the corral (made of rope, if no pole corral was handy), and each rider in turn would tell him which horse to catch. They didn't allow everyone to go charging in with a rope. The roper picked his own mount last. He was quiet and businesslike. Some experienced horses, as they felt a rope, would walk right out to the owner. Others felt they had a reputation to maintain and would fight.

Sometimes a rider asked for a horse not well broken, or just spoiled. When this horse's turn came, the rider would tell the boss. When he caught the horse, two or three men would help to pull him out of the herd and sometimes a rider on a good roping horse would have to drag him out by the saddle horn.

No one with any experience walked up to a horse pulling on a tight rope and put a hand on him. Such a person could get a face full of hoofs. You always made the horse step up to slacken the rope before touching him.

A saddle-horse roper didn't swing his rope; he dabbed it on, or made an easy overhand throw. To swing a rope in a corral full of milling horses excited them and prolonged the whole business. This method of roping is not common now.

It was a beautiful sight to see a man who knew his business catch horse after horse with precision and knowledge, with no fuss or excitement.

There were always a few hangers-on; a homesteader with only one cow; fellows drifting by looking for a job, or people attracted by the commotion. After the regular riders all had their horses for the day, the hangers-on would rope their horses and leave. Anyone riding by was welcome to come in and eat, or to turn his horse into the cavvy for the grazing. If he didn't have a bed, knew the ropes, and wanted to help, he'd go out and night-hawk.

If the outfit was going to move that day, the rango would start to move stuff into the cook wagon. Each cowboy was expected to roll his bed and get it over by the wagon. Big outfits might have an extra wagon for the beds, but usually they went into the cook wagon. The wagons were never drawn by less than four horses or mules, often six. The boss would detail someone to get the cook-wagon team and get them harnessed and this man would stay until the wagon was ready to move out.

The first wagons I remember had only a fly stretching from the chuck box to keep the cook and his food out of the rain or snow. Later it was customary to have a tent. this kept the men out of a storm, but it was pretty sissy for the old-timers, something like wearing rubbers or carrying an umbrella.

The chuck box had a lid at the back of the wagon for working space. The lid was hinged at the bottom and had

Photo by Charles J. Belden, Pitchfork, Wyoming

THE OLD BUCKAROO DAYS HAVE NEARLY GONE, BUT HORSES ARE STILL
NEEDED BY ANY RANGE CATTLE OUTFIT
Chuck wagons drawn by horses are now mostly out of the range picture

a leg so the lid was let down part way until flat, forming
the only table the cook had for mixing dough, peeling
potatoes, or cutting bacon. An awkward person was described as "always getting between the chuck box lid and
the fire." The fire was always close to the chuck box lid
to save steps for the cook. Anyone who got in the cook's
way heard about it "rat now."

If the cook couldn't handle four or six horses, the boss
assigned one of the crew. Most of the good old-time cooks
could drive and liked to. I remember especially Jim Wake-
field and Ed Lundy. They were as proud of their driving
as they were of their cooking.

Sometimes they took a barrel of water on the shelf on
the side of the chuck wagon. If they overtook the crew,
they might serve a noon lunch, but when I first followed
the drive, this was unheard of. A cowboy wasn't supposed
to have any lunch—he rode right on through with no food
until the next stop.

The drive always started *real* early, usually about five
o'clock. That meant that the buckaroos had been busy
since 3:00 A.M. In the summer the sun was the clock—
everybody had the right time and everyone saved daylight.
They'd normally get to the next stop around one o'clock
in the afternoon. If the weather was hot, that would be
plenty long enough. If they did get in early, there were
always things to do: shoe horses, kill and butcher a beef,
tidy up the place if it needed it.

If butchering, the boss already had an animal picked,
perhaps a heifer calf nearly a year old, still sucking. He
would detail two riders to bring the calf into camp, telling them not to run or excite it. They would rope and hold
it while someone would fell it with a poleax, and cut its
throat just after it hit the ground. The cook would come
with sharp knives and a big pan to hold the heart, sweet-
breads, liver, brains, and, in case it was a young calf, the
mar gut.

With the animal down, the cook was the boss. Butchering

HOMEMADE WINDLASS FOR HANGING UP MEAT ON A
DESERT RANCH

The wheel gave enough leverage so that one man could raise a beef weighing
a thousand pounds. The stockade corral shown here was made with what
was at hand—no nails, the uprights bound with rawhide.

was amazingly neat and clean. A good cook wouldn't stand for carelessness. After skinning and quartering the animal, it was hung up to cool. It was wrapped in canvas during the day and hung in the open at night. This just simply was never neglected. If you miss once, the flies can get at it, or if left overnight in the canvas, it will sour. But when handled right, it stays good for a long time, even in hot weather. The dry air and cool nights of the desert made this possible. Meat won't keep that way in a humid climate.

One hour of drive in the morning was worth two in the afternoon. The cattle wanted to go then, and it was better to go with the cattle when they wanted to travel.

The rango rustled wood, built the fire, helped the cook load and unload, looked after the horses in the daytime, did the camp chores. I don't know whether "rango" comes from the Spanish word meaning "arrange," or whether it is from "wrangling." The "rango pan" was the big pan the riders put the dishes in; the cook *never* had to gather up the dirty dishes. If a man left his dishes where he ate, it was an unfailing sign that he was a tenderfoot.

Each rider had five to ten, sometimes more, even up to fourteen horses, and some riders had their own bell mare and neck mule. There were often some itinerant riders with their own horses. They would be traveling through and would stop where riding seemed to be going on.

The neck mule was important. The neck chain was a foot and a half long, with a wide strap on one end, a snap on the other. You buckle the strap around the mule's neck, and fasten the snap to the halter of the horse you want to stay with the bell mare. The strap gave the mule the advantage. He seemed fascinated by the bell. He would stay close to it and the horse he was fastened to couldn't do much about it. The horse couldn't make the mule go the other side of a tree or get tangled in any way. If the horse wouldn't come, the mule would kick him. So the mule trained the horse in jig time to stay with the bell mare.

The owners put in lots of time training the neck mule.

They treated him well, petted him, gave him things he liked, and gentled him so he could be caught. If he ever lost his fascination for the bell, he wasn't any use.

There wasn't too much to do night herding, so we looked at the stars, listened to coyotes, talked, or sang to the cattle. A little bird we called the sage thrush would sing occasionally with surpassing sweetness. We would listen for him and if he *did* sing, it lightened the weariness, refreshed us, and gave joy to the night. The pure, sweet notes that perfumed the night created wonder and peace.

The saddle animals for night herding were brought in after the evening meal when each rider caught his most trustworthy animal, his "nighthawk horse." Usually the guard was split. The first started about eight o'clock when the day herders came in. These guards rode until midnight, then called the second shift. Number of nighthawks depended upon the size of the herd. There were at least two, and larger herds had five or six. One member of the first shift went in ahead to wake up the second group. If only two, they weren't supposed to visit; they stayed on opposite sides of the herd.

When we night herded, we watched the Big Dipper to judge the time. It makes a complete circle around the North Star, so is as good as a clock, and in the desert you can nearly always see it. Total precipitation for the year of five to ten inches doesn't provide many cloudy days or nights.

On night herding you don't light a match to see the time of day, or light a cigarette. The sudden flare of a match *could* stampede a herd and make the whole crew spend days in rounding them up again. A stampede wasn't normal, but it could happen. So we avoided sudden movements or unusual sounds.

The herd was bedded down upon level ground, if possible, not far from camp. If stormy, we tried to find a place sheltered from the wind.

One man was *always* in charge of the nighthawks every night, usually one of the best men in the crew. In black nights, an inexperienced man could get lost and fail to find the herd.

The second guard stayed out until breakfast was over and the day riders had caught their horses and had come out to relieve them. Breakfast was at daylight. In the summer the cooks got up from 2:30 to 3:00 A.M.

Just because a man had been night herding was no sign he'd have it easier the next day. He did his usual work all day long. No portal-to-portal pay or double pay for overtime. Fringe benefits meant that on a slack day you might persuade another buckaroo to cut your hair.

On a few jobs they broke the night into three guards, but this didn't work well. The center shift were often cranky, because they had to get up twice.

The cowboys didn't have much extra time in the morning. It was claimed they could dress so fast because their socks went on from either end.

We carried a bed that cost around one hundred dollars and weighed close to one hundred pounds. A big tarp wrapped around it. The tarp was laid on the ground with enough left over to cover the bed in case of storm. A sort of quilted material served as a mattress. There were two blankets anyhow. The first riders who showed up with sleeping bags were looked at sideways and put down as dudes. It took a horse to carry a man's sleeping outfit. The modern sleeping bag costs twenty dollars, weighs far less than twenty pounds, is so small it can be tied on behind the saddle, and is more efficient than the old beds.

When the cowboy went to bed, he sat down on it; pulled off his boots; put them under the canvas, well back, so they would be dry if it stormed during the night. He then pulled off his pants and sometimes his shirt, and usually used them for a pillow. A few carried pillows, but they didn't pack well, and were not common. Wrapped inside the bed was a small sack with tobacco, a clean pair of socks, and a few things the owner wanted to keep clean and dry.

The tarp was usually made for the purpose, with snaps

and rings so the bed, for packing, would be only half a bed wide, would be snapped shut, and would roll well. In cold weather the cowboy would not unfasten this, sleeping inside, as with a bedroll. In warm weather he would throw the tarp back.

The last thing a cowboy took off at night was his hat. When he got up, the first thing he put on was his hat. Next he put on his shirt, if he didn't sleep in it. He put on his pants last, because he had to stand up to do that. He stayed in his warm nest as long as possible. With me, it became a lifelong habit and even now I put on my pants last. The pants, whether levis or something else, took quite a beating. Saddle, brush, wire fences, rocks, and everything in sight conspired against them. The desert provided few chairs or sofas. So, before getting into the saddle, the cowboy dusted off his seat. Charlie Russell, famous Western artist, never lost that habit. Whether in Westminster Castle, a wealthy publisher's home, or in a corral, he'd *always* dust the seat of his pants when he stood up.

The morning brought out traits not apparent at other times. Some cowboys were grouchy, some silent, some rather dopey until the hot coffee dashed the sleep away. Seth Dixon, of Fort Klamath, would always sit up in bed and, with others still asleep all around, he'd sing. When light first showed in the east and the birds began to cheep, Seth had to burst into joyous song, too. This didn't endear him to some of those with morning grouches, but he couldn't help it. He sang and I liked it. A man who greets each new day that way must have a fine nature inside.

When I was ten years old, I was the rango with the Silver Lake wagon. The ZX wagon on this roundup had a Chinese cook. The cook, of course, was the first one up, then the rango, who had to get the horses in. The Chinese would come to my bed, shake me and he'd always say, "Hey, klid! You glo lango!"

I remember that Halley's comet was the big news when I was eleven and was still rango for the Silver Lake wagon.

Courtesy Schmink Museum, Lakeview, Ore.

CATTLE DRIVE, 1927

Cattle do not look like this now. They are likely to be uniform, and most of them are of a true beef type

The papers were full of it and self-appointed astonomers predicted dismal events when the earth orbited through the fiery tail of the comet. We were to meet the ZX wagon at Benjamin Lake. Bert Wardwell of the ZX came and got me to ride with him to Benjamin Lake the day of the comet, to show him the best route. He came to tell the men the ZX wagon would be delayed. The tail of the comet didn't seem to do much damage out on the desert that day, but I kept wondering when something awful would happen. Something big and terrible and unexpected.

Drives could be with thousands, or with any number down to one animal. There were no trucks, so when you wanted one animal—or a thousand—someplace else, you drove them.

When cattle go to the spring range now, they cut out the weak ones, separate them into classes, cull out all that have shown weaknesses, and improve the quality of the herd. When I was young, they did their culling by leaving the bottom bar up and chasing the herd over it. Those that could jump it were ready to go out on the desert. A few years ago, there was a scientific meeting of Western cattlemen. A college professor was talking of how to cull a herd. An old-time Montana cattle owner commented, "Fer fifty years now I been lettin' the weather do my cullin'. I guess I'll jest let 'er go that way."

Oregon cowboys rode a center-fire saddle, used a riata at least fifty feet long. They used to dally in roping. If they used a hemp rope, it was always three-strand; a four-strand got dishraggy and wasn't so stout.

Cowboys were usually good at remembering terrain. If they got lost when out of sight of camp, they weren't much use to their outfit, so they noticed things, making maps in their minds. When two cowboys met and one tried to describe where he'd spotted a deer, or where a bunch of wild horses were grazing, or where a strange rider had been seen, both of them were soon off their horses. They smoothed off a place in the sand, drew in ridges and swales, and made a sand map. We called this "buckaroo geography."

Noticing things was so natural that illustrative stories grew up. The two new hands on a drive had been told that under no circumstances were they *ever* to change horses. When a man was assigned a horse, he kept that horse as long as he worked there.

Next morning they came to the trail boss, claiming they couldn't tell their horses apart. Busy, distracted, he had to say something, so snapped out, "One o' you dock his horse's tail." This seemed good, but when one rode up on a hill to chase out a couple of strays, they had a little time and each docked his horse. The boss said to roach a mane. Both roached. In desperation, the trail boss told them, "Fer God's

Courtesy Oregon Historical Society

AN OLD-TIME BRANDING SCENE IN EASTERN OREGON
Juniper and sagebrush in the background. Well trained horses keep the ropes taut. Most branding is now done in cattle chutes.

sake, measure 'em!'" Sure enough, the black gelding was a hand and a half taller than the white mare.

When you started on a drive, whether big or little, you never knew what would happen, except that it would be unusual. We started to Fort Klamath driving a bunch of steers sold to Luke Walker. We left from Sink of Peters Creek and were on the road for several days without much sleep. When we got to Wocus Bay on Klamath Marsh, we found a long peninsula that ran out into the marsh with only a narrow neck of solid ground. We put the cattle out on this peninsula and I volunteered to take the guard alone.

I thought I could build a fire on the neck, doze along, and everyone would get needed sleep. I pulled off the saddle, left it at camp, rode out bareback, hobbled my horse, built a fire, and settled down. These were desert cattle; they didn't lie down a second all night. The marsh, the unaccustomed night noises of the birds, the smell of rank and rotting vegetation—these made them suspicious and restless. I chased them back and forth all night long, bareback. Aside from the obvious effect, my pride hurt, too.

When I was a boy, wild cattle were on the desert. They were smart, knew the country, and escaped the riders at roundup. Some did that, year after year, steadily getting wilder. One renowned steer was the last of the notorious wild ones. Such an animal is a menace and costs the cattlemen plenty of money. One truly wild animal will train the others to hide, will break up herds, causing them to scatter, and will become an all-around nuisance.

This particular steer was light red, branded with a Q on the right ribs. He belonged to the Hacklemans on Hampton Buttes, but ran loose for fourteen years. Every cowboy for fifty miles around knew about him. They had tried roping, running, corraling, shooting—everything they knew, and he outsmarted them.

Bill Kittredge and Charlie Pitcher came to our place to stay and ride for cattle one fall. Age eight, I asked them

Photo by Jones Studio, Lakeview, Ore.

BRANDING IRONS COLLECTED BY REUB LONG

Owners are customarily proud of their brands and pass them on from generation to generation. Brands are somewhat akin to coats of arms and are guarded jealously. The picture was taken on the R. A. Long ranch.

if I could go. They said I could if father was willing, and he let me go.

We rode into the Lost Forest country and started to gather cattle. Bill was riding about four miles from the herd when he jumped the big wild steer. He brought the steer into the herd that Charlie Pitcher was driving, with me as helper. We did something not accomplished before. We stopped the steer and held him with the others. We drove to a point near Mound Spring. The steer was getting restless, feeling a touch of claustrophobia.

Bill and Charlie figured they couldn't keep him in the herd much longer. We put the cattle into a natural corral with steep sand dunes on three sides. Charlie watched the entrance. I rode around on top. We didn't have a gun, so Bill rode seven miles to the Green homestead. He came back with a borrowed .30-30, went to the top of the dune, where he could see the renegade, and shot him five times. At the first shot the steer tried to charge, though mortally wounded. He couldn't make much headway up the steep dune.

He had tremendous horns, was built like a buffalo, tapering from a big front to a peaked back end. Bill and Charlie butchered him and gave the meat to homesteaders. We found several bullets in his hide and meat, evidence of past failures to stop him. He was built for speed, rather than meat. We guessed he'd weigh 1,400 pounds.

Similar wild cattle have been found in the Steens Mountain country, some weighing far more than this Q-brand steer, but I doubt if any were so old.

When the range was dotted with homestead shacks, the operations of the large owners got complicated. They looked with suspicion on everyone who lived on the desert, especially if a herd tallied up short on calves. I had a big old cow that gave lots of milk and I put two orphan calves on her, plus her own. One year the ZX had a tough new boss. He came by our place, saw the three calves and called to me,

"What's that cow doing with three calves?" I called back, "She had five, but some S.O.B. stole two." This was the right answer; he rode on.

A Few Things I've Noticed

A big bunch of cows and calves will be lying down after grazing. All at once, as though an alarm had gone off, all the cows will get up and leave for water—all except one. She stays to look after the little calves. I'd like to know how they decide which one is to stay. Maybe she doesn't even have a calf. Perhaps they pay her for baby-sitting.

Two bulls fighting is a right interesting sight, but don't get too close and get in their way. You are just like a sagebrush to them, and they'll run into you without even seeing you. Once I saw a whipped bull run right over a man on a horse.

There are a lot more boys working cows than there are cowboys.

In driving cattle, it's little things not seen by the untrained eye that make the difference between a good and a poor hand. A man's eye takes in only what he knows something about. One who knows nothing about horses will pass one and he knows only that he passed a horse. A good horseman can talk steadily for ten minutes about the same horse that he only glanced at in passing.

Cowboys use the word "work" differently, somewhat as loggers use "buck." Cowboys say, "The boss wants us to work the steers in the north pasture," or "That's a real good workin' horse."

Riatas and Hair Ropes

The remainder of this chapter is written from an interview with my brother-in-law, Leston Linebaugh, rancher of Silver Lake. He is doing the talking now.

"I learned how to make a riata from Charles Ward, buckaroo for Pete French over east in Harney County. We both worked for the ZX in 1907. He made riatas for the whole crew of riders, using only what was at hand. Nowadays they have tools for fleshing and for leather working, but Ward had only his knife. I was just a kid, but I could see that this sort of knowledge would be a handy thing, so he taught me while he was making riatas for the six or eight men in the crew at the White House.

"In those days it was beneath the dignity of a buckaroo to pitch hay or do much of anything not connected with riding. The ZX had a big ranch crew to put up the hay and haul and feed it.

"Ward came here from Warner Valley and was about thirty-five at the time.

"He picked his hide carefully. He wanted an old, thin cow, not an animal such as you'd butcher for beef. The hide from a nice fat animal is not nearly so good for this purpose as that from a thin cow. A hide of solid color is far better than that from a spotted cow. If a hide varies too much in thickness, the strings must be spliced, slow and tedious work.

"He threw the hide in the creek to soften, then spread it out and cut off the corners. Then he cut out one long string, going round and round the hide. He'd get a string about sixty-five feet long and one inch wide. This had the hair still on. In cutting, he avoided the brand.

"He stretched this on the posts of the corral fence, pulling it up tight to dry. He took the hair off with a mower section held straight up to get a scraping rather than a cutting action. This worked better than a knife. Cutting hair is hard on a knife edge, and a man can cut the hide easily if the knife is sharp. It's better to have the long string to work with.

"The string is resoaked and the mower section is used

again to cut off all flesh or fat. He drove the section into a two-by-four with a notch cut in it and scraped off all tallow and flesh.

"The long string is now ready to cut into smaller strings used for the riata. There are machines now, but Ward sawed a notch in a board or plank to hold the edge straight and firm, and drew the long string against a knife held straight up. This cut a small string with a sloping edge. The edge had to be cut straight afterward.

"I always used four of these strands for braiding in order to get a perfectly round riata. If the braiding is done with strings too wet, the riata will be loose when dry. You can't braid it at all if too dry. It's like trying to braid four pieces of wood. You aren't likely to finish a riata the day you start, so wrap in a damp gunnysack overnight.

"Stand up when you braid. Ward taught me how to wrap the strands over my hand so, as more length is needed, they will always pull from the center. Otherwise, you have these long strands that will get all tangled up as you work.

"You must keep the same tension on the strands all the time and you must keep the grain side out. It's better to cut all four strands from the same hide. For a fifty-foot rope have the strings seventy-five feet long, because the braiding takes up about a third of the length.

"Use a dish with soap worked into a paste and keep the strings soaped a foot or two ahead of your work. Ordinary soap, such as Ivory, is all right, but I nearly always used Fels-Naptha. If the strings get too dry, wrap in a damp gunnysack.

"Pull the strings with one hand, braid with the other. If the tension is uneven, the rope will always twist and it will never work right.

"Sometimes you see a riata made of six or eight strands, but neither makes a perfectly round rope.

"When the riata is finished and dried, it must be pounded with a wooden mallet. Some make holes in a stationary beam, then thread the end of the rope through one hole and back through another. By pulling hard, the riata can be pulled through these holes, but it takes more than one man for this job, for the tension must be kept even.

"Perhaps a man *could* make a riata in one day, but buckaroos usually took a week, working only in the evenings. The riata is never treated with oil, wax, or preparation of any kind, but if it should get too limber, rub it well with beef liver.

"A good riata usually costs at least $1.00 a foot, whereas one can buy nylon rope for around ten cents. A buckaroo of my time carried his own riata with him.

"A hondu must be put in the end to start the loop. Metal centers for the hondus can be bought, or a man can roll or braid his own. The rope *must* run through the hondu freely, or you miss too many throws, so homemade hondus were used by the real cowboys who carried a rope to use.

"The length of life of a riata depends upon the user, short of some accident, such as work of a porcupine. When dallied, the riata must be allowed to slip a little, never let it have a hard, sharp, dead jerk.

"A riata is easier on the hands than hemp or nylon. It has lots more life. It is especially good for heeling. A working cowboy is going to be out there in snow or rain. A wet hemp rope dries stiff. But after a lot of using, it gets dishraggy. These are some of the reasons why a regular cowboy used a riata. Besides, he could make it himself, to his own liking.

Hair Rope

"A hair rope is *always* twisted, never braided. It takes two men to make a twisted rope. One man feeds the small strands to another man, who twists them. The hair is pulled out and straightened, then twisted to the right into three small strands. These are then twisted together to the left. Hair of different color may be used to get a two-tone effect.

"These hair ropes are used universally for a McCarty. They are used for reins with a hackamore and are not designed for strength. They are rarely used for tying up, just for leading or reining. Homemade hair cinches are also used.

"The hair is from the mane of a yearling colt or from a cow's tail. Horsetail hair is too harsh and stickery."

BRONC RIDES ON THE HIGH DESERT

R. A. LONG

The Dave Crow Ride

WHEN A DISGRUNTLED HOMESTEADER SHOT AND KILLED Pete French,[1] as the other P Ranch buckaroos watched, all of them unarmed, one of the crew, Dave Crow, took it upon himself to wire Pete's relatives. The nearest wire was at Winnemucca, Nevada, over two hundred miles away. Scene of the killing was near Malheur Lake in Harney County.

The crew had been about to drive a herd of marketable cattle to Winnemucca, so were dressed for traveling in winter weather. The date was December 26, 1897, the time 2:00 P.M. Dave rode from near the Sod House ranch to headquarters at Frenchglen and changed horses. From there he headed for Roaring Springs where he changed horses again. At the Spangleburgen ranch he slept for two and a half hours, then galloped on through Long Valley and on to Fields, where Charlie Fields made him eat some hot chili beans while Fields' own horse was caught and saddled. At Colony he met Melvin Doan, Sam Hall, and Bill Goar and changed horses with Melvin Doan.

He swapped horses again at Denio, on the Nevada-Oregon border, and changed five more times as he galloped on to

---

[1] Some of the facts are taken from *Pete French, Cattle King,* by Elizabeth Lambert Wood. (Portland, Ore.: Binfords & Mort, Publishers, 1959.)

Courtesy Schmink Museum, Lakeview, Ore.

GROUP OF BUCKAROOS IN PAISLEY, OREGON, BEFORE 1920
They rarely wear vests any more. Note the riatas, hackamores, spade bits—all largely out of use now

Winnemucca, pausing at each change only long enough to drink hot coffee.

One horse bucked and he couldn't make much progress. At Denio he got a horse from Ed Bell and rode to Quinn River. There, he said, "I rode into a stable and in the dark stepped off my horse onto an old sow. She had little pigs and I found the manger in a hurry. From there I went to Sod House, Nevada, and again slept two and a half hours. Took a fresh horse and went to Paradise Hill. Here the only horse was an Indian pony on a horse power water pump. I took him, the toughest of all I'd ridden. He took me into Winnemucca at 2:00 P.M., just 48 hours after Pete's death." He was in the saddle over forty hours in cold weather, bearing a burden of horrible news.

There were no highways, so no one knows his exact route or mileage. But he stuck to it, and sent his wire that signaled the end of the one-man cattle empires in Oregon.

Not many men can ride night and day with so little rest. He made no records, either distance or speed, but his perseverence and sense of responsibility command respect.

No one on the way questioned his right, while on such an errand, to take the best horse on the place.

There are several relatives of Dave Crow still around.

Charlie Couch Sat His Horse Well

Charlie was range boss for the Horseshoe-bar outfit, owned by famous Bill Brown. He and his men had some horses under guard at Langdon Springs. He came to our house to ask Mother to make some sandwiches to take to the men.

Mother made the sandwiches and put them in a wide, shallow pan, used to put milk in to let the cream rise. She put a dishcloth around it and drew the four corners together to make a handle for easy carrying.

Charlie was riding a big, fine-looking, bald-faced roan,

a "savina" horse.[2] The land sloped down sharply from our house. Charlie got on and Dad handed him the big pan of sandwiches. This apparently wasn't in the horse's contract. He had a steep downhill shot, and no rodeo will ever show a better bucking job. Charlie sat there with the pan held well out, rode with apparent ease, and never lost a sandwich.

He Rode Red Ears for a Pint

While I was in the second grade, Dad Kittredge had a white horse known all over the desert as "Red Ears," and hard to ride. Some Silver Lake boys bet Charlie Jefferies

[2] I am not sure how this is spelled or where the word came from, but it was in common use on the desert and meant a bald-faced, red roan with white stockings and sometimes a pinto spot on the side or belly. Perhaps it is a corruption of a Spanish word.

GEORGE MENKENMAIER
A Fort Rock boy who became a world-champion rider. Here shown on "Blue Dog" at a rodeo at Redmond, Oregon, in 1957.

a pint of whiskey that he couldn't ride Red Ears and take a drink at the same time. Charlie was pretty good at both these things, but not together.

He rode the horse, drank the whiskey, and vastly impressed an eight-year-old boy. I have never seen better riding anywhere.

Boss Richardson Gets Himself a Job

Boss rode into the ZX wanting a job as a bronc buster. He didn't look like one; his saddle horn was bare, the stitching gone from the cantle, the stirrup leathers tied with broken string. He looked like a rank tenderfoot, and the boys gathered around to help him up after he hit the ground. They led out a horse famous locally—the worst bucker in the caviatta.

Richardson stepped on, the horse broke in two and lived up to his rep. Boss pawed him from shoulder to saddle skirts, looked back at the boys, grinning delightedly, and scarcely even glanced at the horse. That kind of riding is far harder than the rodeo kind, where, at the allotted time, two others ride up and lift the man off. This horse kept on until he didn't have any more in him and Boss just sat on him nonchalantly.

A Boy Twelve Years Old Can Ride All Right

The Foster ranch on Summer Lake was over fifty miles from Cabin Lake to the north. Guy Foster, twelve years old, had to make a quick ride to Cabin Lake to get his grandfather when his grandmother at Summer Lake became alarmingly sick.

He rode to the Hays Ranch near Silver Lake, changed horses, rode on to Cabin Lake. He and the grandfather came back and Guy picked up his horse at the Hays' place.

They arrived the next day, but this made a ride of over one hundred miles for a twelve-year-old boy. As this is written, he is still alive, an old man now. It didn't seem to hurt him any. Child labor of this kind wasn't regarded as particularly noteworthy. I don't remember that anyone cried about it.

Boys Grow Up Fast on the Desert

The first time I went to Diamond Lake to start my dude wrangling work, Holly Schroder, eleven, went with me to help drive twenty-five horses from Silver Lake to Diamond Lake, about eighty miles. They were gentle and fit for dude hire. In a few days, Holly had to go home to Silver Lake.

In early morning I started him on a big black hotblood HF mare, raised by Holly Swingle. He missed the road and went out of his way twenty miles. This made it a

GEORGE AS A BOY NEAR FORT ROCK
He was eight years old. He started riding young, as do most desert youngsters

hundred-mile ride. He got home before dark the same day with no apparent damage, physical or in spirit, to either boy or horse.

The army used to require its cavalry officers to ride fifty miles a day occasionally.

Ed O'Farrell's Christmas Ride

The scene was in a dance hall above a store in Silver Lake. The time was Christmas Eve, 1894. A big Christmas party was going on, complete with dazzling tree, community program, good things to eat, and a general spirit of happy excitement.

Some planks had been placed for seats on upended chunks of wood for a heating stove, and two hundred people— nearly everyone in town and the nearby country—were present. A man stood up to go out, and finding his way barred, he walked along one of the teetering, unsteady planks, thus putting his head two feet higher than normal. Watching his footing, he bumped his head on a huge lamp that swung violently. Kerosene sloshed out.

The lamp was bathed in flame. Francis Chrisman, owner of the building, rushed forward, and did a heroic thing. He unfastened the wires and started for the rear door, bearing the wildly flaming lamp. But spectators fatally got into the act. They batted at the flames and knocked the lamp from Chrisman's hands. It rolled on the floor, leaving a trail of hot fire. In a moment the floor, walls, and ceiling were a mass of roaring flame.

Some tried to get out the door. Folks below, seeing the smoke, tried to reach their children inside. Door and stairway were soon jammed. Warren Duncan kicked out a window at the other end of the hall, coolly helping women and children through the window to a porch roof that soon collapsed. There were other heroes, especially Gus Schroder and Bill Chrisman.

But 16 women, 16 children, and 8 men failed to get out,

and were burned beyond all recognition. Over forty who did get out had terrible burns. There were not enough unharmed persons in Silver Lake to attend the wounded and bury the dead.

Ed O'Farrell became the man of the hour. Long before it was known who or how many had been killed, he was on his way, horseback, riding for all he was worth to get Doctor Daly at Lakeview, one hundred miles away. It was a snowy winter, the middle of night, country roads were snowed in, and snow was four feet deep on the summits. The temperature was twenty below zero.

He got to Lakeview at 4:00 P.M. Christmas afternoon.

There is a sequel. Within an hour Doc Daly had gathered supplies and was on his way with Willard Duncan, in a buggy with the best team in town, called Tom and Jerry. They got fresh teams at Paisley and Summer Lake, where O'Farrell had stopped and alerted someone to have them ready. They stopped for neither rest nor food. A swift ride in a buggy through deep snow in twenty-below-zero weather is not easy to take.

They pulled into Silver Lake at 6:00 A.M. A saloon had been converted into an emergency hospital. Cowboys from ranches nearby were nurses. Housewives brought in all the sheets and pillowcases they owned. These were torn into strips for bandages.

Dr. Daly saved all but three of the badly burned persons, and his methods of healing were later published in detail in a medical journal.

A death list of forty-three in a little town is a ghastly tragedy. No family was left whole. It made mental scars that lasted through life. But some, as Ed O'Farrell, found new stature, and all who came through it with few injuries gave unselfishly of their time and goods for many weeks.

Sumner Houston's Ride from Bend to The Dalles

In 1923, The Dalles had a big celebration. For publicity

they hit upon the idea of a nonstop ride from Bend, 169 miles away, as the route was laid out. Prizes were in actual gold—$700 for first prize, $350 for second, and $150 for third.

Final entrants included Jimmie Taylor, Larry Baxter, Roy Gray, and the brothers, Sumner and Frank Houston.

Sumner got in an hour ahead of the next rider. He made the 169 miles in 10 hours and 22 minutes, leaving Bend at 5:20 A.M. and arriving to claim the $700 prize at 3:42 P.M. This is roughly 16 1/3 miles an hour, or a mile every three minutes and forty seconds. He rode seven horses.

Sumner was most proud of the fact that not a horse limped, nor did he use a quirt or draw blood with spurs. He was a little tired from holding the reins with one hand for over ten hours (he lost a hand in a mowing machine accident in his youth), but was none the worse. He started with a coat and chaps, but discarded them as useless weight.

People kept running out and offering him coffee, pie, sandwiches, and even whiskey, but aside from a candy bar, he didn't accept food and only took a few swallows of water, not wanting any possibility of stomach ache.

This ride is the best record I happen to know of for a distance that great. The pony express schedule called for almost exactly two hundred miles with a day of twenty-four hours, but relay stations were only about ten miles apart. Buffalo Bill, famous rider of his day, said, "Fifteen miles an hour on horseback will shake any man all to pieces."[3] To keep it up for over ten hours was a great tribute to Sumner and to the other riders who finished.

[3] J. Frank Dobie, *The Mustangs* (Boston: Little, Brown & Company, 1952).

ALL IN THE DAY'S WORK

R. A. LONG

I HAD A CRANKY LITTLE BLACK BALD-FACED STOCKING-legged horse called Peanuts that might stampede if you roped anything. At Langdon Springs I found a cow with a face full of porcupine quills. I tried to cut her out and take her to a corral; she ran, and as I started to follow, Peanut's feet hit a slick place on the alkali bank and he fell. When he got up, my right spur caught in my coiled riata. I had split reins and that saved me, because as he kicked at me, I was able to jerk him around. This little game went on for some time, until I jerked the riata strap loose from the saddle.

When I got back on, I decided to rope the cow and teach her good manners, so I tied my rope to the horn. I usually dallied. When I caught her on the dead run she went one way, Peanuts the other. When she came to the end of the rope, I expected Peanuts to be jerked down so I was getting ready to leave him, but the cow went down instead.

In the process I ended behind the saddle with Peanuts bucking. I stepped off on the left side. I landed all right, but things were moving with speed and I hit wrong and broke my instep. I took off the boot, the foot looked about the right shape, color, and size, so I put the boot back on. I hobbled around, turned the cow loose.

By then the foot was hurting in earnest, so I tried to take the boot off and had to work hard to do it. I tied it to the saddle and rode to camp, five miles. It was a solitary camp. I made a bad mistake then, for I turned the horse loose.

That was Saturday morning. No one came by until Monday noon. The foot turned black and blue. I kept it in hot water, but I had to go down a hill one hundred feet to get water, and had to keep a fire going. I remembered a child's wagon by the house, so I put my knee on that and pushed it with the other foot to haul the water and get wood. While boiling water for fifty hours, lots of water will boil away, and lots of wood will be needed.

Leston Linebaugh, my brother-in-law, came by on Monday and took me to Silver Lake.

I had another experience with Peanuts the summer I was nineteen. We took 150 yearling heifers to the desert. I dug a shallow well north of Christmas Lake. I had to pull up water in a bucket and dump it into a trough. A lot of water goes through 150 animals in the summer, so I worked steadily pulling up water and dumping it into a trough. But when snow came, the animals weren't tied down to the well any more and they scattered. It took me weeks to find all of them, two or three here and there for fifty miles around.

I was camped at Rock Springs, seven to eight miles north of Lost Forest. I was reduced to flour with no yeast. You'd be amazed how good dough gods taste if you have nothing else.

I took the cattle from a catch field at Mound Spring and moved to Christmas Lake the day before Thanksgiving, arriving late in the afternoon. I had two horses, riding one and packing the other, both pretty jaded. I caught Peanuts, young then and only partly broken, and turned out the other two. I gathered some other cattle we had around Christmas Lake, threw them in with what I had, and started for Silver Lake that same evening. They drove well, for I had some old cows that knew the route. That night it dropped to thirty degrees below. I had to get to

Silver Lake because there was to be a big dance Thanksgiving night.

I had a terrible time keeping from freezing because Peanuts wouldn't lead. I wanted to build a fire, but he'd try to jerk away every time I lit a match. I taught him to go ahead of me that night. I kept him for years, and until he died he'd walk ahead just fine. I arrived in plenty of time for the dance.

Ed Duffey, working for Kilgores, hauling hay to Walker cabin from Silver Lake with six horses and two wagons, froze his feet that night.

A story tells of the man describing how he was chased by a lion in the Sahara desert, and as he could feel the lion's hot breath on his neck, he saved his life by climbing a tree. A listener objected, "There aren't any trees in the Sahara desert." The storyteller said with dignity and finality, "By God! There *had* to be a tree!"

So in this case, Peanuts wouldn't lead, I'd freeze if I rode, so I *had* to teach him to go ahead.

The spring I was eighteen I broke my wrist. I was running wild horses and finished the summer with my arm lashed to my chest.

I wrangled dudes all one summer with a crutch strapped to my saddle. This was up in the Cascade Mountains where no doctor had located an office. That fall I hunted up a doctor in Bend, and after an X ray, he said I'd broken my kneecap.

In 1902 a horse fell with my brother and broke Everett's leg. A group of students happened to be at Fossil Lake gathering bones of bygone creatures. One of the students was in training for medical school. He set Everett's leg, even though it was a bad break. This saved a hundred-mile trip to a doctor, cost nothing at all, and was the start of a successful medical career. Hardly ever anything works out to benefit everyone in on the deal, as this did.

Incidentally, they hauled away a four-horse wagonload

of fossils from Fossil Lake. I think they went to the Smith-sonian Institution.

One year we had some cattle up in the Bear Flat draws, in the mountains west of Silver Lake. Another man and I hunted out these draws and found three cows and their calves. We got them halfway down, near Ross Springs. The cattle should have been out long ago, because there was a heavy fall of snow. If we hadn't found them, they would have died before spring.

We took turns breaking trail through the snow, the other following with the cows and calves. Night dropped, so we made a fire. A branch from a big pine tree hung down over the fire. I put my wet overshoes on the branch to dry. I dozed off under the tree and an overshoe fell into the fire and burned up. Riding in the cold all the next day with no overshoe left me with a foot badly frostbitten. It aches even now when the weather drops below zero.

Feet are the most important thing in the cold. You want lots of room. You see elk hunters in the mountains hunting in snow and cold with a new pair of high leather boots, laced up tightly. That doesn't work at all, and if these people have to spend the night out, they sometimes lose one or both feet. Two pairs of socks and a rubber overshoe are far more practicable footwear. "German socks" aren't sold much any more in Oregon. These were heavy wool, about like felt. Worn with thin socks inside, and some heavy rubbers over the German socks, they were fine for cold winter weather. Or heavy rubber overshoes over the socks work well, with another pair of socks over the boots. If a man is caught out without overshoes he *can* keep his feet from freezing by wrapping them in gunny sacks.

An expression in our country in the fall is: "Gettin' pretty near time for socks and underwear." I tell that to the hunters that come by in the fall when they seem to be shivering a little. Then I go on, in a reflective mood, "I had a pair of socks once, but the way a man will, I got careless, and one night I stood 'em up side of the bed. Something startled me along toward morning and I jumped out and landed right on the socks. They broke all to pieces."

I bought a fairly large ranch called "the Harrison place." It had a full supply of buildings, for it had been a going ranch for a long time. Then it was vacant and the rats moved in and had a wonderful existence, gnawing into all the buildings and finding unexpected delicacies, such as flour bins, grain hay, leftover seed grain, mattresses stuffed with cotton. I tried poisoning, shooting, trapping—all the things I knew about. The rats outsmarted me on every turn. I killed some but little rats appeared faster than I could kill the big ones.

A neighbor told me that if you caught a full-grown rat, didn't injure him, but whitewashed him and turned him loose, all the rats would think he was a ghost and they'd all leave. That didn't seem to be the sort of thing a person could believe with all his heart, but the remedy was cheap and I was desperate.

So I caught a nice big rat, fat and fierce, and the party began. At that point, several technical points arose. There was no college bulletin on the subject. There we were, out in the middle of the road, quite a group. I was holding the rat, head and heels, there were two hired hands, the neighbor who told me of the remedy, his hired hands, and a couple of other amateur rat specialists. We'd gone to the road to get away from the rat holes in case the rat should jerk loose. No one used the road ordinarily.

I was down on my knees holding him. Such questions came up as whether the whitewash should go on with the grain of the hair, thereby getting a smooth, slick job, or whether against the grain, thereby being more thorough, but leaving him rough and unattractive. Should we let the whitewash dry before turning him loose? Should we mix white of egg, flour paste, or anything in the whitewash to make it sticky? We were acting like scientists making a whole new division of science out of what started as a simple proposition.

A big red car rolled up to our tightly absorbed little group. The driver stuck his head out the window and, not able to see, asked "What in hell is going on here?" I said, carelessly, "Oh! We're just whitewashing a rat." He said incredulously, "You're what?" I said, as though it was an everyday occurrence and I was a little impatient with him, "Just whitewashing a rat."

He said nothing more, and a moment later when I looked up to see what had become of him, his car was just a speck on the distant horizon.

Another time a dapper stranger stopped at the Fort Rock store where I happened to be. He found I was a native and he made no attempt to disguise his contempt for the country—its drab gray color, the wind, sand, and sagebrush, and the *total* lack of rain.

After a time he took another serious look at me, just couldn't stand it any longer, and said, "Do you mean to tell me you actually *live* here?"

I said, "Yes, I live here."

Man: But do you just stay right here all the time?

I: Yes, my business is here, so I stay here.

Man: But how can you *stand* it? Don't you ever want to see what some other place is like? Don't you want to travel?

I: Travel? Why, I'm already here.

I don't lie to people exactly, but it's fun to baffle them. Some of my stories are sort of based upon local events.

In late years I've had a lot of company. One day the chambers of commerce of Bend and Lakeview had a joint meeting. My ranch was the site, for it isn't far from half-way. The Bend group arrived first. I have a large collection of Indian artifacts, so I got that out and we spent an hour looking at all of the stone utensils used hundreds of years ago. I have a few other evidences of past centuries, including a couple of skulls of mountain sheep, common here before white men arrived. The Bend businessmen looked at these with interest.

One said, "Notice how thick the skull structure is between the horns and over the eyes. I suppose that is to enable them to fight, the way I've heard they did, without injuring themselves."

So I told him, "Yes, that is part of the reason. But those thick skulls are on the females, too, and they don't fight. The sheep grazed on mountainsides, too steep and rough for other animals. Often a mountain ledge will follow along for hundreds of feet, then pinch out. That is where the sheep fed. When they got into such a deal, they couldn't back up without stepping off the ledge. These thick skulls saved them. They'd calmly hurl themselves off the ledge, head down, and they could land on the rocks below without harm."

One man had to be sure. He said, "Were you ever so fortunate as to see this yourself, Mr. Long?"

I said, "I almost did once. I saw one feeding on just such a ledge. While I watched he cast himself off. I didn't get to see him land because when he was halfway down, he saw me and turned right around and went back."

These stories have created conversation and have built a questionable reputation of sorts. Con O'Connell lived at Paisley. He said, "I'm a-comin' to belave hahlf the dom lies they tell about Reub Long is true."

Right now cattle are more important to my income than horses. Cattle have no support price, as wheat does, so the price skitters about like a drop of water on a hot stove. A man's success in any one year can depend as much upon the particular day he sells as it does upon his production methods. The two things can combine with weather to make him rich or poor. I am not sure how much difference it makes, though. A bad drought may be in full swing; the poor cows won't give much milk so calves are poor; many calves die; many cows don't conceive, so the owner doesn't have much to sell, and he gets very little for what he does sell; he hasn't enough feed for winter and must buy hay in a runaway hay market; he sits with his head in his hand, wondering how he can hold his outfit together for another year that may be worse; he mutters, "Oh, what a headache!"

But if he can hold on, a year will come when it rains; all the cows have calves and they are big and fat and bring a high price; he has hay to sell, and plenty of extra feed; he takes his cattle to market, gets lots of money, pays off all his debts; has money left, so he asks neighbors in to share his good fortune at an all-night party. The next morning he sits with his head in his hands and mutters, "Oh, what a headache!"

In this desert country funny things happen that make endless entertainment—provided you aren't too wrapped up in your own business to see and hear. In a California county just south of the Oregon border, the district judge had unquestioned legal ability. But the demon rum got hold of him and he was often drunk. In this country that isn't any great thing to hold against a man, but it got so he was drunk while holding court, and this didn't add much to the dignity of the trial.

One year a dry opponent campaigned upon that issue. Before election it was the custom for the Cattlemen's Association to hold a big picnic on the courthouse lawn so the voters could come out of the distant canyons and mountains and meet the candidates. The judge, against all reason, chose this time to get drunk. He stood on the high porch of the courthouse, teetering back and forth, in danger any second of plunging off on his face. The crowd watched, fascinated and fearful, as he barely missed falling while he spoke. His speech is still quoted in the county.

"Voters, my heart bleeds for you as you go to the polls next week to make the fateful cross on the ballot that will decide who will preside at your district court. It bleeds because you must decide between a drunkard and a damned fool. But as you stand in the booth, confronted by this dilemma, I hope you can remember one thing—a drunkard is sometimes sober, a fool never is."

This struck the fancy of the people and he was reelected handily.

THE DESERT WAS KIND TO SHEEP

R. A. LONG

MANY FORTUNES WERE MADE ON THE DESERT WITH SHEEP —and many lost. Before the Taylor Grazing Act, passed in 1934, feed on the public lands of the desert belonged to the fellow who got there first. The sheep are under the command of herders and go in flocks of a thousand or more. A thousand sheep are the equivalent of two hundred cattle. On the desert, two hundred cattle will be scattered over maybe ten thousand acres, but a herder must be able to see his flock all the time. If they scatter, the lambs will soon be adorning the quick-lunch counters of coyotes and bobcats.

The flock, at any one time, will be spread over maybe eighty acres. They may take all the feed and move on to the next eighty. You hear it said that sheep are hard on the range. Actually, they aren't, if the herder knows what he is doing. Most of our best privately owned ranges in eastern Oregon were sheep ranges until recent years.

A good herder can watch the grass and browse, and when it is half used, he will move the herd, thus leaving plenty of unused feed behind him. Cattle do not feed in a band, they do not have daily supervision, so they tend to eat and destroy the feed where they like to gather. They like level land without too many rocks, so they may grievously overgraze a range in one place and leave feed untouched somewhere else.

In the early days, with the range free, nothing riled a

Photo by Bill Cyrus, Hillsboro, Ore.

SHEEP AT A SMALL LAKE ON STEENS MOUNTAIN, 1961

The bands were formerly migrants. They started at lower elevations and gradually worked higher as the season advanced to keep on fresh green feed, just as they have done for thousands of years in Asia. Range sheep numbers are now vastly reduced in the West.

cattleman any more than to try to save feed for later use, only to find from one to twenty bands of sheep on it, the range eaten bare and clean. If the year turned dry, the grass treated that way might die. I want to repeat that with sheep it didn't need to be eaten so closely, because the herder has absolute control, but when the grass belonged to no one, the herder knew that if he didn't get the last spear, someone else would, so there was no point in grazing lightly, as he did on privately owned land.

So the range was pretty well ruined and sheep often got the blame. There were an awful lot of them. Lake County now has about 40,000 sheep, but at the height, 1930, had about 175,000. In addition, unknown thousands came in from Nevada, California, Idaho, and even Utah and Arizona. These were the so-called itinerant sheep.

The desert saw incredible numbers of them, especially in the winter, when the bands weren't tied down to water. There was an entire generation of itinerant sheep owners who had no real headquarters. The range was free, so they could roam at will over much of the West, with two to four dogs their only companions for months. They bought feed if they had to, stole it if they could. They would rent two little patches of privately owned land, maybe one hundred miles apart, and would spend all spring trailing their band to the other field, then devote the summer and fall to trailing back.

Woe to little fields of drylanders on the route, or even flowers and gardens by the homesteaders' shacks.

In lambing time, of course, they had to find some good feed and stay put.

If the itinerants prospered, they'd send to the old country for a nephew or a neighbor's boy, would have him as an unpaid assistant, or apprentice, for a time, then would hire him as herder. Their fortunes were up one year, down the next, but going broke was just an incident, and was rather expected. One could not pay his herder. The wages accumulated until they totaled the value of the band. The owner signed them over to the herder, free of encumbrance, and the former owner became the herder, still unpaid. In time, he owned the band again. He went to his banker, whom he had been neglecting while working as a herder. The banker asked him how he was getting along. He said, "Business is so good now, ba jasus, we's thinkin' of takin' in a pardner."

They would set up camp somewhere and graze out in all directions for a week or two, then move to a new place. Owners of grocery stores in the little desert towns made a living by supplying the herders in the wintertime. They couldn't guess all their needs, but one thing they

Courtesy Schmink Museum, Lakeview, Ore.

A RESULT OF RANGE COMPETITION BETWEEN SHEEPMEN AND CATTLEMEN
The picture was taken near Benjamin Lake shortly after the turn of the century. The sheep in this band had all been shot.

could be certain of would be tea. A pound of tea will last a modern family a long time, but these Irish, Basque, or Portuguese herders would use a pound in less than a tenth of the time. They were out in the wind, cold, and snow, but at the camp was a special kind of sheet metal collapsible stove that would hold a fire well, and on the stove was a big kettle of tea. Whenever the herder was cold, thirsty, tired, or lonesome, he would ride back to camp and drink a few cups of "the drink that cheers, but does not inebriate." Scalding hot, it warmed him, relieved his thirst, and the several trips to get tea helped wonderfully to pass the time. His idea of hospitality was to ask a stranger to his camp to share with him a cup of tea. So tea made up his social life.

An English lord said, "Daily I sink to my knees and give thanks to the Lord I was not born before tea." The Chinese have a regular tea religion, with a complete philosophy based upon it. They regard it as a way of life, not a habit, and these herders, in their lonesome, hard life, came to regard tea and their dogs as their best friends.

The desert herders were grossly misjudged by cattlemen and homesteaders alike. Stories grew up about them. The story was current that the herders went crazy trying to find the long way of the quilts. I have never found any truth in that. First, the herder wasn't crazy; second, if he was, he was that way to start with; and third, most sugans,[1] being handmade, weren't square.

Lake County sheepmen are stable citizens. Many are Irish. A list of the most prominent persons in Lake County would have more Irish names than would be the case in any other county in Oregon. Malheur County would have many Basque names; Grant County's list would have Scotch and Portuguese.

It was the custom to haze the newcomer from Ireland. The new boy in school; the apprentice mechanic sent after

---

[1] Sugan—originally an Irish word meaning a handmade patchwork quilt that weighed around four pounds.

a left-handed wrench; the Easterner with his first job as a cowboy; all the green hands in America in all businesses get this breaking-in training. But it seemed to me the Irish herders carried it too far. One spring at Benjamin Lake I was helping lamb for Tom Cronin and Denny O'Connor. Working for them was Simon Jonto, fresh from Ireland. When someone went to Paisley for supplies, Simon would ask them to bring him a pair of shoes. He was small and couldn't have worn over size seven, but they would bring him two mismated shoes, one a nine, the other an eleven. They wouldn't get him any socks, so he had to fill the extra space with gunny sacks.

He was so anxious to please that he went on a trot all day. Clumping over the rocks with his big shoes, his feet were covered with blisters all summer. He was extraordinarily religious, had never been among rough-talking men, and it didn't take long for the others to find that he was acutely distressed by impure language. They wracked their brains thinking up words, phrases, and stories that would plague him.

Once he got lost in a snowstorm. When he finally came to camp, he said, "I'm the devil's ape, that's what I am. I run all the way so as not to be lahng gone."

One fall I packed water for a sheep camp. They were dry sheep and moved around a lot. The owners gave me a ten-gallon water can that fit into an alforjas. I'd have to fill this can after it was on the horse and then find eighty pounds of rocks to put in the other alforjas to balance the pack. When I got to camp and emptied the can, I'd throw away the rocks. The next day I'd have to find eighty more pounds of rock. I wondered why they didn't get me two cans. It took me three years to decide they were just having fun with me, as they did with Simon Jonto.

If the winter had little snow, camp water might be scarce, and they would hire me and my horse and pack outfit to go two or three miles to get snow to melt for tea and other uses.

Many of the herders were smart. Some did lots of reading and could talk on any subject. Herders were always paid more money than the cowboys drew, so a young fellow saving money for college could save twice as much by herding as he could possibly save in town. He had no board or room expense and no way to spend his money. No other guys were around to call him a cheapskate if he didn't stand his share of the drinks. His summer income was about all saved.

Others saved to buy sheep of their own, and it didn't take long for an Irish or Basque herder to get started with sheep of his own and become a prosperous landowner. A third of the successful landowners in our county started that way.

Still another group saved their money just to accumulate enough to have a glorious spree in the late fall.

Most of the Basques, Portuguese, Scotch, and Irish expected to "make their fortune" and go home. If they didn't make it, they were ashamed to go home and admit failure. But if they did make it, they usually became tied to their land and found it impossible to go home. Some, with romantic ideas of the old country, did go home, intending to stay. They were shocked at the class system all around them. In America they had freedom to grow, regardless of class. So, disillusioned with their boyhood homes, they bade farewell to the old country forever, became United States citizens and proud of it.

A friend of mine dropped into a desert camp a few springs ago. It belonged to a fine sheepman who had taken a band to the desert to lamb. The calendar said it was spring, but spring hadn't found the desert yet. The herder was desperate. There was no feed, it was freezing hard every night, the lambs were dying by the hundreds, and the herder, in his seventies, was coming down with the flu. Besides, the day before he had gotten out his last bottle of medicine and while trying to take out the cork, the bottle slipped from his cold numbed fingers, hit on a rock, and

Courtesy Oregon Historical Society

OLD-TIME HAND SHEARING

A scene impossible to see now. Today, most shearing is done by power clippers. Then, a good shearer was a master hand. He had a frame to hold the shears at exactly the right angle when sharpening them on a grindstone. It was called a "hootnanny." The shearing was done by local groups or by migrants who started in Texas and worked north. These were professionals and they were often Mexicans. Desert shearers were mainly locals.

broke into a hundred pieces. So, in addition to bad weather, dying sheep, and impending illness, he was out of whiskey.

His first question was "And do ye hahve any whiskey?" My friend had nearly a full pint and gave it to him. The old man poured it into a big, heavy camp cup, broke two eggs into it, stirred them up with a fork, and downed it without stopping. As he stirred in the eggs, he said apologetically, "I'm getting too owld to take it straight any lahnger."

The same man, about ten years ago, started to Portland with Elgin Cornett, county agricultural extension agent, and a couple of other Irish sheepmen. They had been members of the National Wool Growers Association for years, and decided to attend the annual convention that year. The convention was in January, and by the time the four reached Klamath Falls, an old-fashioned blizzard was on, and the roads were blocked; it was twenty below zero, and they had to take the train.

They could get only upper berths and the county extension agent, conductor, and the porter got the older sheepman into the berth and explained the procedure. The train was not scheduled to stop until it reached Portland in the morning, so the porters promptly hunted warm beds. In the morning the old man met the county agent and said, "Elgin, I down't think I'll be takin' the train any lahnger. Last night in the middle of it, I hahd to get up and I pushed and pushed on the little button ye showed me, but the damn rascal would never come. And Elgin, 't would have been a verra rough night except by the greatest of good farchun I'd taken me overshoes to bed with me."

Often the desert sheep camps were dry. In the winter snow would serve, but water is far apart on the desert. Canned tomatoes make a dandy substitute. They are both food and drink. A friend, Afton Zundel, raised near Malad, Idaho, tells how he always begged to go with his father to take supplies to the sheep camp out on the desert. Because of school or work, he could go only occasionally. On this

SHEEP ON THE DESERT

Until about 1930 the Oregon desert supplied range for millions of sheep. Numbers are now down to a few thousand in each county. This is a typical desert scene, with sagebrush in the foreground and scattered junipers on the hills beyond.

particular day they got to one camp at two o'clock in the afternoon. The sheep were badly scattered, there was no sign of the herder, and they located him in bed in his tent. Zundel, Senior, said, "Joe! What's the matter? The sheep are going off in all directions."

Joe: Oh, Mr. Zundel, I'm sick.

Zundel: Do you know what's the trouble?

Joe: No, Mr. Zundel, but I ain't been able to keep nothin' on my stummick all day but three cans of tomatoes.

The once vast Western range flocks are now down to almost nothing. One reason for the dissipation of most of the range sheep is the absence of reliable herders. The breed is becoming extinct. Organized sheep owners have been getting a few Basque herders to come over each year, but there aren't enough.

A herder takes twenty thousand dollars' worth of property into the hills and the owner may not see the sheep for months. Whether the year shows a profit or loss depends upon the herder—his loyalty and faithfulness, his judgment and resourcefulness. His day is twenty-four hours. He must move out by daylight; must be quiet so the flock will feed contentedly; must have a map of the area in his head with special attention to water; must know what to do in case of unseasonal snow or dangerous water spouts; must be a good practical veterinarian; must plan every day with wisdom; must be on the lookout day and night for coyotes, bobcats, and, in the mountains, bear. Men with these qualities are scarce.

The sheep don't need much water if they can get snow, or even frost. A band came by the Albert Brooks place late one fall when the bucks were with the ewes. The herder told Brooks he'd lost two bucks—to please look for them. A year later Brooks found them in the lava beds where they'd spent twelve months. They had lived on snow, frost, and dew.

James K. Wallace camped with an old Basque herder some years ago and wrote about the experience for the journal of the National Wool Growers. Since then it has been published widely.[2]

The Basque Sheepherder and the Shepherd Psalm

By James K. Wallace

Out on the Nevada desert Fernando D'Alfonso, the Basque, roams with his sheep. He is a herder employed by one of the big sheep outfits of the West, which has over thirty bands of one thousand ewes on the open range in charge of competent shepherds. D'Alfonso, now over sixty years of age, withered by years of exposure to the sun and wind, came to this country from the mountains of northern Spain over thirty years ago and is rated as one of the best sheep rangers in the State, and he should be, for back of him is the definite history of twenty generations of Iberian shepherds, while there are legendary tales of direct ancestors who herded sheep in the Pyrenees sheepwalks before the time of Christ.

D'Alfonso is more than a sheepherder, for he is a patriarch of his guild, traditions and secrets of which have been handed down from generation to generation just as were those of the gold beaters, the copper workers, the Damascus steel temperers and other trade guilds of the premedieval ages. Despite his long absence from the homeland, spending most of his time far from human habitation and from usual means of modern communications, he is still full of legends, the mysteries, the religious fervor and the belief in symbolism of his native hills.

---

[2] Published with permission of the National Wool Growers Association, Salt Lake City, Utah.

As I sat with him one night under the clear, starry skies, his sheep bedded down beside a pool of sparkling water and we preparing to curl up in our blankets and go to sleep, he suddenly began a dissertation in a jargon of Greek and Basque. When he had finished, I asked him what it was he had just repeated. After much dreamy meditation he began to quote in English the Twenty-third Psalm.

No biblical writing, other than the Lord's Prayer, has been so widely memorized as has this beautiful poem, and out on the Nevada desert I received the sheepherder's literal understanding of the inspirational word picture.

"David and his ancestors," said D'Alfonso, "knew sheep and their ways, and he has translated a sheep's musing into simple words. The daily repetition of the Psalm fills the sheepherder with reverence for his calling. He can look into the eyes of his charges and see the love and affection which David saw. Our guild takes as the lodestone of its calling this poem. It is ours. It is our inspiration. It is our bulwark when the days are hot or stormy; when the nights are dark; when wild animals surround our bands. Many of its lines are the statement of the simple requirements and actual duties of a Holy Land shepherd in the care of his flocks, whether he lives at the present day or followed the same calling six thousand years ago. Phrase by phrase it has a well-understood meaning for us."

He maketh me to lie down in green pastures:

"Sheep graze from around three-thirty o'clock in the morning until about ten o'clock. Then they want to lie down for three or four hours and rest," said D'Alfonso. "When they are contentedly chewing their cuds the shepherd knows they are putting on fat. Consequently, the good shepherd starts his flock out in the early hours on the rougher herbage, moving through the morning onto the richer, sweeter grasses, and finally coming with the band to a shady place for its forenoon rest into the best grazing of the day. Sheep, while resting in such happy surroundings, not only have had the benefit of the good late eating but have the atmosphere on the fine green pastures around them, giving the natural incentive towards contentment and growth."

He leadeth me beside the still waters.

"Every sheepman knows," said the Basque, "that sheep will not drink gurgling water. There are many small springs high in the hills of the Holy Land whose waters run down to the valleys only to evaporate in the desert sun. Although the sheep greatly need the water, they will not drink from the tiny fast-flowing streams until the shepherd has found a place where rocks or erosion have made a little pool, or else has fashioned out with his own hands a pocket sufficient to hold at least a bucketful."

He restoreth my soul: he leadeth me in the paths of righteousness for his name's sake.

"Holy Land sheep are led rather than driven in their wanderings in search of browse. They exceed in herding instinct the Spanish Merino or the French Rambouillet," according to D'Alfonso. "Each one takes its place in the grazing line in the morning and keeps the same position throughout the day. Once, however, during the day, each sheep leaves its place and goes to the shepherd. The sheep approaches with expectant eye and mild little 'Baa,' whereupon the shepherd stretches out his hand and the sheep runs to him. He rubs its nose and ears, scratches its chin, whispers love words into its ears, and fondles it affectionately. The sheep, in the meantime, rubs against his leg, or, if he is sitting down, nibbles at the shepherd's ear and rubs its cheek against his face. After a few minutes of this communion with the master, the sheep returns to its place in the feeding line refreshed and made content by his personal contact."

Yea, though I walk through the valley of the shadow of death, I will fear no evil: for thou art with me.

"There is an actual Valley of the Shadow of Death in Palestine and every sheepherder from Spain to Dalmatia knows of it. It is south of the Jericho road leading from Jerusalem to the Dead Sea and is a very narrow defile through a mountain range. It is necessary to go through this valley to get from the old-time feeding grounds of David and his tribesmen to those of Abraham and his descendants. Its side walls are over fifteen hundred feet high in places and it is about four and one-half miles long, yet is only ten to twelve feet wide at the bottom. The grade of the valley slopes from about twenty-seven hundred feet above sea level at one end down to nearly four hundred feet below sea level at the other. The valley is made dangerous due to its floor being badly eroded by waters from cloudbursts, so that actual footing on solid rock is so narrow that in many places a sheep cannot turn around. Mules have not been able to make the trip for centuries, but sheep and goat herders from earliest Old Testament days have maintained a passage for their stock. Gullies, often seven and eight feet deep, have been washed in many places. It is an unwritten law of the shepherds that flocks must go up the valley in the morning hours and down towards the eventide, else there would be endless confusion, should flocks meet in the defile."

Thy rod and thy staff they comfort me.

"About halfway through the valley the walk crosses from one side to the other at a place where the two-and-one-half-foot-wide path is cut in two by an eight-foot-deep gully. One section of the walk is about eighteen inches higher than the other, so in their journeying down the valley, the sheep have to jump upwards and across, while on the opposite trip they jump downwards. The shepherd stands at this break and urges, coaxes, pets, encourages and sometimes forces the sheep to make the leap. As a result of slippery walkways, poor footing, or tiredness, sheep occasionally miss the jump and land in the gully. The shepherd's rod is immediately brought into play. The old-style crook is encircled around a large sheep's neck or a small sheep's chest and it is lifted to safety. If the more modern narrow crook is used, the sheep is caught just above the hoofs and lifted up to the walk. Many wild dogs lurk in the shadows of the valley looking for prey, and when they are encountered the shepherd's staff comes into active use. After a band has entered the defile, the lead sheep may come onto a dog. Unable to retreat the leaders baa a warning and upon hearing this, the shepherd, skilled in throwing the staff, hurls it at the dog, often one hundred and fifty feet away. In all but rare instances, he succeeds in knocking the dog down into the washed-out gully where it is easily killed. Climatic and grazing conditions make it necessary for the sheep to be moved through the Valley of the Shadow of Death for seasonal feeding each year, so they have learned to fear no evil, for their master is there to aid and protect them."

*Thou preparest a table before me in the
presence of mine enemies.*

"This statement seems to convey a boastful, rather pagan thought of gloating over the hunger of others while those in the favor of Jehovah feasted. However, David's meaning is a simple one," said D'Alfonso, "when conditions on the Holy Land sheep ranges are known. Poisonous plants abound which are fatal to grazing animals. The most noxious is a species of whorled milkweed. It sinks its roots deep down in the rocky soils and its eradication during the centuries has been impossible. Each spring the shepherd mu be constantly on guard as the plant is on some of the best feeding ground. When found the shepherd takes his awkward old mattock and goes on ahead of the flock, grubbing out every stock and root he can see. As he digs out the stocks he lays them on little stone pyres, some of which were built by shepherds in Old Testament days, and by morrow they are dry enough to burn. In the meantime, the field being free from the poisonous plants, the sheep are led into the newly prepared pastures and in the presence of their deadly plant enemies, they eat in peace."

Thou anointest my head with oil; my cup runneth over.

"This phrase has been interpreted many times as symbolic of fullness of reward for well-doing. Literally, however, it is the statement of a daily task of a professional shepherd in the most time-honored calling. At every sheepfold there is found a big earthen bowl of olive oil and a large stone jar of water. As the sheep come in for the night, they are led along the side of the wall to the gate in one end. The shepherd lays aside his woolen robe and his staff, but rests his rod across the top of the gateway just higher than the backs of the sheep. As each passes him in single file he quickly examines it for briars in the ears, snags in the cheek or weeping of the eyes from dust or scratches. When such conditions are found, he drops the rod across the sheep's back, and it steps out of line and waits until all the sheep have been examined. Out of his flock of two hundred and fifty ewes, the shepherd may find one or a dozen needing attention," said D'Alfonso. "Each sheep's laceration is carefully cleaned. Then the shepherd dips his hand into the olive oil and anoints the injury gently but thoroughly sparing of the oil. Along with the treatment, love words are poured into the sheep's ears and the cup is dipped into the large jar of evaporation in the unglazed pottery, ever half full but always overflowing.

The sheep will sink its nose down into the water clear to the eyes if fevered, and drink until fully refreshed. Then it is allowed to enter the sheepfold and the next injured sheep is treated.

"When all of the sheep are at rest, the shepherd places his rod in the corner, lays his staff on the ground within reach, in case it is needed for protection of the flock during the night, wraps himself in his heavy woolen robe and lies down across the gateway facing the sheep, for his night's repose.

"So," said D'Alfonso, "after all this care and protection can a sheep be blamed for soliloquizing in the twilight— as translated into words by David?"

Surely goodness and mercy shall follow me all
the days of my life: and I will dwell in
the house of the Lord for ever.

INDIANS IN THE DESERT

E. R. Jackman

IN MODERN TIMES INDIANS WERE SCARCE IN THE DESERT, but back when glaciers melted and filled the desert with huge, freshwater lakes, this area had more Indians than any other part of Oregon. At least more Indian artifacts have been picked up here than elsewhere.

Apparently the lakes were marvelous hunting grounds. They made perfect nesting places for hundreds of thousands of birds of all kinds—not only ducks and geese, but egrets, swans, cranes, and every kind of swimming or wading fowl that existed in pre-white-man Oregon. Fish were in the lakes. There were many necks of land, or peninsulas, that ran into the lakes, where Indians could camp and fish and hunt on the same trip. In such spots, hunters for Indian articles sift the sand through coarse screens, and have carted away stone objects by the thousands. It is likely that many thousands are still buried in the desert sands around the borders of forgotten lakes. There are mortars, pestles, arrowheads and spearheads, stone knives for skinning and working skins, cooking pots, and stone war clubs. Lake County was the permanent home of large numbers of Indians about ten thousand years ago. Before horses came, about 1750, the Indians couldn't carry many stone objects. Where they are found is where Indians lived.

In caves in several places in the desert, throwing sticks were und, such as were used by primitive tribes in Australia. e nine-thousand-year-old sandals found in a cave on

Reub's place are different from those found in any other Indian campsite in North America. No Indian tribe has made such sandals in modern times. Tribes completely un-

Photo by Jones Studio, Lakeview, Ore.

ARTIFACTS OWNED BY R. A. LONG

Except for the pestle, used for grinding food, the other articles were of unknown use. The stone at the right has a human face carved near the top. It does not show in the picture.

known to history must have lived along the shores of the great lakes.

In many places in the desert, from Horse Ridge east of Bend clear across to Hart Mountain, are numerous drawings on smooth faces of rocks. Some are evidently maps, directing others to water holes. Some, such as one on the antelope refuge on Hart Mountain, depict hunting scenes. Others may have had some religious significance, or perhaps a thinking Indian doodled, absentmindedly.

In Klamath there is a quarter of a mile of Indian work chiseled into a cliff that formerly stood in Tule Lake. As the lake rose and the waters covered this unsolved mystery story, members of some unknown tribe apparently stood in boats and laboriously recarved it. Here was an Indian tribe

Photo by Jones Studio, Lakeview, Ore.

INDIAN ARTIFACTS OWNED BY R. A. LONG
A knife, fleshing tool, and spearhead used by Indians a thousand years before Columbus
came to America.

that could write! Perhaps they wandered into the sanctuary of the pleasant Klamath Basin, with its lakes, good hunting and fishing, and wished to record their wanderings.

This long record is a series of wavy lines with dots over and under—a form of writing. Since no American tribe advanced to the writing stage—not even the highly superior Incas—here is a mystery thriller. Present-day Indians are as mystified as white persons. Of course, this huge, perpendicular cliff with smooth walls attracted the notice of recent Indians, who painted typical Indian drawings over the older chiseled record.

In modern times no Indians lived in the desert, so it was

Photo by Merritt Parks, Fort Rock, Ore.

A CAVE ON THE RANCH OF R. A. LONG. THE AREA IS NOW A NATIONAL MONUMENT

Careful digging has revealed over seventy sandals, stored there by Indians about one hundred centuries ago. This is the earliest indication of commerce or trade in either North or South America

not claimed by any tribe. In winter, when deer could live there and use snow for water, large numbers of these animals drifted to the desert to escape the deep snow in the surrounding mountains. That brought Indians of all adjacent tribes for an annual hunt, as armies of hunters now descend upon the special hunt areas.

The Indian winter hunters liked the lava beds. At least in the lavas are dozens of circular lines of stones used for fastening down their tepees, called "tepee rings" for want of a better name. These rocks are usually about the size of the crown of a hat, or a football. They are always in a circle the diameter of a tepee. Perhaps, in the chaos of the lava beds, it was easier for skillful hunters to trap deer in the winding paths between the waves of lava. These paths support native shrubs of all kinds, offer protection from the winds, and probably the deer liked such areas as winter quarters.

This is a poor place, though, for white hunters. The rough, formless face of the lava waves will cut a man's shoes to pieces in a few hours. The pliant, yielding surface of moccasins doesn't cut so easily. The Indians didn't have horses. Horses cannot navigate over the lava very well, either. It cuts their hooves. Most white hunters have neither the patience nor the know-how to hunt in the lava beds.

Winter hunting in our part of the desert brought in at least these tribes: Paiutes from the east and southeast, Warm Springs from the north, Klamaths and Modocs from the south. It is possible that it drew tribes from farther away, such as the Wascos and Umatillas, or even Umpquas and Rogues from west of the Cascades. At any event, since no tribe claimed the desert, here was a place where the various tribes could meet, trade, run races, or have games. The extent of trade among the tribes was far greater than is generally supposed. When a tribe near the ocean received a supply of goods from a sailing ship, some of the trade articles showed up in a few months far in the interior.

Indian tribes of the Northwest developed a trade language

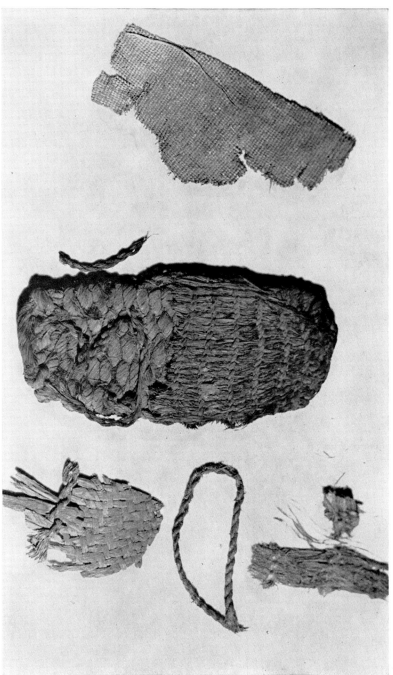

Photo by Jones Studio, Lakeview, Ore.

A SANDAL (AND PORTIONS OF OTHERS) UNEARTHED IN THE CAVE ON R. A. LONG'S RANCH

Radiocarbon readings show an age of approximately ten thousand years. The sandals were made of sagebrush fibers, and were held by cords around the ankles, tied in front, exactly as sandals are fastened today. For a complete story of these sandals, see *The Sandal and the Cave: The Indians of Oregon*, by Dr. L. S. Cressman, University of Oregon, Eugene.

manufactured by necessity, just as pidgeon English was a trade language throughout the far-spaced islands of the Pacific. In the Northwest it was known as Chinook jargon. Reub's father knew it and could talk with most any Indian he met—of whatever tribe. The various tribes all had their own languages, developed through centuries, and, for the most part, could not understand each other. But when they met at The Dalles at the great annual salmon-fishing fair, or on the desert to hunt deer, or at an obsidian mountain to get arrowhead material, they talked in the tongue of commerce and trade—Chinook jargon.

This intertribal language, sort of a pre-white-man Esperanto, has been preserved in written form,[1] but it has been impossible to preserve it exactly because many words had meaning determined by gestures and emphasis, just as our slang word "yeah" can mean almost anything, depending upon the way we say it.

The Chinook jargon was made up of mostly Chinook words because the Indians of that tribe were great traders, and their location, at the mouth of the Columbia, gave them ready communication to both interior and coast tribes. But some words in the language were manufactured to imitate sounds, and some came from other tribes. Later on the language picked up English, French, and even a few Spanish words, modified by Indian language difficulties. Like the Chinese, they had no "r" sound, so made it "l." Neither did they have an "f" sound, so our "fire" became "piah" in the jargon.

Those who think Indians have no sense of humor are just ignorant of Indians. Reub tells of one year when he was riding on the spring roundup. Jim Hays was the elected boss of the Silver Lake chuck wagon. The rango of the crew was an Indian boy of maybe fifteen. He brought the horses in each morning and the roper caught the horses to

---

[1] Thomas Edward Harper, *Chinook: A History and a Dictionary* (Portland, Ore.: Metropolitan Press, 1937).

Courtesy Lake County (Ore.) Chamber of Commerce

THE DESERT HAS DOZENS OF THESE INDIAN PICTURES CARVED OR PAINTED ON STONES

Some were records, some were maps, and others were used in ceremonies—and probably there were Indian doodlers, pre-civilization artists

be used that day, as described in Chapter 7. The entire day's operation depended upon having the horses in on time.

The boss fell into the habit of ribbing the Indian boy. The crew got a kick out of it, and the boy's credulity seemed unlimited. One night he asked if the lakes on the high desert had fish in them. The boss said, "Oh, sure! They're just full of fish. When the lakes dry up, the fish crawl up in the juniper trees and wait until the winter rains fill the lakes again." The men nudged each other and grinned behind their hands.

Next morning the Indian boy didn't get in with the horses. They waited and waited, the boss getting madder by the minute. The best part of the day for rounding up or driving cattle is in the morning, and here the best of the day was slipping away. Long after he was due, the Indian boy brought the caviatta in, and the boss lit into him with every blistering word he could dig out of his well-stocked word cache. When he stopped for breath, the Indian boy said, "No fish in trees. Me look." The boss started again, but halted suddenly at what just could have been a look of overplayed innocence on the face of the boy. He looked around at the men, said gruffly, "Get your horses," and he didn't guy the boy any more.

One of America's truly great storytellers was Charlie Russell, of Montana. You have seen Charlie's pictures of horses, Indians, coyotes, soldiers, and trappers. They form a vivid and vital history of the early West. He tells of meeting a cowpuncher with a hate on toward the Indians. "They're no good and never will be. They don't *think* like people. They got no sense of values. Only yesterday I met an Indian who somehow had got a good outfit. Good saddle, bridle, pony, everything. You know what that crazy Indian wanted to do? He wanted to trade that good outfit of his, worth a hundred dollars of anybody's money, for a two-dollar bottle of whiskey he saw in this jacket pocket. Now that's just like an Indian—no sense at all. They can't never get along." So Charlie Russell said, "Did you make the trade?" The cowboy looked surprised, almost injured: "Hell, no. That's all the whiskey I had!"

There are still many Indians in Oregon. One of them told me about the Indian brothers, Jock and Charlie, who were inseparable. They indulged in no useless talk, and they would come to town on Saturdays, stay together all day without saying a word. One day, as they lounged at a counter and drank cokes for hours without speaking, Charlie suddenly turned and hit Jock on the chin, knocking him down. Jock raised himself on his elbow, thought hard, and said in a voice holding only a puzzled note, "Just what was you alludin' to, Charlie?"

Near the little town of Bly in Klamath County lives an

Photo by Merritt Parks, Fort Rock, Ore.

INDIAN TEPEE RING, PHOTOGRAPHED IN 1962

The pre-white-man Indians, while hunting in the lava beds, evidently held down the edges of their tepees with rocks such as these. Dozens of rock circles can be found in the area.

Indian who was not satisfied to accept the social security offered by the Indian Service. He developed a nice little cattle layout with about seventy-five cows. One day he sent word around that he was going to brand and mark his calves next Friday. In isolated communities this isn't exactly a ranch chore—it is a social occasion. So the neighbors gathered in. The day was unseasonably hot and breathless. In a few minutes dust hung heavy and part of the crew preferred to sit on top of the high log corral while others wrestled calves in the stifling and sticky dust below. At the end, the calves were all turned out, the dust settled, and the Indian rancher drew himself up, pointed slowly to the house and announced with ancient dignity, "All Indians who work in corral, go to house—and eat. All white men who work in corral, go to house—and eat. All Indians, all white men, who sit on fence—*sit* on fence."

Oregonians have wondered why Indians were more numerous in the desert than in western Oregon. In the eastern Oregon desert, summers are hot, winters cold, and it's a long time between drinks. In the pleasant valleys west of the Cascades, life must have been quiet and easy before white men made it complicated. Streams were everywhere and were full of fish, grass grew tall in the prairies, the temperature was remarkably uniform—but Indians were few there. Maybe primitive life needed adversity to sustain it. The Blackfeet in the Montana mountains and the Navajos and related tribes in the southern desert were intellectually and physically superior to many of the tribes living in easier surroundings.

In the early days every old-timer had some sort of a run-in with Indians. Friends or relatives of his had been killed or had lost property. He had no faith in them. The only good Indian was a dead Indian. It didn't matter that for every Indian atrocity there was an atrocity by whites. Those things didn't count. But ranchers would hire Indians to make fence, dig ditches, or make roads. But they wouldn't eat with them. Many ranches had an "Injun table." The expression is still heard, though it has lost its original meaning. When a man is in bad with his wife, or with the boss, he'll say resignedly, "I expect I'll have to sit at the Injun table."

Some of us were hunting elk southeast of Pilot Rock. An Indian there didn't hunt the way we did. He came horseback, tied the horse to a tree a few hundred yards away, then sat down with his back against a big yellow pine. He just sat there all day. He said he always got an elk there.

One of our party, Paul Gilliland, got an elk down in the deep canyon of Meadow Creek. An elk is a big animal, and carrying it out on your back takes most of the day for four or five men, or it takes one man five days to get the four quarters, the hide, and the head. So Paul went to the Indian, whom he knew, and asked if he could rent the Indian's horse. The Indian agreed at once, in the most friendly manner. This was the conversation:

Paul: Wait a minute. What are you going to charge me for the horse?

Indian (Speculatively): Some Indians charge twenty-five dollars.

Paul (Outraged): Well, of all the. . . .

Indian (Hastily): No — no — not me — me no charge twenty-five dollars. Me good Indian. Some Indians charge ten dollars.

Paul (Loudly): I'm not a-goin to——

Indian (Hastily): But not me. Me your friend. Me no charge ten dollars. Some Indians charge five dollars.

Paul: I'll give you fifty cents.

Indian: All right.

Reub tells of the Indian who came to the blacksmith shop at Silver Lake for a horseshoeing job. He told the blacksmith, "You shoe only hind feet. He can see where front feet go."

The old feeling between white man and Indians is almost

gone. There are some remnants in the dregs—the lowest classes of both. Such men as Will Rogers, who lost no chance to brag a little of his Indian blood, are partly responsible, but time irons out such things. I was a visitor once in Chile. The Spaniards conquered the Indians with fire, sword, and Bible. The conquered believed in God or else. But one tribe of Indians just simply refused to be conquered. They were the Araucanian Indians, who lived down toward the southern portion of Chile.

Even today these Indians maintain much of their old ways, dress, and customs. But, so far as I could see, every Chilean is proud of these Indians and whenever you meet a Chilean who can show an Araucanian limb on his family tree, he tells you at once, "Sir, I am part Araucanian!" It is likely that by another generation, that will be exactly the feeling in the United States. As in Will Rogers' case, there is a little of that feeling now, and by 1990, I suspect that every American who can qualify, will hasten to tell you, "My mother was one-quarter Nez Perce," or "My grandfather was half Umpqua."

Indians like to spoof white men. I know of one old Indian who can neither read nor write, but occasionally he goes to a city. When he gets to, say San Francisco, he takes out a plumb bob on a string, walks out in the street, oblivious to the traffic, carefully holds up the plumb bob, sights it along the corner of a tall building, takes out a book such as surveyors use, and pretends to make notes. He sights the plumb bob again, to check his reading, nodding in a satisfied way.

In no time at all, there is a crowd watching, and as he steps back on the walk, some of them try to question him. He refuses to say a word.

Learn from Indians

A friend of mine was deer hunting. He is one of the best hunters I know. He came to the edge of an open hill-

side and sat down in the dense shade of a bush, systematically examining the entire rock-strewn mountainside. He
sat there motionless for thirty minutes in utter silence. De-
ciding to move on, he rose and to his amazement, an Indian
with two boys stood behind him. He had heard no sound.
He asked about the boys. The Indian said he took each
of his boys hunting at seven years of age. The boy was not
allowed a gun, but he must walk silently behind the Indian
and step exactly where he stepped. My friend said, "When
can your boy have a gun?" He said, "When he is fourteen.
He can go alone. He won't need me." Thus he trained
each boy for seven years before allowing him to carry a
gun.

An Indian friend told me that from the age of ten he
was raised by an uncle who owned a small gold mine. The
uncle and his squaw were childless. From his isolated mountain valley it was a three-day trip by team and wagon to
the nearest town. Once a year the uncle and boy mined
enough gold to buy a year's supply of needed goods. The
gold was put in a fruit jar. They hitched up a four-horse
team, and made the three-day journey to town, camping
at night.

At the town, after buying the year's supplies, the uncle
bought a quart of whiskey for himself and a quart of rum
for his squaw. This purchase, at the time, was strictly
illegal, either to buy or to take upon the reservation.

On the return trip, the squaw sat in the back of the
wagon with the tent, groceries, and horse feed. The uncle
and boy sat on the wagon seat. The quart of whiskey lasted
the uncle all year and was taken only as a warming tonic in
emergencies. But the squaw, fearful that her rum might be
discovered and confiscated, sat quietly among the groceries
and drank the entire quart. She then became hysterical.

The uncle stopped the team, handed the lines to the boy,
got down, helped his squaw down, climbed up, and drove
on, leaving his wife to walk. At night they camped, put
up the tent, prepared a good meal. The uncle carefully

banked the fire so it would last. When his squaw arrived, some time after midnight, sober but tired, he got up, heated her belated supper, and treated her as an honored guest.

This went on exactly the same for the ten years my friend lived with them. Not once, in that ten years, did the uncle say one word of censure to his wife. He did not even refer to conduct he must have regarded unfavorably, since he was not a drinking man. They lived together with dignity and politeness, unmarred by a word of faultfinding.

Later, when the uncle was very old, my friend asked him about this attitude, and he explained simply, "It is not good to shame a squaw." The old man also explained about his mine. He said, "If you had money in a bank, you would not take it out all at one time. The mine is my bank. I take only what I need."

Wisdom is where you find it. It should not be confused with schooling.

In *Gold and Cattle Country* is Lum Short's story of the Klamath Indian who was leaning against a big tree early in the morning as Lum rode by. Late that afternoon Lum rode back and his Indian friend was still there. Lum rode over, said, "George, what you thinking about so hard?" The Indian said, simply, "All time see black horse with white face. Never see white horse with black face." Now, to my mind, that is a good story, because you can't tell anything about it. It is likely that the Indian had the thought, stopped to check up in his mind the horses he saw yesterday, the day before, and so on back. But maybe his answer was only his way of saying that his thoughts were none of your damn business. Or, knowing of Lum's interest in horses, he *could* have replied so as to bother Lum and get him to thinking.

Indian Religion

In his way, the Indian of the Pacific Northwest was an extremely religious person. In most of the tribes it was the

custom to send boys out into the wilderness to stay until
they had a religious experience. They must not eat at such
times, or build a fire for comfort. They might drink water,
but only to keep alive. After some days of travel and fast-
ing, they commonly came into contact with their personal
spirit, who stayed with them and watched over them all
of their lives. This spirit might be that of a dead person,
or it might live in some animal, or even in a plant. This
highly personal religion was sacred to an Indian and was
not to be cheapened by talk about it.

In addition to their personal guardian angels, there was
an overall Great Spirit who looked after all beings on earth.
He presided over a happy hunting ground quite analogous
to our heaven. He might become angry with an entire tribe,
leading to their weakening or total destruction. If you
think that is silly, read the Old Testament.

But what happened to the individual was more likely
to reflect the efficiency of his own guardian spirit. He was
represented by feathers, porcupine quills, fur, or something
tangible, as many white persons carry a crucifix or other
symbol. The warrior's self-made weapons were fashioned
from the advice of his personal spirit, and his actions were
often guided by a seance with this spirit. In a fight, he
should go up a certain draw, or start at one specific time
and wear a peculiar ornament—all advised by the Indian's
guardian angel. If he had bad luck on the hunt or in warfare, he could usually trace it to some way in which he
had disobeyed his angel, or his "power," as he often called
it. This "power" was more closely knit to him than superstition. It was a part of him—too sacred to mention. Good
and bad spirits were all about him—and for all we actually
know about it, maybe they are.

Lum Short, of Klamath Falls, told me about an Indian
friend with three daughters. The Indian told him, "Three
years ago the medicine man came to me and said if I no
give him $500, my oldest daughter die. I didn't pay him
and she die. Last year he say if I no give him $500, my

second daughter die. She die. Today he tell me if I no pay him $800 my last daughter die. What you do?" Lum said, "I think I'd shoot the ———!" The Indian nodded and the next day the medicine man was found with a bullet hole neatly placed in the middle of his brow. Lum said, "The crime was never solved."

I know of at least one Indian who seems to have some abnormal powers. He has repeatedly told with success where to look for lost persons, dead or alive. Some sort of extra-sensory perception, E.S.P. Perhaps some Indians live a little closer to natural feelings and can sense things vague to us. Or, as with most seers or fortune-tellers, maybe their seeming successes are only good guesses, stated in such general terms that they are right in some respects, even when wrong.

The Speech that Settled Oregon

This is about a speech made by an Indian from the Flathead Valley in Montana. This valley is not part of the desert. But it was a speech that led directly to the "Oregon fever" that prompted the huge immigration to Oregon, starting in 1843.

This valley is west of the main range of the Rockies and the Indians living there were peaceable, friendly to the whites, and to everyone else. The towering backbone of the continent, the Rocky Mountains, separated them from the fierce warriors to the east, the Blackfeet. But about 1770, the Blackfeet acquired horses. Suddenly their fierceness was given wider scope. They could sweep out hundreds of miles and get back again. As foot soldiers, they had developed a technique of living based on following the food supply from mountain to plain and back. This confined them to a small area. A man, or a squaw, can't carry robes, tents, stone pots, and babies, very far.

But as cavalry they could go anywhere, even with their tepees and stone utensils. So they swept across the Rockies, killed or enslaved the peaceful Flatheads. By 1830 the latter tribe was reduced in numbers and in spirit. They called a solemn conclave to hear suggestions. Maybe now we'd call it an economic conference. Anyhow, their wisest men talked, and out of all this was sifted a conclusion that their gods were impotent or had deserted them. Where, then, could they get other gods? Only the white man seemed able to stand against the Blackfeet. Therefore, the gods of the white man must be superior; therefore, they would adopt the white man's god. What could be more logical?

They elected four of their members to go to the nearest council house of the white man and ask to be led to his God. It was reputed to be hidden in a book greatly treasured by the white man of wisdom. The four chosen were judged to be their wisest men, still young and resourceful enough to withstand a long journey.

They stole through the entire Blackfoot domain—east and south of Glacier Park, thence across the wide prairies to St. Louis. This was in 1831. Of all the towns in America, St. Louis had the least to offer in a spiritual way. The population ran heavily to river rats, prostitutes, swearing teamsters, trappers in for their yearly spree, and all the frontier riffraff that would gather to gamble, cheat and steal.

Into this setting came the four Indians, looking for God. Most of those they met regarded all Indians as treacherous murderers. They considered it no crime to kill an Indian, and as for humbling or insulting him, there was no such thing. How would you insult a rattlesnake? So the four were laughed at, ridiculed, tormented, and belittled in every way that cruelty could devise. Two of them died. Eventually, the remaining pair found their way to the ex-governor of Missiouri, William Clark, of the immortal Lewis and Clark team, then Commissioner of Indian Affairs.

More than twenty-five years before, Clark had been befriended by the Flatheads—helped in every way possible, and those Indians regarded him as dependable and under standing. Clark looked out for his Indian friends. He gave them everything that he thought they could use, stopped (so far as he could) the indignities heaped upon them, and tried to make them welcome. But he only dimly understood the reason behind their presence. He did not lead them to God.

Finally, in resignation and despair, the two left, their mission a failure. When they bade farewell to Governor Clark, a reporter was present. We cannot know now whether his report of their speech was accurate, or whether it sprang from a moment of inspiration, but the story electrified the nation. Even now, with the story completely out of its time and place in history, its picture words robbed of their poignance by our lack of understanding, it carries a tone of anguish and sadness almost unbearable.

Here it is, as printed at the time.[1]

"We came to you, over a trail of many moons, from the setting sun. You were the friend of our fathers, who have all gone the long way. We came with our eyes partly opened for more light for our people who sit in darkness. We go back with our eyes closed. How can we go back, blind, to our blind people? We made our way to you with strong arms, through enemies and strange lands, that we might carry back much to them. We go back with arms broken and empty. The two fathers who came with us— the braves of many winters and wars—we leave here asleep by your great water and wigwam. They were tired with their journey and their moccasins were worn out.

"Our people sent us to get the white man's Book of Heaven. You took us where they worship the Great Spirit

---

[1] The fascinating and moving story of the Indians and the speech have been the subject of much speculation by historians and others. Marcus Whitman, in his published journal, refers to them as Flatheads, as does Jason Lee in his official mission record. Fontanelle, frontier trader who seems to have guided them to St. Louis, said they were and also gives another tribe as having contributed members, who, except for one man, turned back at Council Bluffs. These were doubtless Nez Perce though Fontanelle called them Napierson.

The speech is generally thought to be the work of someone else, perhaps a clerk in Clark's office who is reputed to have sent it east to George Catlin at Pittsburgh. But no one disputes the effect when printed in eastern papers. It *did* galvanize the churches of all creeds and it *did* result in starting the western movement down the Oregon Trail. It *did* give character to the early citizens of Oregon, as compared to other western states. They were better educated, motivated by higher ideals, and certainly were steadier and more sober.

with candles, but the Book was not there. You showed us images of good spirits, and pictures of the good land beyond, but the Book is not among them. We are going back the long sad trail to our people. When we tell them, after one more snow, in the big council, that we did not bring the Book, no word will be spoken by our old men nor by our young braves. One by one they will rise up and go out in silence. Our people will die in darkness, and they will go on the long path to the other hunting grounds. No white man will go with them, and no Book of Heaven will make the way plain. We have no more words."

In no time at all, every little hamlet in New England and the Atlantic States had missionary societies raising funds to bring the light to these poor, groping people about to go on their long dark path without the Book of Heaven to light the way.

That speech settled Oregon and made it part of the Union. First came Jason Lee, Reverend Spalding, Marcus Whitman, and their group, but reinforcements followed, and for the nine-year period from 1834 to 1843, there were more missionaries in Oregon, counting their families and lay members of the mission, than there were all other Americans combined—all fired by the speech of an unlettered Indian. In America's history there have been other great speeches by Indians. All of them carry the same spirit of dignity and submission to forces beyond their control, but none of the others had such a galvanic effect upon the nation. Without it, Oregon now might have belonged to some other nation.

THE COYOTE

E. R. Jackman

The coming of the white man to north america doomed the buffalo, the passenger pigeon and several other birds; the lordly elk was pushed from the prairie into the highest and most rugged of our mountains; the American great bald eagle is extinct in many places; the cougar is on the way out; the grizzly bear is mainly a memory; and the big gray wolf has been driven into Canada. But that disciple of the devil, Señor Coyote, with his sly humor, his irritating ability to survive, is still with us.

Unknown races of Indians have come down from the North, made mystic writings here and there, and disappeared. Spaniards, Russians, French, and English explored with incredible will and energy, and left. Fur traders pursued the beaver up every little stream and lovely mountain valley in the West—and departed. On our deserts the homesteaders came and moved on.

The coyote has observed all of these comings and goings. The hand of every man has been against him and thousands in the West, even now, carry a gun in the car, "in case I see a coyote."

Scientists have labored with test tube and crucible to concoct ever more lethal poisons to eliminate him. Sportsmen have bred dogs of superior speed and cunning in order to catch him. Bounties by hundreds of thousands of dollars have been paid to tempt the ranch boys and professional trappers to bring in his pelt. Our dress designers periodically make coyote fur fashionable, and for a few years his skins command a fine price. The government hires professional hunters to poison and trap him and dig out his dens to destroy pups. Lately, devilishly lifelike calls have appeared; the squeal of a terrified rabbit; a calf in pain; a lamb, lost and afraid—all devised to lure a coyote to his death.

In spite of this steady, persistent effort of thousands to banish him from the prairie, if you sit outside on a quiet evening at the edge of any of North America's deserts, you will soon hear, from the rimrock, or distant hill, the eerie, long talk of the coyote. He must be talking. It isn't howling or screaming; it isn't a mating call, for it goes on all year. I know of no other sound so descriptive of the desert. It is wild, remote, something elemental from the beginning of time, out of harmony with civilization.

In spite of his depredations upon deer, sheep, birds, poultry, and young calves, desert dwellers come to have a grudging admiration for this one wild creature that refuses to bow to man's dominion. Such persons go out at night, especially on cold, still nights in winter, to listen to him with a kind of inner delight.

Indians probably come close to understanding what he is saying. Almost every Indian tribe in the West has myths and folklore about him, often with an almost affectionate tone to it—much as we have toward the immortal "Br'er Rabbit" stories of Uncle Remus. The coyote takes a larger total place in Indian mythology than any other animal. He is usually depicted as wise, cunning in an elfin, mischievous way, and he makes trouble for the other animals.

Some Indians claim to understand what he is saying and interpret his widely varying notes in terms of things important to both—storms, droughts, the presence of game. White men have been dominant in our desert for only ninety to one hundred years. Before that the Indian who couldn't interpret signs and sounds soon became a dead Indian. He heard the chatter of a jay and knew whether it meant friend or foe; wind in the trees meant fair or foul weather; the cha-cha-cha of a tree squirrel told him things he needed to know. So it would be strange if he couldn't interpret some of the many notes of the "prairie tenor."

Our farm in the Flathead Valley of Montana stretched to the base of the forested foothills. About two miles west of our house was a high perpendicular rock cliff that seemed to be a favorite talking place for the coyotes. They are so expert at changing their voices that no listener can tell how many singers are in the barbaric chorus. On still nights our whole family would go outside and listen. Usually the a cappella singers would be on the cliff and the two-mile interval between us was as nothing. They might have been no farther away than the barn, so clear was every note.

The eerie, indescribably lonesome sounds could have been coming down to us from some strange creature left from another age, doomed to roam forever, looking for more of its kind. Our spines would tingle, and to shake off the slight foreboding, we would hurl wordless imprecations to him. This seemed a challenge and all coyotes in that end of the county would rise to it, their words echoing back and forth from hill to hill and rock to rock.

One night a strange thing happened. After the others had quieted, one special coyote broke into maniacal laughter, sounding exactly as a screaming, hysterical woman might. This was too scary for any of us to try to imitate. There was only the one long, high, crazy laugh, then silence. That sound was far from the usual coyote sounds, too far apart to be identified with it for sure. In a few weeks we heard it again, a high, demented laugh, half scream. Like reading "The Fall of the House of Usher," it was a poor thing to go to bed on.

Sometimes the sound would come again the following night, but often it would not occur for weeks and sometimes months. We heard it for three years. I have not heard anything like it since. Coyotes also talk it up about dawn, but the crazy laughter did not come down from the

Photo by Joe Van Wormer, Bend, Ore.

THE WILD DOG OF THE DESERT, THE COYOTE, SNIFFING HIS WAY

He lives in a world of smells

hills then, only at night. It would be nice and grisly to report that it always foretold disaster or death, but it didn't foretell anything except a quickly caught breath on our part, and a quick scamper into the warmth and light of the house.

I imagine those coyote conversations, night and morning, mean the start and end of the hunt. Maybe at night each is telling where he will be hunting, just as a group of deer hunters agree "I'll take the north canyon, you and Bill circle behind to see if I scare anything over the hill, and Frank and Henry can circle to the west and go up Cotton- wood." And when the human hunters get together at the agreed rendezvous, there are always stories to tell. "We'd have got that big four-point that Henry scared up if I'd only had sense enough to be behind that lone juniper in- stead of in front where he could see me."

The morning coyote talk, always more yippy and argu- mentative, is in the nature of placing blame: "You and your big feet! Why did you have to step on a rolling stone just as I was set to grab off that rabbit?" Or, "Yellow Skin and I had worked that doe to perfection. She was about to charge me while my partner was behind a big sagebrush ready to snaffle off her fawn, and then you— half a mile off your course—came plowing in, awkward as a man, and spoiled the whole thing." In the mornings there is less of the mysterious quality to the coyote noise. It sounds more like talk and less like lament.

The Coyote's Name

There aren't too many Indian words that have come into common use all over the world where English is spoken. We have local use of such words. In Oregon one hears "skookum," "cultus," "potlatch," but you don't hear those words in Pennsylvania. In the Southwest there are many Mexican or Indian words, but they aren't used in Maine. Names for nearly all horse gear are derived from Mexican

terms, but these are either outright Spanish or a corruption
of Spanish—not Indian.

The word "coyote" is an exception. To be sure, we have
corrupted the original *coyotl* of the Southwest Indian into
a word easier to say. Northern Indians had other words
for this wild dog of the desert, such as *Talapus,* in Chinook
jargon, or *Telima,* the Yakima Indian term.

The coyote entered into the consciousness and folklore
of the Southwest Indians far more than in Oregon. The
animal wasn't thick originally in western Oregon, and he
wasn't so pervasive among the tribes in the northeast, along
the Columbia River, such as the Nez Perce. The Paiutes
were in every inhabitable place in the desert lands of Idaho,
Oregon, and Nevada. These Indians knew the coyote well
and he appears in their myths, folklore, and tribal customs,
just as Señor Coyote does among the Apaches, Navajos, and
Mexican tribes.

The Mexicans have a saying, "Next to God the coyote
is the smartest person on earth." Señor Coyote is seen in
their pictures. His picture is not common in Oregon Indian
art. The Aztecs in Mexico had a coyote cult, complete with
ceremonies, symbols, dress, and ritual.

"Coyote" is the name the Southwest desert Indians used,
and he is typically a desert animal. White men daily play
a deadly game of cops and robbers with him, and this has
had one effect—it has dispersed him to every place in
America where there is a lonely hillside suitable for a den
among the rocks or under low-hanging brush. His nightly
curses on mankind now echo along the canyons of Hollywood. He taunts the trappers in the woods of Maine, and
barks into the abandoned mine shafts of West Virginia.
His derision of the human race spreads over the frozen lakes
of Michigan and Minnesota. He hates man with good reason,
but often chooses to live near man because there may be
more food there. He disdains all of man's fetishes, such as
our great god, Time. He worships only one thing, smell.

He, like his name, has spread from the desert to most

of North America, and enters into our conversation everywhere. *A Dictionary of Americanisms*[1] has 1,946 pages of collected usages of words, many of them not in the ordinary dictionaries. It records over twenty ways in which Mr. Coyote has permeated our language. These words are listed in Appendix F.

In addition to these nationwide uses, every part of the West has uses not common elsewhere. For example, in the Columbia Basin, before scientific dry farming, every now and then someone with a gambling nature would drill wheat into the stubble, with no summer fallow or other land preparation at all. If it rained frequently, such a person might harvest a crop at very little expense. This was "coyote farming."

Indian Coyote Legends

Probably it was pure coincidence that the various tribes along the Klamath River looked at the coyote as the embodiment of a friendly deity. These tribes were not related to each other, and some were completely different. The Hoopa tribe, for example, were closely tied to the Navajos and were an island of a different Indian culture. The Modocs, at the head of the river, had no blood ties with the tribes down the river. But all of them had legends giving the coyote supernatural power way back in the beginning of time.

The Shasta Indians[2] told how the coyote brought fire to them from far in the East. It was in the form of a fire stone. The Sun had nine brothers, all shedding intolerable heat, burning up the earth. The coyote killed them, leaving just enough heat from the one remaining sun. This

---

[1] Milford McL. Mathews, ed., *A Dictionary of Americanisms on Historical Principles* (Chicago: University of Chicago Press, 1956). See Appendix F.

[2] This and some of the other legends are from the authoritative work, published in 1877, *Contributions to North American Ethnology*, by Mr. Stephen Powers. (Washington, D.C.: Government Printing Office, 1877.)

brave and resourceful spirit then had another problem. The Moon had nine brothers, too, shedding ice and cold. The coyote went far to the East, killed the nine, thus keeping everyone from freezing.

Another small tribe in California tells of the early man who, out of anger, set the world on fire in the North and perished with it. The coyote, seeing the smoke from far in the South, raced northward and put out the fire. He then made a sweathouse and split a large number of little sticks, which he put in the house overnight. These changed into persons, thus repopulating the devastated land. Perhaps this story, handed down for generations, resulted from the great explosion that blew off the top of the mountain, making a huge cup for Crater Lake.

A coastal group, the Poneo, had a tribal story that wicked Indians were changed to coyotes, but when they did some good deed, they were changed back to men again. These animal-men spirits did heroic things, such as establishing lakes and springs.

A tribe living in the middle regions of the Klamath River was called the Karok. They were particularly full of coyote fables. One long story dealt with those foolish coyotes who went to dance with the stars. They could talk with stars and begged them to come close to earth, take the coyotes with them and dance in the skies. This did not turn out well for the coyotes. The author thinks this was inspired by watching falling stars or meteors. Perhaps these occurred spectacularly some evening, just after the coyotes' evening serenade.

Another Karok legend told how the coyote outwitted some female devils at the mouth of the Klamath, opened an obstruction there, and let the salmon come up the river. These Indians had a culture based upon salmon, so the author thinks that at some distant past age, some obstruction formed at the mouth, keeping the salmon out; when it was removed and salmon again appeared, it must have been a time of rejoicing, and it became necessary to account for the miracle.

The Karok also have a story about the origin of species —a sort of a Darwin account turned around. The Supreme God, Kareya, made all the animals and man, but being too busy to complete the details, he left man to distribute the various attributes to each. He had their characteristics laid out, as one might have a stock of goods in a store. The coyote, through trickery, planned to get there first, but overreached himself, and got there last. The man gave the greatest power to the cougar, the second greatest to the bear, and so on down to the frog, who had a small, miserable power. But one power was left, and man asked, perplexed, who was missing. It was the coyote, who was asleep, having stayed awake all night to be first in line.

The coyote got little indeed, but the man prayed to Kareya for him, and Kareya gave him the best power of all—cunning. The grateful coyote has been a friend of man ever since.

The Pit River Indians, south of the Oregon line, had the coyote and the eagle making the earth and creating all the growing things. In this story, he went to the *West* to get the fire, whereas the coast Indian legends had him going to the *East*, perhaps evidence that they considered the flaming volcanoes to be the source of fire.

These stories are typical of hundreds of Indian legends, common in virtually all Western tribes. The stories show different attitudes toward the coyote, but are so numerous that it is evident that the coyote filled a large place in their religion, folklore, spoken tales of adventure, and mythology. Even on the Oregon coast, where coyotes were not at all numerous, the coyote had a place in the dim past where mythology blends with history, superstition, and mere story-telling.

What Coyotes Eat

The internal privacy of the coyote has been invaded by (fittingly enough) the United States Department of the Interior. From 1931 to 1935, government personnel analyzed the stomach contents of 8,339 of the ubiquitous "prairie wolves."[3] Results were classified by time of year and region, so the eating habits of this wild dog are an open book, though they are practiced mainly at night.

As might be expected, many rabbits ended their careers inside the coyote: jackrabbits in the plains, cottontails in the foothills, and snowshoe rabbits in the mountains. All were grist to his mill, and they made up 33 per cent of the content of all stomachs. Overall percentages were:

Rabbits	33 %
Carrion	25 %
Rodents	10 %
Domestic livestock	13.5%
Deer	3.5%
Birds	3 %
Insects	1 %
Vegetable matter	2 %
Other animal matter—baits, etc.	1 %

The diet of the young pups ran heavily to immature rabbits—as soon as the pups were old enough to eat things other than spoon victuals, but not old enough to forage for themselves. This is a fair division: old rabbits for old coyotes, young rabbits for young coyotes.

Carrion would also be expected. The coyote performs something of a Health Department chore by cleaning up all carrion on the open range. Most of us who hunt elk

---

[3] Some of the material for this chapter was drawn from Charles C. Sperry, *Food Habits of the Coyote* ("Fish and Wildlife Service, Wildlife Research Bulletin No. 4," U.S. Department of the Interior) (Washington, D.C.: Government Printing Office, 1941).

or deer have had the experience of returning in a day or two to the place where we had dressed an animal and finding very little left to mark the spot. They seem to like the innards better than the meat. Maybe they know of the Wisconsin work showing the greater vitamin content of the insides. I was in Brazil about ten years ago and was intrigued by the translated Brazilian name for the numerous turkey buzzards, "The Brazilian Sanitary Police." Some claim that coyotes learn to watch the buzzards, waiting patiently until the circling ends in discovery of carrion. Then they steal the food, while the buzzards sit watching without enthusiasm.

The percentage of carrion in the stomachs varied by months. It was largest in the winter. Other kinds of food are in shorter supply in the winter and the weather serves as a relentless and cruel weapon in nature to insure the death of the unfit. Then, with natural food scarce, with cold and wind to drain the energy from the wasted bodies, is the time of death for the old, the infirm, the irresolute, and the weaklings. Deer, antelope, cattle, horses, even the coyotes themselves, surrender the vital spark as the impersonal cold worms its way to the insides of the hurt or weak. Then comes the coyote, to use the carcass for his own survival, the Oregon Sanitary Police.

Still another reason for more carrion in winter is the refrigerator function of the weather. In summer, bacteria, beetles, and flies destroy a dead animal in a few days. The deep freeze of winter will preserve it for months.

There are numerous rodents on the desert. Some of them are mice, wood or pack rats, Kangaroo rats, Columbian ground squirrels, "Picket pin" squirrels, marmots, pocket gophers. The biologists class porcupines among the rodents, too. Coyotes eat all of them with gusto.

Many amateur naturalists, and some professionals, believe that the coyote has a place in preventing the occasional explosion of population among rabbits and mice. This theory has little to stand on. These explosions have been going on since biblical times, just as with insect plagues.

In 1958, when eastern Oregon had a mouse plague, every paper in the area had triumphant "I told you so" letters from citizens who blamed the millions of busy mice upon the fact that coyotes had been destroyed by overzealous stockmen or government hunters. Coyotes number something like one animal per section, but the mice in the infested areas ran up to 6,400,000 to the section. It was not noticeable that there were fewer where coyotes were thick.

These mouse and rabbit plagues have occurred in years when coyotes have been exceptionally numerous.

Of all domestic livestock, lambs are the favored dessert of the experienced coyote gourmand. Recent drastic decline in range sheep numbers can be blamed in places upon the lamb losses. In free land days, a death loss of 15 per cent or more a year might be endured because of the low cost of grazing, but modern conditions, including high taxes, make survival of a business impossible if subjected to losses even half as great.

The range lambs are beginning to gambol joyously at the same time that the coyote pups are demanding more and more food. A mature coyote can easily carry a lamb several miles, if need be, to present to her overjoyed pups, as an indulgent parent gives candy to his children. Or, if carrying o'er hill and dale is wearisome, the coyote can eat the lamb, then disgorge it near the den as a kind of pre-digested snack, a four-footed motorized market basket.

From my own boyhood, I can remember with pain the look on my mother's face when she found her precious flock of turkeys killed, apparently by one coyote, and just for fun. She said quietly, "One more dream gone." The turkey money belonged to her and forty to fifty turkeys gave her about all the money she had to spend during the year. This animal came boldly in the day and destroyed the flock close to the house.

Most cattle aren't much afraid of a coyote. I have watched

coyotes among cattle many times. Even cows with calves will keep on grazing, not much concerned. If a group of coyotes, though, can catch a cow and calf in deep, crusted snow, don't bet on the cow.

In the same way, a deer that delays migration and gets snowed in, will be a dead statistic before spring. In trying to preserve an antelope herd in Oregon, coyotes have been the single, most disturbing factor. A herd not hunted should increase fast, but they do not. Coyotes become too expert in snaffling off the fawns.

In the beautifully written book, *Where Rolls the Oregon,* the author, Dallas Lore Sharp, tells of the unequal fight between an antelope mother with two fawns and two coyotes who were expert hunters, each helping the other and each knowing exactly what the other coyote would do. This volume was published in 1914. Since then, many have seen similar things, nearly always ending in tragedy for the antelope, unless the witness interfered.

In the bulletin mentioned, *Food Habits of the Coyote,* the author classifies the food eaten. He says that 80 per cent of the coyote's food, such as rodents and rabbits, is a detriment to the human race and that only 20 per cent of it causes us losses when destroyed.

The trouble, though, with such a classification is that one man may lose five thousand dollars' worth of sheep, or a poultry grower may be put out of business, while another farmer may have no loss at all. Also, when a certain coyote gets lazy and decides to eat tame animals, he may dine exclusively on them, and forget all about the other 80 per cent of statistical food. Statistics are a weak argument to present to a man ruined by coyotes.

Their food changes with the seasons and they have an exceedingly varied diet: snakes, lizards, insects, fruit of all kinds, juniper berries, eggs, animals of every kind, protein-rich grass in early spring—they can eat anything and everything that has nutritive value.

Many of the same persons who shed tears over the killing

of a doe are equally worked up over the killing of a coyote. If coyotes were allowed to get as thick as nature would allow, we wouldn't have many deer or antelope. One can say triumphantly, "What about before white men came?" The answer is that we didn't have many deer then. Deer are at least ten times as numerous in Oregon now as they were seventy years ago. The covered-wagon folk didn't find many deer in Oregon. Neither did Fremont in 1843, nor Peter Skene Ogden in 1826. Even the fur trappers, who were often solitary hunters on the most remote streams, didn't find many deer in Oregon in most places.

Perhaps killing off the cougars had more to do with this enormous increase of deer than the thinning of the coyote population, but the fact remains that we have far more deer in Oregon now than at any time in the past.

Coyote hunting has been an exciting spare-time job for many ranch boys. In some counties ranchers had specially trained dogs and they'd ride out with the dogs and have a coyote hunt, without the ritual and ceremony of an English fox hunt, but with far more risk and excitement. Another sport developed, too. Reub commented on this:

"Ever since the first cowboy rode into coyote country with his coiled riata on his saddle, cowboys have been trying to rope the elusive wild dog of the desert. I have tried it many times, but if Lake County had to depend upon me to keep the coyote numbers down, we'd have all been hip deep in coyotes. I caught a few.

"You don't often catch a coyote away from the brush and there always seems to be a big sagebrush between you and him. He is a past master of dodging; he must have a D.D. degree, Doctor of Dodging. He will duck to one side, stop and run in the opposite direction. Unless you have a mighty well-reined horse, by the time you get turned around, the coyote is a hundred yards away and going strong.

"Most horses will follow a cow and turn with her, but not many horses see any sense in following a coyote. After a few turns, your horse gets mad or disgusted and loses all interest in the silly game. So the coyote gets away, laughing at you and your horse.

"If you do get a good throw at him in the open, you either miss or he jumps through your loop. A scheme that will sometimes work, if you have a good horse in a big open country, is to stay behind the coyote and whip him with your loop every chance you get. Maybe he'll come to bay, back up against a sagebrush and try to fight. I think his dignity is offended and he won't take any more undignified lashings in the rear. This doesn't hurt him much, but I can see it doesn't build him up.

"It's easier to run over him than to rope him. A horse won't step on him if he can miss, but the coyote is dodging in every direction and the hard-running horse can't always avoid him.

"One reason why the coyote nearly always gets away is that he is running the race for bigger stakes."

Another coyote-hunting scheme is to shoot them with a shotgun from a low-flying plane. Orville Cutsforth, of Lexington, asked me to go hunting with him. He says you get the coyote to running, then drop down with the plane flying in the same direction he is running, and, as you go by, the hunter must shoot at the tip of his tail. The superior speed of the plane carries the shot forward so that you hit him in the head.

This type of hunting has its risks, but I ran onto an airplane hunter on the desert in California who asked me to go with him. I cautiously asked how he did it. He'd start one to running, then dip down sharply and break the back of the animal with his wheels. I thought my life insurance company might not recommend this too highly. I didn't go.

From the earliest Indians right down to the latest tourist, the coyote has been an object of intense interest to everyone who strays out on the desert.

Every class views him differently. The naturalist has a

fierce protective interest; the passerby has lively curiosity; the sheep owner is desperately antagonistic; the wife of a rancher looks at him with sorrow and pain. If, like some politicians I know, he can stand anything except to be ignored, he should be well satisfied.

THE LITTLE FOLK OF THE DESERT

E. R. JACKMAN

THE OLD LAW OF COMPENSATION WORKS WITH CERTAINTY. It is inexorable and lacks justice, is often cruel, but it shows no favorites. The automobile, for example, erases distance, quadruples a man's efficiency, but it robs us of ability to see. We whiz through the desert at seventy miles an hour and say, "My, what a waste. Absolutely nothing to see for the last three hundred miles." In the horse days, every cowboy or sheepherder knew more about his surroundings than the smartest pavement traveler now.

Reub's father, shy of book knowledge but long on observation, said, "There are three rules that apply to the desert birds and animals:

1. A hare runs, a rabbit hides;
2. A bird takes food to its young, a fowl takes its young to the feed;
3. A squirrel feeds in the daylight, a rat feeds at night."

The desert is teeming with life, all engaging in the starkest drama known, the fierce struggle to live. It has been said that evolution is merely an unceasing attempt to find forms of life that can fit into every cranny of this earth. Mother Nature has done a remarkable job toward that goal.

Most of the small animals of the desert are not seen by the traveler, but each of the desert counties will have perhaps ninety different species of mammals, maybe two hun-

Photo by Jim Anderson, Oregon Museum of Science and Industry, Portland

LUPINE

Photo by Jim Anderson, Oregon Museum of Science and Industry, Portland

INDIAN PAINTBRUSH

Photo by Jim Anderson, Oreg
Museum of Science and Industr
Portland

MARIPOSA LILY

Photo by Jim Anderson, Oreg
Museum of Science and Industr
Portland

MOUNTAIN LILY

Photo by Jim Anderson, Oregon
Museum of Science and Industry,
Portland

DESERT PRIMROSE

DEATH CAMAS

GREAT HORNED OWL

WILD SALSIFY

FERRUGINOUS ROUGH-LEGGED HAWK
It lives mostly on rabbits, squirrels, and mice, and should be protected

dred or more different birds, a dozen reptiles, insects by the hundreds, and thousands of plants.

To get some inkling of the animal life, find a place where there is a rod or two of smooth sand. Toward night take a board and level the loose sandy soil, making a surface free of all tracks. Then go to bed in the back of a station wagon.

At first you will be wrapped in a blanket of stillness, but soon you hear the dozens of little desert folk. Scratchings, squeaks, whirs, small cries of terror, create an impression that minute chaos is erupting—all of this in an area apparently devoid of life. If there has been no wind, examine at daylight the smooth sand-parchment sheet you prepared. Every square foot of it will record travels of little animals.

The Indians knew these animals because they had time to study them. The Paiutes, mainly desert citizens, had a name for each. They ate many of them, and white persons who have had enough bravery to try have testified that most of them are delicious. It is said that he was a brave man who first ate an oyster. It would perhaps be an act of equal heroism to eat a civet cat (little skunk), or a nice plump mouse.

Many persons have starved to death in desert, forest, or prairie abounding in edible plants and animals. The Indians lived in such places for thousands of years, with a diet complete with what scientists have found best for us. They did what came naturally. They looked at the life around them. They watched the squirrels, mice, rabbits, deer, porcupines; saw what the animals ate, and tried it. In the main, animals' tastes are similar to ours. Not identical—but usually if an animal, with every sign of enjoyment, eats a plant or another animal, we can eat the same thing without harm. The Indians ate high up on the wilderness with an astoundingly varied diet.

Scientists long ago began to study what they call "ecology," the relation of plant and animal life to environment. In doing so they soon noticed that some animals, plants, and insects lived only in the desert; others couldn't exist there; others lived only in the high mountains. So, to keep from repeating forever the environment in their descriptions, they divided the earth's land area into seven primary life zones, each with several subzones. Oregon has five of these primary seven.[1]

Kinds of Desert Mammals in Oregon

Our desert is what they call the "Western arid division of the upper Sonoran." Some of the small mammals of this life zone include: three kinds of rabbits and hares; three kinds of squirrels; nine different mice; two gophers; two skunks; the Kangaroo rat and the wood rat, neither of them really a rat; the Nevada desert fox; and several kinds of bats that mainly inhabit lava caves.

The larger animals are: badgers, bobcats, coyotes, porcupines, antelope, and mule deer. We once had buffalo and mountain sheep. When Malheur Lake went dry, dozens of buffalo skeletons were exposed. On Hart Mountain on a smooth, vertical rock face, is an Indian drawing of three rams, plainly mountain sheep. We have the Mutton Mountains in Wasco County, Sheep Mountain in Grant County, and Sheep Rock in central Lake County, named for the mountain sheep, plentiful in eastern Oregon only a hundred years ago.

We had the prairie gray wolf, too, at one time. One skeleton was found in the south ice cave southeast of Bend. A few others were killed as late as 1920. The sheep disappeared from the desert around 1880. The buffalo vanished before the white men came. Paiute Indians said a bad winter cleaned them out. There was no well-defined route for seasonal migration from north to south as the plains buffalo had, so they adopted eastern Oregon for a year-round home. It proved to be a poor winter resort.

---

[1] See Appendix G for the names and brief descriptions.

Rabbits and Hares

1. ROCKY MOUNTAIN SNOWSHOE HARE

A person who hasn't hunted and eaten these, especially when he was young, has missed a special boyhood thrill. Wait for a snowstorm, followed by clear weather, then head for the timbered hills. The hares will be pure white then and hard to see. Watch for their bright black eyes, or for movement against a spruce or fir with branches clear to the ground. They make the best eating of all wild rabbits, especially in the winter. To me, as a boy, they tasted better than chicken, and I expect they still would.

They are well named because they can skip over the snow, even if not crusted. They have long feet covered with hair and can outrun a coyote in loose snow. They depend so heavily upon their invisibility that they sit humped up, perfectly motionless, and let a man get close to them. They then explode in a shower of snow and normally get away before the hunter can figure out the right end of the gun.

They aren't a typical desert animal, being partial to woods where they like brushy, thicket-type growth, but they occur along the edges of the Oregon desert, close to timber, especially where a string of brush may run out into the desert along a stream course.

2. OREGON JACKRABBIT

In 1915 the desert homesteaders complained bitterly about the jackrabbits eating up their gardens, flowers, and fields of dryland grain. If a man had a little water for irrigation, and seeded alfalfa, the jacks had a ball. They ate in it all summer, and when winter came, they would dig out the crowns and eat them to three or four inches below the ground. The alfalfa didn't enjoy this and entire fields would die.

In Harney County, homesteaders appealed to the county

court. The court, accustomed to the jacks but not so accustomed to drylanders, tried to shut off complaints by posting a five-cent bounty. In the one year they paid for 1,029,182 jackrabbits, or a total of $51,459.10. This cured the court—the bounty was removed because most of the homesteaders paid no taxes, and stockmen didn't enjoy paying money to drylanders. This was the only source of income to many of the homesteaders.

It was common practice for a homesteader, after he proved up and got a government patent to his land, to carry this around in his coat pocket, or file it in the Montgomery Ward catalog. If he recorded it, his taxes started at once, but until then it was officially still government land. If he sold his homestead, or mortgaged it, he had to prove ownership by recording and lost his tax immunity.

Many of these folks lived on the rabbit bounty and greeted its removal with loud displeasure. The rabbits were the primary ingredient in many a stew. The desert wives traded knowledge on how to prepare them in new and tempting ways. Reub, when I asked him if they were good to eat, said, "Good to eat? If they hadn't been, I'd never have weighed over forty pounds."

There were big, organized drives in those days. All the homesteaders would get together, form a huge crescent, and drive the jacks in front of them into some predetermined spot with close-mesh wire on three sides. The drives netted 2,000 to 5,000 jacks. They were killed with clubs. With rabbits running in every direction, shooting was too dangerous. Dogs and boys enjoyed it, the neighbors had the pleasant feeling of cooperation for the benefit of all, the women served hot coffee and sandwiches, and everyone felt good about it except the jacks.

Jackrabbits got their name from the long ears that naturally reminded someone of the ears of a jackass. They are not at all homebodies; their housekeeping is sketchy. They have a scooped-out place under a bush. Even when thick, so that a person along toward evening can see hundreds of them, they act like total strangers, each pursuing his own rabbit business as though he were the only jack on the premises.

Sam Boardman, father of Oregon's park system, had a keen zest for living and I always talked with him when I saw him. At the beginning of the state's highway system, he begged the fledgling Highway Commission for funds to start trees along the Columbia River Highway where it runs through the desert for one hundred miles between The Dalles and Pendleton. They couldn't see it. In those days Sam had little income and few prospects. He lived at Boardman. He kept at the tree idea and finally induced Bob Withycombe, superintendent of the Union Experiment Station, to furnish trees.

Sam planted Russian olive, Ailanthus, and black locust all along the highway, hauled water and started them nicely. This was from 1922 to 1925. I was traveling the highway one day and found Sam placing little rings of desert cactus around each tree. I stopped to ask. He said, "After I'd plant a tree, I'd come out in a few days to water it and I'd notice a young jack would come loping over the prairie. He'd see my tree and think to himself he'd never seen that before. So he'd hop up to it, smell it, then sit down and start to eat the bark. I s'pose they've got to live like everything else, and if it takes my trees to keep 'em alive, they're going to eat, but I'll be damned if I'm going to have the ———— sitting down to it!"

This habit of eating bark on young trees has enraged most everyone who has tried to make a home in eastern Oregon, even within the towns. The protection, of course, is a high sleeve of stout metal screen around the trunk.

Since Mark Twain described the jacks "kicking the miles behind them," the speed of the long-eared breed has been a Western legend.

They can outrun a lone coyote, partly because they are artful dodgers. The coyotes learn to circle them, and two coyotes can outmaneuver one jack by relaying. One runs while the other rests. I doubt if this is instinct on the coyote's part—it must be brains. Vernon Bailey[1] says they can do thirty-five miles per hour.

The jacks rarely make a noise, but I heard one scream in fright as a bobcat sprang on him, and the noise was the purest expression of terror I have ever heard, a fine mood setter for a horror film.

Desert dwellers, plants or animals, have one thing in common: they economize on water. The jacks do not need it —they live by thousands far away from any water. There are innumerable desert stories about them. "It's so dry this year that all the jackrabbits are carrying their lunch." "We had a five-inch rain yesterday—that is, five inches between drops. And you know what? It killed the jacks by the thousands! Ran 'em to death trying to dodge the drops!" Scientists say that desert animals can break down carbohydrates, separating the water from the carbon, so they do not need any H_2O from stream or pond.

The jacks offer a human health hazard when they are too thick. Tularemia will appear and one can see sick jacks everyplace he looks. That's a real good time to let them alone. Humans can catch tularemia.

After that it will take some years to build up another population so thick that all the desert roads are paved with rabbitskins.

They are night prowlers, like most of the desert mammals. They thereby avoid heat. On our mile-high deserts, nights are cool. I have seen over 100° temperatures at noon drop far enough to cause a sharp freeze at night. Changes of 70° between midday and midnight are not the rule, but are common.

Jacks have a wide-ranging appetite. Anything green that grows is on their grocery list. They like grass, hence compete with domestic animals. They will gather for miles

---

[1] Vernon Bailey, *The Mammals and Life Zones of Oregon* (U.S. Department of Agriculture, Bureau of Biology, "Survey of North American Fauna," No. 55), Washington, D.C., 1936.

around to welcome the advent of an alfalfa field into the community.

Scientists, when asked "When is a rabbit a hare?" say that hares are born with eyes open and are born with fur, whereas rabbits are born naked with eyes closed. The hares live above ground and have no real home, whereas the rabbits make burrows and spend much time underground. So jackrabbits are hares.

At least two types of jacks live in Oregon, distinguished by color of tail. The white-tailed jack has mastered the art of camouflage better and turns nearly white in winter. In that respect he resembles the snowshoe rabbit, but the latter is primarily a timber dweller, whereas the white-tail is a desert denizen. The white-tail is noticeably larger than the black-tailed jack, is more prolific, and is better to eat. The names aren't quite true. The tail of the black-tail is black on top, white below. The other's tail is white top and bottom. The white-tail may weigh up to thirteen pounds, whereas the black-tail that weighs seven pounds is a big fellow.

They have similar habits.

3. Sagebrush Cottontail

Most every boy raised in the West has hunted these cunning little animals, and has eaten them. They are true rabbits, not hares. They cannot outrun any predator, so hide in brushy areas close to their burrows. Many hunters, sneaking up on a deer, have been startled enough to jump and warn their intended prey when a little cottontail scurried from underfoot and dashed into the sagebrush.

Other wild animals and birds know that this appealing animal can be graded "choice." He is mainly nocturnal, but is often scared up in daylight when he disappears, as by magic, as one watches. He is rarely in sight for more than three jumps.

Since his range is limited to a small area around his burrow, the cottontail usually makes trails or runways under the brush and follows these on his nightly searches for food. Farm boys learn to find these trails and hang miniature snares, or lassos, in them with the loops held open. Such a trapline, though, must be visited every day, and even then birds or four-footed animals may have found the snared rabbit and appropriated him.

As compared to the big jacks that weigh five pounds or more, the cottontails weigh two pounds or less, fully furred.

4. Pygmy, or Sage Rabbit

These entrancing little bright-eyed creatures are animated bundles of soft fur. True desert dwellers, they have burrows that must take many, many days to dig. Their favorite location is under a large sagebrush, and centuries of persecution have taught them to have auxiliary entrances. They will pick out a spreading, healthy sage of such a size that a coyote, digging hungrily on one side, cannot see the other side of the bush. So, as the coyote digs, the little rabbit slips out the other side and scurries silently away, helping the coyote's disposition not at all.

A person wonders why these miniature rabbits have not been domesticated. Now that villages are growing in sagebrush lands, inhabited by persons seeking nature and avoiding the clang and clatter of civilization, perhaps such a business will spring up.

The soft, furry little desert dwellers live on sagebrush and are reported to have a strong taste on that account. Even jackrabbits are better to eat, while cottontails and snowshoe rabbits are good enough to grace any table. But there is no wild creature more deserving of the overworked word "cute" than these dwarfs of the rabbit tribe. They tip the scale at about a pound, fighting weight.

Chipmunks

Here is a jolly, playful, inquisitive, easily tamed group of animals that charm youngsters whether red-skinned or white. They are miniature squirrels, but are differentiated from the other members by having stripes on their heads. Most squirrels do not have real stripes on the body either, but the golden-mantled squirrel does.

A man in Alaska has made an excellent income for himself and contributed handsomely to United States tax coffers by packaging and selling seeds of Alaskan wild flowers. I imagine a family with a flare for advertising and a feeling for living things could develop a fine income by raising, exhibiting, and selling the common desert plants and animals. I am offering this marvelous money-making possibility free —not even green stamps are needed. But I warn any takers that they won't succeed unless genuinely interested in their merchandise. They must be scientist and naturalist, must have keen observation, and must have the elusive group of virtues called "personality." But if such a person (or family) exists, he will surely have chipmunks as a most salable product.

Here is an odd feature of animal life, pointed out first by Vernon Bailey, I think: The animals that do not hibernate usually store food for winter. Food storers are not friendly with others of their kind. They do not believe in socialism in any form; their creed is "what is mine is mine."

Food storers are thus rugged individualists dedicated to private enterprise. They kill, if they can, any other animal that covets their stored food supply. Animals that have solved the winter food problem by convenient and inert winter hibernation are likely to be sociable with others of their race. What do they have to lose? Zero isn't divisible.

Maybe there is a moral here somewhere. It can be religious, political, or in the realm of social behaviorism. Religionwise, the "more blessed to give than receive" doctrine— common to all great religions—is contrary to the creed of

the animal food storers. Maybe, though, the theory of lay-
ing up treasures in heaven instead of upon this earth is
merely an extension of the theory of the storers, substi-
tuting intangible assets for the tangible. As to ethics and
social behavior, we do not find too much in nature to delight the starry-eyed of the world.

William Wordsworth's oft-quoted lines apply well to most
of the animal kingdom:

> . . . The good old rule
> Sufficeth them, the simple plan,
> That they should take who have the power,
> And they should keep who can.

This seems to be wandering away from chipmunks. Two
of the kinds found in the desert are listed here and described
briefly. Oregon has a dozen other chipmunks, but most
of them are woods creatures, not adapted to the desert.

1. KLAMATH CHIPMUNKS

Highly colored. Stripes are: three black, two brown, two
gray, two white. A lot of stripes for such a tiny creature.
They live in the foothills adjacent to the desert, as much of
Klamath County is. They like conifer seeds, are easily tamed
and lose their fear of man quickly. But if you like to have
them around your woods cabin, you'd better have a lot of
food boxes lined with tin.

2. SAGEBRUSH, OR DESERT CHIPMUNK

Very small, a true desert dweller. If you need to describe him with just one word, it would be "slender." He
has an abnormally long tail. His stripes are: five black,
two light gray, two dark gray. His long tail helps in balanc-
ing him as he climbs about the sagebrush branches, eating
the small sagebrush seeds. For this gift from the sage, he

returns the favor by eating any small worms found on it. It takes a dozen of him to weigh a pound.

Squirrels

1. GOLDEN-MANTLED GROUND SQUIRRELS

These resemble chipmunks and are usually called that. They are common in timber all over eastern Oregon, but are found in the desert adjacent to timber. They are larger than chipmunks, and their bodies are chunkier. They weigh up to half a pound. They have four black and two white stripes. Outside the striped area they have a distinctive

Photo by Joe Van Wormer, Bend, Ore.

THE GOLDEN-MANTLED GROUND SQUIRREL

Called a "chipmunk" by most persons, this is one of eastern Oregon's most charming citizens. He is playful, easy to tame, and is a jolly little friend. But do not leave bacon or butter within his reach.

beautiful golden color, maybe closer to what we speak of as "old gold."

They live in underground burrows, but climb about with dexterity. Where a chipmunk will regard you with great nervous activity, this pretty little squirrel will sit motionless on a stump or fence post for a long time watching you with interest. They tame easily, and even the wild ones will come up to a person and beg for peanuts. In places where people gather regularly, such as parks, these squirrels are practically on the dole, and refuse to do regular squirrel work.

Long ago they voted for daylight saving time and do no gallivanting at night. They have large cheek pouches that they fill with most any food a man will offer and store it away until a day when peanut donaters are absent.

Their appetite ranges widely. They take up residence where, as the race of man goes by in swift automobiles, it kills all kinds of wildlife that may venture onto the highway. The little scavengers then come out and eat the meaty parts of the unlucky birds or rodents.

They do no real damage at all, beyond such things as stealing or contaminating butter unwisely left within their reach, stealing baits from traps, and nibbling at bacon. Anyone who wants an interesting sight around camp may have it by leaving a large bacon rind or a big slice of watermelon within the squirrels' reach. They will eat on it for a time, then feel the need for a bath. If dust is handy, they will wash their paws and faces in it with great vigor and thoroughness, just as a human might after eating corn on the cob.

The sight of the beautifully colored little squirrels, their lack of fear, their antics, playfulness, and actions, are surely ample pay for any small annoyance they may give.

2. Antelope Squirrel

In Oregon these clean and dainty little squirrels are found

only in the desert. They are about the size of a large chipmunk, but with heavier, more muscular bodies, much shorter
tails, very short ears, and large cheek pouches. They have
one broad white stripe along each side, thereby distinguishing them from chipmunks with several stripes. They are
pure white underneath, cinnamon color on back. Their
tails are white underneath, and as they run they curl the
tails over their backs, giving a flashing white appearance to
the rump, as viewed from behind. Hence, the name, antelope squirrel.

They believe in talking it over, with a shrill cry almost
like a whistle. They are out in the daylight and are attrac-
tive. They do no conceivable harm and any camper who
amuses himself by shooting them has scant regard for the
out-of-doors. Don't trust him. He'd probably poke things
into babies' eyes.

3. OREGON GROUND SQUIRREL

These gray squirrels are mainly desert folk, but they like
open spots such as warm south slopes, inside the timbered
lands. They are only half as large as the meatier Columbian
ground squirrel, depend upon their burrows for protection,
and do not store much food. They have cheek pouches,
just in case, but do not use them much. Some men carry
empty brief cases, as a status symbol.

These squirrels are one up on the labor unions, pressing
for a five-day week. The squirrels have achieved a five-
month year; they are inactive above ground from July to
the next March.

They are tough on rye fields, newly seeded spring grain,
new grass seedings. A person who trustfully scatters seed
on top of the ground in a squirrel-rich field may do so
optimistically, but he is soon misting optically. The squirrels from all around regard such fields as specially prepared
for them and within a few weeks no seed is left. Even when
the grain is covered, they learn that drills leave it in nice

straight rows, that they follow, happy to find such a systematically arranged food supply.

There is an old rhyme, outlawed now by DDT and other alphabetical combinations. It referred to the farmer and seeding. It went:

> One for the rodent
> One for the crow
> One for the worm
> And two to mow.

Such prodigality sufficed fifty years ago, but any present-day farmer with such a philosophy is soon a regular customer at the county welfare office.

4. Speckled Ground Squirrel

This species claims the desert for home. He is mainly gray, but has small white spots over him. He is very short-tailed. His clan were taught military lore by an evolutionary general, because, when a coyote or man appears, or a hawk is seen, the first to see the danger gives a warning whistle and all the little squirrels within hearing spring to attention, arms at sides, all smiles wiped from faces, heels together, chests out, shoulders back—a field full of toy soldiers.

They do not store food, do comparatively little damage, and hibernate most of the year.

5. Sage Squirrel

These little animals are the size of the golden-mantled squirrel and are in the desert in the extreme southeastern corner of the state. They have short tails, short legs, and are gray. They do not need water and the Paiute Indians say they are excellent for human food.

Maybe, if we ever get into an atomic war, we will need to know such things. If supermarkets were destroyed, along with wholesale groceries, trucking lines, and railroads, the deserts would be the best place to live, but what would the survivors eat? Answer—sage squirrels. Each county's civilian defense organization should be listing edible plants and animals found in the county.

Several other squirrels occur on the desert, some restricted to small areas.

Woodchuck

February 2 is "Groundhog Day" and Missouri even made it such by legislative act. If the groundhog, breaking his hibernation, and venturing from his rocky den, on that day sees his shadow, he will know winter will stay in the land for six more weeks, but if the day is cloudy and no shadow is visible, then he has done the right thing in coming out, for spring has sprung. This beguiling bit of unnatural history was imported, duty free, from England and Germany early in our national life. Its only advantage is that millions of people, through it, learn of woodchucks—persons who would never hear of the animal were it not for this gentle and appealing superstition.

The woodchuck is poorly named. He does not live in the woods, though he might reside in a big pile of wood. He is called "groundhog," too, and that isn't a good name, for he prefers to live in rocks. Vernon Bailey points out that we should chuck these names and call him "rockchuck," which would at least identify his preferred home, even if he doesn't chuck any rocks, either.

He is big, gentle, fat, slow, and peaceful. He may weigh up to ten pounds, does not store food, hibernates, gets too fat in the fall to keep his waistline, and the Indians considered him one of the best of all animals for adorning a dinner table.

Before public welfare programs, when hungry persons had to go out and forage some food or stay hungry, many frontier citizens tried eating them and found the meat rich and delicious. The word "groundhog" was fastened on them because, as the hog does, they get fat if food is plentiful.

They den up late in the fall and are not typically desert animals. In Oregon, though, they are sometimes found around the edge of the desert.

The predatory animals and birds just dote on them. They resemble a ground squirrel, but are more highly colored, are clearly more yellow than gray. Their danger signal is a sharp whistle, unlike the various chirps of other rodents.

The proper name of this usually harmless animal is "marmot," but scientists probably won't be able to change his common names from the misleading "woodchuck" and "groundhog."

The Pack Rats

There are several of these trade rats or pack rats in Oregon, but some are not found in the desert. Humans dislike them because of their strong, musky odor that fills deserted cabins that hunters would like to take over. They are not much afraid of humans, and when the hunters have gone to bed, the busy rodents see to it that their human guests get very little sleep. They run across the beds, and even over the faces of those trying to sleep. Shoes thrown at them may hit another hunter, but the rat is soon back. If a man in such a cabin has trustfully piled his money, watch, extra bullets, and good-luck pieces on the floor, his first act in the morning is to look accusingly and speculatively at the other men in the group, wondering which is a kleptomaniac.

In the primary grades, I went to a country one-room school. In the middle of the school year, pencils, erasers, rulers, pens, and all the small adjuncts of education began to disappear. The teacher gave us talks upon honesty and said she wouldn't tell the parents of the guilty child if he would just quietly return the stolen articles. This had no effect except to make everyone in the school, about fifty, a suspect. Such a thing is terribly hard on morale, and inevitably it happened that someone publicly accused an-

Photo by Jim Anderson, Oregon Museum of Science and Industry, Portland

KANGAROO RAT

Photo by Jim Anderson, Oregon Museum of Science and Industry, Portland

TURKEY BUZZARD

The correct name for this sanitarian of the desert is "turkey vulture."

Photo by Glenn Lorang, Dishman, Wash.

WILD BUCKWHEAT

Photo by Glenn Lorang,
Dishman, Wash.

WILD ASTER

by Glenn Lorang, Dishman, Wash.

DESERT HAWK'S-BEARD

Photo by Glenn Lorang,
Dishman, Wash.

PENSTEMON

Photo by Charles Conkling, Portland, Ore.

STEENS MOUNTAIN, SOUTH OF BURNS, OREGON

Here, near the close of day, the sheep are brought together to spend the night in
Blitzen Gorge.

other child of being the thief. This made school a kind of hell for the accused. He was shut out of games, had to eat lunch alone, and no one walked home from school with him.

When the year was nearly over, the long stovepipe in the room got out of plumb and the teacher sent two of the bigger boys into the attic to fix it. They found a neat heap of all the stolen articles. That was my first experience with pack rats. I have had many others since. I have often wondered if such wrongly accused children suffered any permanent character erosion.

These pilfering rogues are maligned and wrongly accused, themselves. We call them "rats" and the word carries damnation by humans. Countless thousands have killed them for no other reason than their name. They are *not* rats at all, and neither is the common kangaroo rat of the desert.

A little boy, with other children, caught a pack rat away from its home and killed it in a frenzy of activity. Unknown to him, the minister was calling. He ran to his mother excitedly yelling at the top of his voice, "Mamma! We caught a dirty ol' rat an' we kicked him an' gouged him an' hit him until . . ." and here he noted the minister and finished piously and primly ". . . until God called him home," holding up the discarded body as proof.

So the cleanly, pretty, and vastly interesting little Neotoma is classed as a "dirty ol' rat" and killed without mercy. Their nests are clean as can be, the animals are clean, and when they take over an empty building, they, by common consent, pick out a room, or a corner, for their excrement. They often live in rimrock or rock cliffs, and here, too, their sewage disposal unit is located outside the home.

Geologists, without benefit of training in the subject, often find a black, asphalt-like layer in the rock and get excited about it, burning, tasting, and applying other amateur tests. Such places mark outhouses of unnumbered generations of wood rats. Time, weather, and moisture decompose the naturally dry pellets into gummy black formless material. In the same way, wood rat urine, deposited in the same place over many years, will make a white layer, resembling lime.

They do not multiply very fast and are not heavy eaters, hence they do no harm to crops. They make fine pets because they do not seem to suffer from loss of freedom.

Oregon has several species of the little creatures: the bushy-tailed rat, Nevada wood rat, desert wood rat, and others. They are distinguished mainly by color and size, for all have the same habits.

Most of them weigh less than a pound and build small nests, hardly large enough for the individual rat to curl up in and keep warm. They do not talk things over between themselves, unless thumping with the feet is some form of Morse code unknown to humans. They do not hibernate and do not store much food, either. They have small piles of berries or leaves picked while green. Sometimes their soft, neat little nests are inside large mounds of twigs, sticks, thistle heads, burlap bags, wool, or whatever they can find. Presumably these "houses" are for protection and warmth.

Kangaroo Rat

The kangaroo rat is a tastefully decorated night-foraging, extremely busy little rodent that leaps on its hind legs, using its front legs neatly for gathering food, holding it while eating, and for putting away food in its underground pantries, cupboards, and granaries.

Its homes are conspicuous. Of all the desert animals, it seems to need a highly visible home, instead of making it inconspicuous as many of the smaller kinds do. The jacks don't even have any homes at all; they just camp out and avoid taxes. But the kangaroo rats have homes built up a couple of feet above the surface around them. They may be two- or three-story, split level, or ranch-type, depending upon the ratty architect.

These houses have several doors, always above the level

of the adjacent land, so that melting snow or running water won't come in the front or back door, making a mess of the furniture. Food for winter is stored in special compartments, carefully segregated. The salads are never mixed with the cereals. Wheaties are kept separate from the proteins, each in a little room off one of the main hallways. Sleeping quarters are normally the rooms farthest away from the doors. To confuse would-be burglars, there are many dead-end streets.

As compared to the homeless, careless, and carefree species, such a jackrabbits, the little kangaroo rats are busy, busy, busy. Their homes and winter food supplies weigh heavily upon their consciences, and they never take time off to call on the neighbors, listen on a party line, or chat with a passerby. Every day is a work day with no forty-hour week nonsense. The amount of stuff they store is incredible, running into many bushels—often far more than they could eat in a lifetime. They do not heed the biblical warning "Lay not up for yourselves treasures upon earth." Storage of seeds, leaves, small pieces of stems cut up for better handling, is accomplished by carrying the load in the cheek pouches.

A kangaroo rat is geared for desert life. He needs no water, lives off the land around him, and doesn't see any good in water. He hates it as much as the grimiest small boy, who has been defined as a loud noise entirely surrounded by dirt. He hates the light, too. He comes out only on rainless nights when the moon has been abstemious, or, at least, isn't full.

But he is a fierce little fighter. John Scharff, of Burns, tells how the CCC boys, who were organized somewhat along army lines, would develop squad morale and were forever seeking contests. They would go out with flashlight and gunny sack, capture kangaroo rats, take them back to barracks and match them in fights to the death—no holds barred. Betting was lively. If one group had a kangaroo rat that had cleaned up on the champions of other groups, thus acquiring a "rep," their willingness to bet on their fighter was limited only by the size of their pokes.

These rats measure a foot long, from nose to tail tip, but the tail makes up about 60 per cent of the length. The kangaroo mice look much like them, but are dwarf replicas, though both try to gain stature by hopping on their hind legs, thus appearing taller than if they dropped to all fours. They do no harm and the man who would deliberately destroy them should be shut up somewhere.

Mice

Although mice are the commonest mammals over most of the earth, there is a curious lack of stories and legends about them. Walt Disney, in an inspired moment, created Mickey Mouse and charmed young and old of all nations with stories of his cocky, clever, and humorous little animal. One titled Englishman said, "I would rather have created Mickey Mouse than to have ruled a nation." I know of no such folklore about mice as we have about other wild animals. No athletic teams are named "The Mice," though we have "Badgers," "Bobcats," "Wolves," "Beavers," "Ducks," and "Bears" all over the gridirons, diamonds, and basketball courts of the land.

We have "Hickory, dickory, dock," wherein a mouse ran up the clock, but nothing happened thereafter. As legends go, it is mighty slack drama. The plot is thin, nothing to compare with the wolf pretending to be Red Riding Hood's grandmother.

Some of the numerous mice on our desert, as listed by Vernon Bailey, are:

1. Oregon grasshopper mouse. It takes ten of him to weigh a pound, but he can lick his weight in other mice anytime or anyplace. He has no real home but wanders all around in search of food. He feeds at night on any unlucky insect that comes his way and will clean a house

of insects in short order. Mormon crickets are his chosen food if there are any around. Pity that he doesn't like ants.

He has a short, thick tail, a reddish-brown back, a snow-white belly, with the white extending up the sides a short way.

These little mice must have watched a wolf back in history somewhere, for they point their noses to the sky and try to howl.[2] Bailey says that in alarm or protest they also bark as a tiny terrier their size might do.

2. Deer mouse. These white-footed and light-footed little wraiths of the night are common over the Oregon desert. There are several kinds, differing in color, size of ear, and length of tail. They are real desert species, not needing water. They eat berries and seeds, are nocturnal, usually live in underground nests, are timid and harmless. Their tails are rather short, but one kind, the Idaho Canyon mouse, has a long hairy tail. All of the kinds eat insects and they are the short-tailed, white-footed mice that are trapped in buildings on the desert. They do little damage and considerable good. Some kinds are so small that it takes eighteen of them to weigh a pound.

3. Meadow mouse. This is the villain that in 1958 over-ran all of eastern Oregon. As the name indicates, they prefer irrigated or subirrigated lands, so aren't true desert types, but when they assume plague proportions, they crowd out onto the desert. They can completely ruin a stand of grass or alfalfa in one winter. In the recent outbreak, one Klamath grower offered to bet all comers that if they threw a silver dollar out into his field of alfalfa, it would fall into an open mouse hole. He nearly always won.

No one would object much to this mouse if he weren't so prolific. When unchecked by disease, or by natural causes of death, they can mount up to many thousands to the acre. They are especially fond of legumes, and during the winter when other food is scarce, they may kill an alfalfa field.

They do not believe in the old rhyme about one for the

[2] E. Raymond Hall, *Mammals of Nevada* (Berkeley, Calif.: University of California Press, 1946).

rodent, one for the crow, one for the worm and two to mow—the rodent will take all five. They are also hard on bunch-type grasses, such as orchard and crested wheat grass. The grasses with creeping root stocks aren't so susceptible to damage.

They have several litters a year, but they do not breed in winter. They are mighty good trenchermen and consume their own weight of food in twenty-four hours. If a large man ate as much, he could put down the hatch two full-sized one-hundred-pound sacks of potatoes every day.

Predatory birds and animals find them tasty, so coyotes have a fine time catching them on the big wild hay meadows in Harney, Lake, and Klamath counties. Hawks find it profitable to soar endlessly over the meadows after the hay has been cut, dropping swiftly out of the sky many times a day to catch a meadow mouse.

These are dark-colored mice, sooty color above with lighter gray below. They tilt the scales at the rate of nine per pound—fighting weight. The grasshopper mice can do them in if the fight is fair.

4. Oregon creeping mouse. This is a pygmy among the mice, just as we have pygmy rabbits on the desert. They are short-tailed, light gray, do not get far from their burrows, and feed in daylight hours. They live in all of the sagebrush country, but one will hardly notice them, they are so small, so gray and timid. They do not make runways, as most other mice do, so creep around among the sagebrush, mostly unnoticed by everyone except the rattlesnakes, that seem especially fond of them.

5. Oregon gnome mouse. This truly engaging little dark-gray animal with the cream-colored underside and a light stripe along his sides, is related to the kangaroo rats and pocket mice, in that he has fur-lined cheek pouches. The most distinctive thing about him, though, is his abnormally large head, that gives him the gnome cognomen. His eyes, too, are unusually large and very bright, so that, peering

from under a sage plant, or from a burrow, he could be some desert-dwelling elf in rodent form.

He runs by hopping on his hind feet, using his delicate, quick little hands mostly to stuff seeds into his cheek pouches, and to remove the seeds for storage in his underground granaries.

He is nocturnal, does not hibernate, and spends the daylight hours asleep in his burrow. Perhaps to keep out heat, he usually closes the burrow entrances from within—a sort of go-into-a-hole-and-pull-it-in-after-you technique. He is gentle and not afraid of humans.

It takes about thirty of him to weigh a pound.

Photo by Joe Van Wormer, Bend, Ore.

COCK OF THE DESERT—THE SAGE GROUSE

At mating season the cocks meet at strutting grounds and do their stuff. They inflate the neck sacs, strut, stamp, dance, and threaten, but they seldom fight.

Pocket Gopher

Several species of these live in Oregon. They aren't real desert animals, since they prefer meadowland that is moist enough for easy digging, but has enough clay to hold together without caving in. They dig tunnels hundreds of feet long and use them for life if not disturbed. At intervals they dig a side branch, bring it to the surface, and bulldoze the soil out in little piles that are a menace to mower sections. In gopher country, mower sickles must be changed at least twice a day and maybe three or four times.

On irrigated lands they get in their worst licks. A little stream may start down the long run to the next lateral and never arrive. It may find a gopher burrow and follow it for a hundred feet or more, only to break out and flood a part of the field already irrigated, or perhaps run onto a neighbor's field. If it's tearing along underground at too much speed, it may carry soil with it and cause a disastrous washout.

Gophers are extremely fond of alfalfa roots and can soon ruin a field. One of the advantages of the new grazing alfalfas is that they can generate new shoots from the roots below the crown. Standard hay types die if cut off below the crown. In isolated little valleys where an alfalfa field is a summons to every gopher for a mile or two around, the owner will do well to seed Nomad, or one of the other varieties that can replenish the stand.

Several kinds of gophers exist, but the main species is the Townsend pocket gopher, though I doubt if they know much about the Townsend plan.

In the winter the little workers don't stop. They make tunnels through the snow, then fill those tunnels with soil from underground runways. This makes, in appearance, long ropes of soil winding around over the land under the snow. The snow melts, the long ropes freeze, get compacted, and when all of the snow is gone we see whole hillsides covered by these casts of earth, a little smaller than a fire hose, but larger than a garden hose.

In irrigated lands, the owner is almost forced to notice gophers, especially if he is growing alfalfa. County extension agents explain gopher control to someone almost daily.

BADGERS AND SKUNKS ARE NICE PEOPLE

E. R. JACKMAN

The California Badger

ONE OF THE DESERT'S MOST DISTINCTIVE ANIMALS, THE badger, has been saddled with a California name. In the early days of the state, when a man either rode horseback or didn't venture out, now and then a man and horse would come to grief when the horse stepped into a badger hole. This didn't happen often, because a horse can smell them and instinctively avoids their burrows.

But, since it *has* happened, the badger gets blamed and people's hands and minds are turned against him. Some of my best friends are badgers. For some poor reason, the word "badger" is used to describe a process of vicious annoyance of another person.

Badgers aren't mad at anyone, and avoid trouble. A dog, though, may mistake this attitude for fear, and think, "What fun! I'll badger this low-slung, inferior little beast." Whereupon the dog gets a surprise fully as instructive as his first encounter with a skunk or a porcupine. The badger's fur is long and dense, his hide extremely tough; a thick layer of fat lies beneath the hide. It is impossible for the dog to get a death grip. When he thinks he has one, he is nonplussed when the badger turns and grabs him by nose or foot, or rakes his face with sharp claws activated by leg muscles far stronger than those of the dog.

The badger, bedeviled by a dog, loves to seize the dog's

nose, then slowly back, step by step, dragging the astounded dog after him until they reach a burrow, which the badger sinks into. The dog meanwhile has frantically applied brakes to all four wheels, but the only result is to sink the badger's teeth still farther into the tender nose muscles. It takes the dog a long time to recover his enthusiasm, but it seems to be all in the day's work with the badger. He harbors no grudge.

If caught young, the badger makes an ideal pet. My brother, who lived near Malin in Klamath County, had one for years. He was affectionate, extremely clean, and not destructive. He got along well with the numerous dogs and cats on the ranch, never bothered chickens, turkeys, or ducks, and was pleased and happy whenever anyone noticed him.

William and Irene Finley[1] tell of their tame badger that was interesting enough, but would bite the ankles, legs, and hands of his keepers. The full-grown one of my brother, Harry, never offered to bite and was friendly and charming.

They are born gypsies, or nomads; they sleep where night overtakes them. Digging is their best talent and they make their living that way, taking their pay in squirrels. If they live where the ground freezes, they hibernate, but if they can dig, they see no reason for wasting time all winter.

Their legs are short, their bodies flat. The same architect who designed the turtle must have made the original blueprints. They are muscular in the extreme. Once I tried to cook one. I had heard they were good to eat; the meat looked and smelled good. I cooked him all day and still he was too tough. A pressure cooker might have subdued him. There is no need to starve, though, if a badger is around. He weighs twenty pounds and that would keep a person for a week.

Right now, 1962, badger fur is rather valuable, large ones from the desert selling up to five dollars. An enterprising

---

[1] William and Irene Finley, *Wild Animal Pets* (New York: Charles Scribner's Sons, 1928).

person could develop a market for the little ones as unusual pets.

They are the world's champion diggers. One case is on record of a badger that started on level land and dug himself out of sight in one and a half minutes.[2] They aren't much afraid of humans, or of other animals, either. They have none of the incurable wildness of the bobcat or the coyote.

Great Basin Skunk

The Paiute word for skunk is *Poonuche*, which might well be the exclamation of any person upon his first encounter with that fragrant animal. The Chinook jargon word is equally good—*pipiupiu*.

A straight-thinking, logical bachelor in central Oregon, at the Grange meeting, blamed the poor clover seed crop upon the large number of old maids in the community. His argument was: they all keep cats; the cats keep mice in the fields cleared out; the skunks, unable to find enough mice to eat, turn to bumblebees for food; the bees pollenize the clover—hence, the inevitable conclusion, "if we bachelors want good clover seed crops, we've got to marry these old maids." This somehow introduces an ugly commercial aspect into the holy state of matrimony.

These beautiful, well-dressed animals, with their immaculate fashionable black and white formal clothes, make charming pets. They aren't naturally suspicious, so if caught young, they show man neither fear nor resentment. He hasn't "broken nature's social union," so far as they are concerned. They gambol around, playful as kittens. They like attention and show genuine affection for children. I knew a farm family near Grants Pass who had two fully-grown skunks. They were not kept locked up, were allowed

---

[2] Joseph Grinnell, Joseph S. Dixon, and Jean M. Linsdale, *Fur-Bearing Mammals of California* (2 vols.; Berkeley, Calif.: University of California Press, 1937).

in the house, and as long as I knew them, never once—er—ah —became unscrupulous.

These still had their scent glands; others who wish them for pets remove temptation. No tame skunk has ever taken advantage of his friends in this dastardly manner, but sometimes the dog of a visitor will push a skunk too far. City dogs do not like the results, and neither do the owners who must take the dogs home in family cars. If anyone thinks that dogs have no emotions except hunger and thirst, he should see a dog, mortified, ashamed, and dejected after he has bothered a skunk. He is a social outcast and knows it.

Another kind of skunk is the pretty little civet cat, or spotted skunk. He is adorned by a huge, fancy, plume-like white tail. He has a white spot on his forehead, one on each cheek, and several on his rump. He is small, but oh, my! He can throw his objectionable perfume clear across a room. In the early days in the West, a story grew that his bite always produced hydrophobia. This is pure nonsense. He can contract rabies from the bite of a rabid coyote, but he is far less likely to have it than is the family dog.

He loves the rimrock, where he prowls only at night, seeking such rodents as he can find. Except for an occasional skunk that takes up a permanent residence around the farmstead and stays as long as the chickens hold out, they do ranchers far more good than harm.

Their fur is usually in demand, and skunk farms are in existence. Right now, though, 1962, the price for skins is way down. It takes a good one to bring fifty cents, whereas they were worth dollars a few years back.

Another use for them is to spirit one into the one-room country schoolhouse as a kind of initiation for a new teacher. This seems to upset her a great deal, and education in that community grinds to a halt for a day or two.

No sight is so captivating as a family of six or seven baby skunks as they follow their mother, single file, across a country road. They are irresistible.

A long association with the strong skunk fragrance creates unawareness. In our valley lived a professional trapper. He caught skunks nearly every day. He was at our farm one day, and as we carefully maneuvered to keep upwind from him, he discoursed.

He said, "Trouble with most people is they don't understand skunks. Skunks don't want to waste their smell on humans—it's to protect 'em against coyotes and bobcats. If you know that and when you catch 'em, you finish 'em off quick, you can handle 'em and never even get a whiff. I handle 'em all the time and you'd never know it. One has never let loose on me for a long time now." Which was all right, except that we could detect his presence easily at one hundred yards.

We were a hospitable family in a hospitable land, but he was one person we scarcely dared ask in at mealtime.

The skunk's effective defense has robbed him of his proper place in literature. He is playful, extremely beautiful, responds to kindness, is not vicious, and should therefore be loved by humans. But no poet sings his praises; no moralist finds in him a lesson to guide us along the good path. He is unloved and unsung. For him no minstrel raptures swell. In Bartlett's book of famous quotations, there are eighty-one references to the sky—none at all to the skunk.

Porcupine

From Shakespeare's time the porcupine has intrigued poets, dramatists, and writers because, in all nature, there isn't anything else exactly like him, though some plants do pretty well, operating on the same principle. In *Hamlet*, the melancholy Dane says, "I could a tale unfold [that would cause] each particular hair to stand on end, like quills upon the fretful porpentine." Shakespeare lived in 1600 and in the 360 years since then the old English word somehow slid into "porcupine." The association with pigs, indicated by the change from "porp" to "pork," probably came about due to the grunting habit of this unique animal.

He can't see very well, his gait is slow and lumbering, he never discovered the trick of hibernating, his IQ can be

Photo by Jim Anderson, Oregon Museum of Science and Industry, Portland
THE PORCUPINE IS UNIQUE AMONG ANIMALS BECAUSE OF HIS DEFENSE
"He ain't mad at nobody," but all other animals carefully respect him

questioned, his mate has only one or two little ones a year —yet he has increased so that organized campaigns against him are carried out yearly.

There is a persistent belief that state laws protect him "because he is the one animal that a lost man can overtake and kill for food, thus saving countless people from a miserable death." That has only one fault. Oregon has never had such a law and probably no other state ever had it. The statement has truth—an unarmed man *can* catch and kill one, and they are good to eat. The Indians ate them, coyotes and bobcats eat them, and I have heard of hunters who tried them in a crisis and claimed they were good.

The Indians roasted them whole, without trying to skin them. The animals were roasted until the quills and skin were crusty and came off easily. I imagine this gives far better results than any sort of frying-pan treatment. In Argentina, where they truly love beef, they barbecue the animal with the hair and hide on, and claim it is better that way. No doubt it is, so if anyone wants to cook a porky, in a scientific mood of inquiry, I'd advise the Indian system. The porky is awfully hard to skin and probably the meat, in the process, will get contaminated from hair or soil.

The porcupine is scarce in western Oregon, but is overly plentiful in and near the timber all over eastern Oregon.

Children are warned, "Now stand back—they can throw their quills." This isn't true. The animals can slap the tail with some force and can thereby drive the quills into any animal within reach, but the quills are fastened in, the same as hairs, and they can't be thrown.

The quills are decorative, black tips on white bases, and the Indians used them for ornaments on ceremonial clothes. The black part has a large number of minute barbs. They are shingled back, so the tip can penetrate, but cannot be pulled out easily. The barbs swell when moistened, making it still harder to pull them out. Every movement of the body tends to work them in, and every now and then one

finds an animal on the desert dead or dying from an over-
dose of quills. The trouble is mostly in the mouth. It may
be so full of quills that the coyote, dog, or cow cannot eat.
But the quills may work in and puncture some organ that
doesn't work well when punctured. Or sores develop around
the quill and get infected.

A young horse, inexperienced and curious, will often
smell of a porcupine and get slapped in the nose. If you
examine the hind feet of the horse, you will often find
quills there, too. This shows, as clearly as though you had
witnessed it, that the surprised and angry horse had retaliated in the only way he knew, by whirling and kicking,
thereby getting quills in both ends.

Most dogs learn from one experience and thereafter go
out of their way to avoid this animated pincushion, but an
occasional dog harbors a fierce resentment and attacks, in
an ungovernable rage, whenever he sees one. The dog can't
seem to get the hang of things, because he snarls and bites
the hand of the man who is trying to remove the tormenting
objects.

If a man has a pitchfork handy, he can remove the quills
without help by slipping a tine on each side of the dog's
neck, then pushing the tines into the ground. The dog is
then helpless and the man can use both hands in pulling
out the quills, providing he sits on the dog.

Porcupines cause damage by eating the inner bark of
young pine trees—especially at the very tips of the trees.
They girdle the growing tip, causing the tree to send out
several new limbs, thus making a bushy tree of little commercial use. This tree damage has been plentiful enough
to lead to organized porcupine hunts with community prizes
for the person who kills the most. Most foresters secretly
hope that the campaigns will succeed only enough to thin
the numbers, not to exterminate the race. This bark-eating
habit is only practiced in the winter. In the summer they
eat broad-leaved plants of all kinds. They seem particularly
fond of ladino clover. I have seen many seed fields eaten

and trampled down so badly that the seed crop was destroyed. They like alfalfa, too.

Once Mel Burke, of the United States Forest Service; Garnet Best; and Art King, Extension Service; and I, were on a trip into the high Wallowas to make some grass plant-- ings and grass fertilizer trials. We camped the first night in a deserted cabin high up on Lostine River. In the middle of the night we were awakened by a shot, and Garnet came in with his mutilated bridle reins, chewed into pieces by a salt-loving porcupine. He held up the pieces of reins for us to view by flashlight. "Oh, well," said Mel, "it could have been a lot worse—it could have been mine," and he settled back into his warm sleeping bag.

In the morning I was getting breakfast when Mel came in and said, "Last night I said it could have been worse, and by ——— it was!" He held up his saddle cinch, completely gnawed in two.

This shows another kind of nuisance damage. The porkies will gnaw on anything that tastes of salt. Pitchfork handles, salt boxes carried into the hills horseback, floorboards around the stove, mangers in barns, saddles—the animals seem to be salt famished. This weak point is used in destroying them by mixing salt and strychnine and putting it in their "resting trees." They pick out a resting tree while doing their bark destruction in the winter. They return to this tree day after day. One can spot the trees by the large number of pellets below, by the moth-eaten appearance of the tree against the sky, and by the litter of needles and small twigs on the snow. Poison baits are nailed on the side branches ten or twelve feet above the ground and out a short distance from the trunk.

Moderate tree damage is of little concern because there are usually too many trees anyhow, but the animals are not at all skilled in selective harvesting and in any one place they may ruin all the trees.

Common sense would say, "Let's eliminate 'em." It isn't good to eliminate any part of nature's plan. Nature, at times, isn't a bit scrupulous about this herself. She eliminated hundreds of animals in Oregon and many more hundreds of plants by changing the eastern Oregon climate from near tropical to "arid upper Sonoran." Survival of the fittest is a pretty fair scheme, as long as it is carried out with reason and restraint, but in eastern Oregon, back at the dawn of history, the rule was "death to all, then let's start over." I think that's going too far. Maybe the whole thing was aimed at preparing for us a gigantic object lesson about nuclear weapons, because in northern Russia, prehistoric big elephantine creatures were killed so suddenly and given such a quick freeze that they are found standing upright in the ice and frozen mud that covers them.

The Bobcat

The Paiute Indian name for this free-wheeling pirate is an expressive *Too-hoo-oo.* He is pretty, but not cooperative. He is found all over the desert wherever there is food. His tufted ears, distinct sideburns, rich buff-colored fur with black spots, his absurd short tail, looking as if bobbed on purpose—all of these things make him handsome and noticeable. Ranchers or owners of service stations occasionally keep one in a cage, and strangers, beguiled by the beautiful big kitty, will try to pet him. After that their friends refer to them as Old Three Fingers.

Mostly they live in the rimrocks, preferring caves with narrow openings. They forage at night, but I have seen many in the daylight. When a person comes upon one suddenly, the cat will spit just as a tame cat does.

The food of bobcats includes all kinds of birds, and every animal, tame or wild, that they can kill.[3]

They like birds' eggs, large insects, and domestic cats. The latter seem to give bobcats an insufferable smug satisfaction. They are willing to stop at any time, no matter

---

[3] For a list of things found in bobcats' stomachs, see Appendix H.

how busy, to polish off a domestic cat. If bobcats are thick around a ranch, tame cats aren't.

There is a famous old limerick:

> There was a young lady from Niger,
> Who smiled as she rode on a tiger;
> They returned from the ride
> With the lady inside,
> And the smile on the face of the tiger.

Any pet cat that smiles, with friendly intent, upon a bobcat is soon inside.

At one time Oregon paid a bounty of one dollar on them. Now a lone dollar wasn't too much incentive, for, to collect it, one had to make a trip to town, sign forms, exhibit the scalp, and spend quite a bit of time. Most ranchers who killed them didn't bother to collect. Neither did deer hunters. Sheepherders, with flocks to look after, just couldn't run off to town. Government hunters were barred from collecting. So it can be assumed that most dead cats went bountyless. But from October 1, 1913, to December 31, 1914, bounty payments by counties were:

> Harney 1,039
> Malheur 595
> Lake 452
> Crook 182
> Baker 104

The fur isn't too durable, though handsome in color and design. Government hunters are required to save the skins, which are shipped to central markets and sold at auction. The price they bring is almost always too low to justify the work and expense. One man in Portland saw the skins selling at give-away prices, so arranged with tanners and a glove factory to buy some of them and make them up as gloves. I have had half a dozen pairs and have given them as gifts. They are perfectly marvelous for driving, can be

Photo by Joe Van Wormer, Bend, Ore.

A HANDSOME BOBCAT ON HIS DAILY DESERT TOUR FOR FOOD

He will eat almost anything that moves, and other wild animals don't pal with him much

washed, and are a pleasure to wear because of their soft flexibility and the way they fit the contours of the hand. If a glovemaker could get enough hides so that he could stock them regularly and have a complete line of sizes for men and women, he could surely have a flourishing business.

This year, 1962, ordinary sizes of bobcat skins from Oregon are worth about two dollars, and large skins sell for twice that. The paler colors from eastern Oregon are worth more than the highly colored fur from western Oregon.

Among wild and tame animals the bobcat is a social outcast. He trusts no one and has no animal friends. A coyote won't eat a bobcat, although the coyote may take the edge off his appetite by eating one of his own kind. Jays and magpies will often warn a man of the presence of a bobcat. They also warn rabbits or other intended prey and the cat feels no good will toward these birds.

Antelope

A popular song of over one hundred years ago had as its chorus:

> I'll chase the antelope over the plain,
> The tiger's cub I'll bind with a chain;
> And the wild gazelle with its silvery feet
> I'll bring thee for a playmate sweet.

Folks have been chasing the antelope over the plain ever since. They are truly plains dwellers and are the swiftest of our wild animals. When a motorist spies an antelope on the smooth bed of a dry alkaline lake, the temptation to try out the speed of the animal is almost irresistible, and many Oregonians have checked this point. They all say that a mature animal can hit a mile-a-minute pace for a short distance. Antelope can outrun a coyote with ease and take time out to make derisive remarks if so inclined.

The coyotes manage to keep antelope numbers down by ganging up on them when the fawns are young. Working together, one coyote can often manage to get the fawn while another keeps the mother busy. When the fawns are young, the mothers stay with the young only long enough to feed them, then leave, sometimes going as far as a quarter of a mile away. This is a protective device, because the mothers have hidden the young ones and told them not to move. A lurking coyote may see the mothers shifting about; they will not see the little fawns. The fawns have no scent detectable to a dog or coyote.

Something else keeps numbers down. Loss of fawns at weaning time seems heavy. Maybe it is nutritional. Not many are killed by hunters—less than five hundred yearly in Oregon.

Antelope are unusually handsome, tastefully decorated in a two-color arrangement. The rump has a large white patch, and when danger threatens, the hair on the patch rises, reflecting the sunlight with an on-and-off effect. Cahalane[4] has called them the desert heliograph. When watching for them, you want to look for three things: dust rising where you see nothing at first; movement against the sage; the white, flashing signal. It seems that nature played them a dirty trick to camouflage them and then give away their location by the white flag, reflecting the sun. But probably the signal can be seen by other antelope from farther away than a man or a coyote can see it, so it may help the species, even though it betrays the individual.

The white flashes help the State Game Commission when making the annual game census. They fly their planes fairly low, going away from the sun. The observer counts the glistening spots of the antelope over a wide area ahead of him. By making counts over the same courses yearly, they estimate numbers and decide how many hunting permits to issue.

Active scent glands release a strong musky odor that

---

[4] Victor H. Cahalane, *Mammals of North America* (New York: The Macmillan Company, 1947).

warns other antelope. There is no such thing as disturbing one animal without alerting the entire herd.

Every writer about this beautiful animal has commented upon the large black limpid eyes. Though an antelope is only a sixth as large as a horse, the antelope's eyes are as large as the horse's. The body is richly tawny, with pure white markings on the throat. The eyes are set wide apart, giving them, in effect, a wide-angle lens; by turning their heads a little each way, they can see the entire landscape.

A man can hunt deer successfully on foot and alone. With luck and some knowledge of deer, he may get his buck every year. It is unrewarding to hunt antelope that way. It is a team job for men just as it is for coyotes.

Deer and elk have solid hat racks, called antlers, shed annually. Cattle, sheep, and goats have hollow headgear called horns, because originally they were used as such. These hollow horns must last for life. Powder horns, horns such as Little Boy Blue used to blow on—such things explain the name horn. It wouldn't work well to make a powder horn out of a deer's antlers. The "cow with the crumpled horn, that tossed the dog" over the barn, had to use that same old crumpled horn as long as she lived. But the antelope, alone among the horned tribe, get new horns each year.

At the base of the horn, the antelope has some permanent horn stubs, as a man has permanent starting places for his fingernails. The old horn coverings loosen and are pushed off by the new horns growing from below. The horns that we see are really protection devices for the permanent small horns attached to the skull bones, somewhat as a thick, heavy glove is a protection for the hand. So the permanent horn stays, but the covering is discarded yearly. Very handy. Quite smart of the antelope to figure out such a scheme.

You rarely find an antelope horn that hasn't been gnawed on by nearly every other four-footed creature. They must be "horns of plenty" in the minds of other wild animals, for the discarded horns seem to make good chewing. Wild

THE ANTELOPE, OREGON'S MOST BEAUTIFUL WILD ANIMAL

The distinctive markings camouflage him so that he is hard to see except when running

animals chew on deer antlers, but don't put their hearts into it, and you can find deer antlers that lie for years undisturbed. Ranchers, service station owners, and others, occasionally make deer horn fences, but an antelope horn fence would attract every porcupine for miles around and a man would be fresh out of fence in no time.

Does have one or two fawns. They have learned a smart trick in that they hide the fawns, if they have two, one hundred yards apart so that if the ever-seeking coyote or bobcat finds one, the other may escape. The mother knows the "bird with the broken wing" trick, too, and when her remarkably keen eyes see a coyote near, she will deliberately lead him away from the fawns by pretending injury or lameness. Since every predator has had the experience of finding an injured antelope and dining on her handsomely, he licks his chops, feels that this is his day, and falls for the trick regularly.

A lone coyote has no stomach for a contest with an uninjured antelope. He knows she can outrun him anyhow, and if she wants to stand and fight, she may kill or maim him with her sharp hoofs. But he is always on the lookout for young fawns and wounded animals. Hunters in the desert naturally take many long shots, can't see the results clearly, often cripple an animal, watch it run out of sight, and decide they have scored a clean miss. Coyotes and bobcats vote overwhelming approval for such business.

Antelope have several scent glands that give messages to others of their species. There are even glands between the hoof claws. As you chase an antelope over the plain, in her track in the sand she leaves the time of day; name and address; telephone and social security number, in case another antelope comes along and wants a pen pal.

Antelope have some of the habits of sheep. In their wild state, sheep are gregarious, with a strong herd instinct. This has been lost in some breeds by confinement within fences for hundreds of years. The fine wools, though, herded in flocks in Spain, and long before that in the ranges of North

Africa and in the Holy Land, still retain the old instincts of the wild herds, and if they lose the herd, they are restless and ill at ease.

If you see a lone antelope, he is most likely a buck, because the does like company. Now and then an antelope will take up with a group of cattle and will graze and go to water with them for weeks—apparently just for the pleasure of their company. Maybe they have mutual friends, or haven't yet heard all of each other's jokes.

Horses on the desert can survive the winter by pawing the snow away from the grass. Cattle, sheep, and antelope have never learned much about this. The antelope, free to travel, and able to go through a wire fence on the dead run, tend to concentrate in winter on those parts of the desert where snow doesn't get deep. If snow comes, they can live on the leaves of sagebrush or greasewood. The latter is common on the alkali flats. Perhaps, because of their habit of grazing on brush and weeds that grow in alkali, they do not seem to need salt so much as some wild animals do.

The antelope of our plains has always been here. No other continent has any close relative, whereas deer much like ours are found nearly everywhere. The prehistoric fossil animals dug out of the colorful green claybeds along the John Day River include forbears of our pronghorns. They were native to Oregon forty million years ago. The vast and overpowering forces that destroyed camels, horses, elephants, gigantic pigs, and dozens of other animals, spared the antelope.

Perhaps the secret is transportation. Through the ages of history, those races of man that established any kind of supremacy in transportation, sea or land, were able to prosper at the expense of other tribes. It was only when the Indians obtained horses that they were formidable. The Spanish were great when they ruled the seas. So, when successive waves of lava covered eastern Oregon, they destroyed the rhinos of the day, but the fleet antelope could retreat to the east or south, looking back over his shoulders at the fiery, roaring waves of destruction behind.

The geese and ducks had good transportation, too, the open road of the sky. So they escaped. Later the Cascade mountains shoved their peaks into the sky and took the moisture from the ocean breezes. That turned much of eastern Oregon into a desert. Large, slow-moving animals that needed a bale of hay every few minutes in order to live, gave up the ghost. Some person unknown to me once wrote:

> The Great Auk stood upon one leg,
> Sighed twice and three times winked;
> Then turned and laid a phantom egg
> And murmured, "I'm extinct."

The antelope escaped the phantom stage barely in time. His transportation facilities enabled him to cover more terrain and find enough food, so he lived on into our time.

Maybe our present vast concern over the conquering of space is an unreasoning instinct bred into us by history. The nations that have the best transportation grow great and survive—the others perish, or live in the shadow of their larger neighbors, and at their sufferance, getting intolerable inferiority complexes.

Man had two metallic weapons that nearly caused antelope extinction. Their triumphs over lava flows, earth convulsions, the deadly chill of the ice age, and the searing heat of desert, gave them no training when men appeared with rifles and plows. The rifles could kill from a distant hill and the plow robbed them of their best feeding grounds. Fortunately, antelope refuges were created in the nick of time. Our own two-hundred-thousand-acre Hart Mountain Antelope Refuge now provides the best place in Oregon to see them. Right now, 1962, the refuge is also making an experiment in returning the wild sheep to their former home on the desert. I hope it succeeds with sheep as well as it did with antelope. They kept the antelope, our most beautiful game animal, from following the great auk into oblivion. At least this is true in Oregon.

Antelope are hunted only by special permits obtained in an annual drawing. Only about five hundred permits are sold yearly, the number going up or down slightly as the fawn crop grows or lessens from year to year. The last figures I saw, 1959, showed a kill of 448 out of an estimated population of 12,000. Probably coyotes and bobcats, not known to hunt by any such lottery system, accounted for far more than men. Those animals have a twelve-month hunting season and are more experienced than any of our human interlopers among the antelopers.

MULE DEER

E. R. JACKMAN

DEER WERE FORMERLY NOT TOO PLENTIFUL ON THE DESERT except in the winter. Coyotes can run on the crust, whereas the small feet of the deer break through, and a deer in three feet of snow is helpless. A coyote can walk up and help himself. So deer, as the snows start, leave the mountains and timber and either go to the desert, where snowfall is light, or, in some places in Oregon, go to low elevations.

This forced migration has some bad features. Most of the winter and spring range is privately owned, so hundreds of Oregon ranchers sacrifice from 10 per cent of their feed on up to 20 per cent to the deer. Thus, a man with 200 cows and a gross income of $14,000 a year, could be taking in $3,000 more, were it not for the deer. The effect upon his net income in such cases is drastic. Of his $14,000 gross, he is pretty lucky if he has $4,000 net. The $10,000 that goes for expenses is for taxes, hired help, fertilizer, irrigation, depreciation on machinery, and dozens of things. But those go right on, no matter what the income. If he could keep fifty more cows on the feed the deer eat, the income from the animals could be banked with very little added expense. So fifty additional cows, if kept on the same land, might double the net.

Many hunters are frightfully angry if asked to keep out of certain fields—yet that rancher may be paying out of his pocket $3,000, or even up to $10,000, to feed the deer. Most city hunters wouldn't want to pay that much for a hunting license. If the State Game Commission had to buy all of this winter and spring feed, raised on privately owned land, a license would cost $300 or more.

Reub says that many people are so busy hunting, they don't have time to kill a deer. Jack Tippett, of Wallowa County, was out on his range the first day of elk hunting. Hunters were there in great numbers. A corpulent man stopped to talk. His clothes and gun were expensive.

Sportsman: Lots of hunters around.

Jack: I haven't noticed any.

Sportsman: That's funny. I see them all over.

Jack: Oh, I've seen plenty of stump sitters and trail runners. I haven't seen any hunters.

The mule deer is Oregon's best game animal. Elk are too big; antelope are not numerous enough. Both are, in effect, raffled off by the Game Commission. Anyone in Oregon who can legally buy a license can hunt deer. For years the annual take by hunters in this state has been larger than in any other state. In 1961 it totaled 163,939, with 265,326 hunting licenses sold. About a quarter of the total kill was in the desert counties.

The State Game Commission gets raked over the coals yearly by hunters who failed to get their deer. The papers are full of wrathy letters condemning the Commission from hell to breakfast. In spite of the large yearly kill, there are just as many deer next year. In our hunting party of about a dozen, we count the deer we see—as nearly as we can. We try to eliminate duplicates. We have been hunting in the same place for thirty-four years, counting 1962. Deer numbers are increasing, if anything.

This is in an area where the pioneers, both immigrants and trappers, reported a great scarcity of deer. Early-day cattlemen tell of riding for days without seeing a deer, and at night, if someone reported he had seen one, they all gathered around him, asking questions. Riders now take deer so much for granted that no one says anything about them—each rider is likely to see from a dozen on up to a hundred.

It seems to me that the Game Commission is doing a job almost miraculous in its success. With thousands of additional hunters each year, deer numbers are not decreasing.

The big majority of hunters are courteous and well behaved. Perhaps 2 per cent are the dregs of humanity. The things they do are unbelievable. Each year some will go into a pasture of perhaps five thousand acres where the only water is pumped by a windmill into a metal tank that carefully meters it into a trough for maybe fifty cows grazing there. Not seeing a deer, they will pass the time seeing from how far away they can shoot a hole in the water tank. This drains all the water, and if the owner doesn't happen around soon, the cattle may die from thirst. The precious water is also taken away from the birds and wild animals that live within a few miles.

Others will shoot cattle, sometimes, apparently, just for the fun of it. A hardware store in Portland, one fall before hunting season, showed a picture of wire cutters in their ad in the *Oregonian,* with the caption "Why drive a mile around to a gate when you can go through for $1.25?" They apparently sold many cutters, because every year ranchers find their fences cut. Gates are left open, or even rammed with jeeps or weapon carriers to break them down. The rancher's cattle will usually find the hole and scatter for miles. Ranchers who lose cattle, or find them painfully wounded, have no kindly feeling for the perpetrators.

A few years ago a woman and her husband were hunting out of Burns. They went to a certain mountain where they knew the terrain. The husband said he'd go up the draw to the left if his wife would take the right draw. Each was to watch the ridge between, and they would meet around noon up above where the draws joined. It worked as planned. A fine buck came bounding over the hill and the wife dropped him with one shot. She tied her tag to the antlers and was dressing her deer when a big man with

Photo by Joe Van Wormer, Bend, Ore.

A FOUR-POINT AND DOE MAKE A QUIET GETAWAY

Sagebrush and rabbit brush aren't normally eaten much by deer. These animals like the open brush country because of other feed that grows there and because they can see enemies.

brand-new hunting clothes came up with an open knife, cut off her tag, threw it into the sagebrush, and tied on his own. The Burns woman, too astonished to argue at first, said, "What do you think you're doing with my deer?" The man said, "It's my deer now."

This lady from Burns was of sterner stuff than most. She said, "The hell it is, mister," and placed a shot carefully through his shoulder, below the bone. He began to yell, a car appeared on the road below, four companions came and led him away, the woman retrieved her tag, and went on cleaning the deer. She explained to her husband, "I didn't want to kill him, but I wanted to teach him never to do a trick like that again."

The hunting licenses in Oregon say on the faces, "Although fish and wildlife are publicly owned resources, enjoyment of the opportunity to fish or hunt on private land is a privilege that can be granted only by the landowner." But only last fall a man told me, "I've bought a license, and I'm a taxpayer, and by God that gives me a right to hunt anywhere I damn please and I'll beat hell out of anyone who objects."

Such persons, as stated, are in the minority. Most hunters are anxious to do the right thing. After hunting all day, or maybe three or four days, without seeing anything to shoot at, a few get to have a strange distortion of vision, so that anything they see takes on the shape of a deer. I know of one who shot at two quarreling magpies; horses are shot, even out in the open; each year many cattle are killed; and a fellow hunter can even look like a buck deer. I don't know how a test could be prepared so that such dangerous persons could be kept at home. Apparently they really do see a deer in such cases. The man who shoots through brush at anything that moves, is a hazard of a different kind. He knows when he shoots that the movement he detected could be any other kind of animal, including man.

This distorted vision is probably a result of an overactive

imagination combined with unaccustomed weariness. A few years ago a man killed another man. The victim was sitting down, his back against a big pine tree. He was tying a shoelace. The shooter came into the clearing about a hundred and fifty yards away. He was in full sight of the sitting man and he swore that the man appeared like a deer to him, antlers and all.

I am not a very good shot. One year I had missed several deer and Chet Craddock, of Burns, then ranching, said, "Don't worry about that, there's an awful lot of room around a deer." I nearly always get my deer, though, because even now, sixty-eight years old, eyesight not so good, reflexes slowed down, and unable to cover much ground, I can still see them. Reub, nearly the same age, says, "Many of my friends complain that as they get old, their eyesight is failing. Mine is getting better every year. All my life I've had spots before my eyes, but now I can see 'em lots more plainly."

In the first place, there is luck about it, just as in card playing. One year Cliff Smith of our party will see the most bucks, the next year Otis sees them wherever he goes, and the following year they seem to be anxious to have Rearden see them.

Some things help me in hunting. Other hunters will have a completely different list. Here are a few things I would tell a new hunter, or one not accustomed to hunting mule deer in the open sagebrush hills:

1. Stand still a lot. Deer don't notice a stationary object. Better yet, sit down, if you can still see that way. It's easier to hear a running deer if you are in contact with the ground.

2. Whenever you stop, try to stop in shade of a tree, brush, or rock. Deer always do that if they can. The hunter can learn a few tricks from watching them. They learn quickly that shade is a good camouflage.

3. If cattle or horses are in sight, watch them. Horses, especially, will nearly always point out a deer to you. Cattle aren't so good at it, but if most of them stop grazing and

all look in the same direction, probably they see a man. If you know the man is there, you are more likely to see a deer he may scare out.

4. In hunting in open country, approach the top of every hill quietly, and when you can see over the ridge, don't show anything below your eyes. Look over the gulley or little valley, or mesa, real thoroughly before you get in sight.

5. Try to learn to shoot at some particular part of a deer, not just at the deer. You'll get more deer that way; you'll spoil less meat; fewer wounded deer will get away; and you'll soon find where your mistake is in aiming. I try to shoot just behind the front leg, others take the neck or backbone.

6. Don't shoot at the antlers. The urge, especially if the deer is running, is almost irresistible, and most hunters overshoot. You rarely bag a deer with big antlers that are intact. One or more points have been shot off. It had to happen that year, because he grows new antlers every year. The dictionary says a deer has "periodically deciduous frontal appendages."

7. Never pull the trigger unless you are "on." Sounds silly, but many excellent target shooters regularly miss by pulling the trigger after the deer has run past the sight.

8. Use a scope or carry glasses. Many old-time hunters scorn such an aid, figuring if they can't get a deer without such things, they'll go without venison. The large ears of a mule deer can often hide the antlers completely. Also, you can spot other hunters; can watch deer on a distant hill; can pick out coyotes or bobcats; can distinguish deer from horses or cattle in the distance; and you can see what's going on. Glasses add much to the enjoyment of a day in the hills. I'd rather use glasses than a scope.

9. For mule deer or elk, use a gun with plenty of shocking power. A .30-30 doesn't have enough, especially for hunting in the open where you often take long shots.

10. *Always* track a deer you have shot at. A deer running downhill can travel two hundred yards if shot through

the heart. Every year hundreds of deer in Oregon are wounded, unknown to the hunter. He shoots, the deer doesn't even hesitate, and he says, "Shucks! I missed again." Quite often mortally wounded deer do not bleed on the outside, so absence of blood isn't always evidence of a miss. If you are a good hunter, you are a good tracker.

11. This is the last rule. Learn how to take care of a deer after you get it. A man who leaves the hide on, then puts the deer on the outside of his car, along the engine or over it, on a warm hood, is sacrificing good venison to vanity.

Types of Hunters

From fifty years of hunting, associating with hunters, meeting with and watching hunters, and knowing thousands of them, maybe I am qualified to classify this subspecies of Homo sapiens. First, hunters *tend* to be the elite men of the community, although as a rule, the very small percentage of brutes are usually hunters. The latter are hunters for the same reason that they may be thieves, or bullies, or men obsessed by cruelty. There is something out there to take, and by ———— they are going to get theirs. But so few of these brutish kinds exist that we don't need to pay much attention to them. It's the 250,000 others in Oregon that I am talking about.

First, a remarkable change has occurred in Oregon in deer hunting camps in the past thirty years. Before 1930, a woman in camp wasn't unknown, but she was a rarity. If you met a woman in the forest or out in the sagebrush, you would mention it to every other hunter. Women just simply weren't normal if they got out and really hunted. A few men always took their wives with them because the ladies were afraid to stay home alone, or because they didn't mind cooking for the men, or because they regarded it as a sort of vacation.

Now I think that maybe 75 per cent of the camps have

women who hunt. Some are excellent shots. One lady
hunted with our group as long as she lived. Her eyesight
was marvelous, and year after year she saw more bucks
than anyone else. She was a fine hunter, and a great person to have around. But, as mentioned, this was unusual.

The women, though, must be classed the same as other
hunters; they fall into the same groups.

Classification

1. The Head Hunters. They want a trophy head. They
come from all over. Mainly they have money enough so
they can afford to go where they hear the trophy heads
are found. You find more of them in the high mountains
than in ordinary places. They hire outfits, pack in, and
will spend days learning the habits of some old mossy back
buck that lives above timberline. They study shade pat-
terns, wind currents, muzzle velocities, bullet weights, and
manage to become scientists, with their own learned vocabulary. This is a harmless but expensive kind of insanity. I
have always wondered what their wives thought of them.

I have met a few of these dedicated souls and I can't
remember that they said anything about their wives. I
have a somewhat blurred mental picture of a timid little
woman doomed to flit forever, thoroughly cowed, in the
presence of frightening heads of huge snarling beasts ringing the walls. Such a home couldn't be too restful. To get
peace of mind, she'd have to go down to the boiler factory.

2. The Meat Hound. These are more numerous and more
dangerous. The Head Hunter will never shoot a fellow
hunter, but the Meat Hound might. Some of these are
extremely good hunters and know exactly what they are
doing. They are more likely to be poor than rich, but this
doesn't follow inevitably. If a man lives in a deer neighborhood, and he has some growing children, and the price
of beef is high, a deer can possibly be his cheapest source
of good nourishing meals. With most of us, if we figured

in all of the costs, our venison might run up into an alarming figure—on a pound basis.

The Meat Hound may be a different breed. He may have promised his poker-playing friends that he'd throw a champagne and venison supper for all hands. Or he may be one of the success mad who can't give "no" for an answer when someone asks, on his return, "Did you get a deer?" Such a man *must* kill a deer and have some meat to prove it. Try to learn the distinguishing marks of this type and keep out of their sight. As the days go by and they have no deer, a kind of madness falls upon them and they get to pulling the trigger when they see a movement on the hillside.

3. The Escapist. With this man, hunting may be the only way he has of escaping from the cut and dried procedure of his daily task. While hunting he can emerge from the labyrinth of civilization, from the web that the machine has woven, and can pretend at least that he is living in a more primitive world, where his own stamina and cunning are all that count. If one of this species happens to be experienced and a good observer, he will be one of the best of all hunters, for he is putting into the game every ability he has. For the time being, he is the elemental man out in the wilderness seeking food for his tribe. When he returns to his home he will slip back behind his desk and bow meekly to the overwhelming forces civilization uses to control him.

4. The Professional Sportsman. This man belongs to a cult. He worships the Great God Sport. He may be fully initiated, or merely a novice. He reads the magazines, belongs to a club. He may be a fanatic or only a faint believer who joined because it's the thing to do among his set. Please spare me from the fanatic, for he has taken what should be relaxing, something good for the soul, and he makes a flaming issue out of it. He quarrels with those who do not subscribe fully to all the tenets of his faith.

Between him and a normal hunter there is all of the difference between a man who occasionally takes a glass of
wine, and the habitual drunkard. It's a difference in degree,
and a profound difference in temperament. These folks are
not the best hunters, but they usually are not the poorest.
They have professional standards that keep them from destroying property and shooting wildly. But they may not
know much about deer. They may not have the right kind
of mind and may be unable to tell opinion from authority.
They get up in their clubs and deliver orations based solely
upon limited observation. They write letters to the papers.

5. The Social Hunter. This species regards the animal
hunt very much as he might the annual trek for huckle-
berries, or the clamming trip to the beach. He is out for
enjoyment. He isn't trying to prove anything and he isn't
mad at anybody. He makes up our most numerous hunting group, and by and large our best group. He is the
average American citizen. He wants to do the right thing,
and if he does the wrong thing, it is due to inexperience.
Some of our best and poorest hunters are in this class, depending largely upon years or personal traits, such as observation, nervousness, patience, eyesight, hearing, endurance,
enthusiasm, tolerance. The right combination will make
a good hunter. If a poor hunter to start with, he will become better each succeeding year.

6. The Perfectionist. This man is a trial to the other
hunters, and if he is also assertive, he may be impossible.
But he is a good hunter. You don't see him making shots
through the hams or the paunch. He doesn't shoot at does.
If he shoots at a deer, he nearly always gets meat and it
isn't spoiled. Wounded deer do not get away. The others
can learn things from this man if he doesn't aggravate them
so much that they wouldn't take any idea of his on a bet.

7. The Amateur Naturalist. There are several subspecies,
but these folks actually aren't out there to get a deer. They
take rifles and may get their share of deer, but that isn't

their purpose. They hunt because everyone would think them queer if they just wandered around out in the hills without any plain purpose. Actually, that's what they want to do. I am not talking of photographers, artists, writers, and professional naturalists. I am talking of farmers, saw-mill workers, lawyers, and persons of all trades who get more enjoyment out of being in the hills than out of any other one thing. They get it just by being there. They have to hunt as an excuse.

You can't imagine a man going to his boss and saying, "I've just got to have a week off to wander alone out in the woods." The boss would be calling in a psychiatrist. But the same man may meet a highly cooperative spirit when he says, "Boss, a few of us have always gone deer hunting this week, and if you can spare me, I'd surely like to go."

I suspect that a lot of folks who hunt don't give a royal hoot whether they get a deer or not.

There are splinter groups, or schisms within these seven major classifications, and perhaps I've missed some. My deer hunting has been mostly in the sagebrush. In mountain country or in the thick woods of western Oregon, probably there are classes unknown to me. All of those listed, except the Head Hunters, show up regularly for the desert hunting.

Deer hunting is wonderful, even if you don't get a deer. The more you learn about it, the more you enjoy it, the same as any other sport. Those who know nothing about football don't enjoy a good football game.

But there is something special about deer hunting. The clear, bracing air of fall; the brilliant, jewellike fall sunshine; the flaming patch of quaking aspen that unexpectedly comes to view in a hidden pocket; the intricate engineering of the beavers in a nearly dry watercourse; the badger or porcupine awkwardly getting away; the stories the tracks reveal; the whole scene much as it was when Lewis and Clark came this way over 150 years ago; these things make deer hunting rather wonderful, and deer hunters as a group are fine, tolerant, helpful people.

HOW TO GET ALONG

R. A. Long

WHEN YOU LIVE WHERE MOST EVERYONE ELSE HAS FAILED, you learn to recognize an acorn when you see it. The plants that grow on the desert all have some way of hanging onto water. As a boy grows up there, he must learn to postpone wants, economize on needs, and keep his liquid assets from evaporating in the dry desert air. His wants must be few and his needs less. Fat isn't any good out there on a man or a horse, and it shortens the life of both.

My business, most of my life, was with horses, and there are all kinds of horse businesses. I tried all of them except racing. In addition, I tried sheepherding, trapping, dairying, dryland farming, surveying, dude wrangling, moving-picture making, working for the government, and running a pool hall. Once, in a pinch, I even trained and promoted a prizefighter.

This chapter is about some of the acorns I managed to pick up while rooting around.

Archie Warner and I went to John's Marsh, near Sycan River, to lamb out Lannes Klippel's sheep. We had four hounds in camp to scare the coyotes off. I came in from "flagging"[1] some ewes and lambs and got my breakfast at 10:00 o'clock. Someone ahead of me had left the lid off the bean pot. I found all four of the hounds in the beans,

---

[1] A flag of white muslin is tied to a willow stick stuck into the ground. A series of these flags is set around a little bunch of ewes with newly dropped lambs. These flutter in the wind above the sagebrush and scare the coyotes away for a while—long enough to let a man get breakfast.

real happy. I kicked them out of the tent and put the lid back on. Shortly after, the boss came in and helped himself liberally to the beans.

When he found he was playing second fiddle on the bean pot to the dogs, he was so mad he told me to pack up my bed and get on my horse and never come back. Archie, loyal to me, quit.

With only two horses, we put both beds on my horse, with me on top of the pack. Archie drove the packhorse, with me on it, to Silver Lake, forty miles away. The horse had no bridle or halter, and there I was, on top, with no control. The horse would stray off into the mahoganies or pine thickets. Archie would come whooping after him, swinging his romal, and would drive the horse back to the trail on a dead run. I didn't dare dodge the brush because unless the weight of a pack is divided evenly, your pack is soon underneath, and then, with the horse bucking and running, it is scattered over the mountainside.

It was great fun for Archie, and maybe for the packhorse. I put it in my book as the wildest ride I ever took.

Archie was strong and fast, and it was necessary for him to do everything better than anyone else. I was sixteen and he was twenty-six. I admitted he could beat me at anything so we got along fine. We decided to go into business.

We heard the butcher shop at Silver Lake was for sale. We agreed to buy it, but we'd keep an ace in the hole by having Archie shear sheep up on the Sycan. He gave me three hundred dollars to buy the shop. I couldn't buy it for that money, but could buy the pool hall. I rode out to where Archie was working and reported. He said to go ahead, he didn't think much of the butcher business anyhow—too many flies. They didn't bother the billiard balls.

We became the hopeful owners of these things: safe, back bar, a whole lot of glasses, miscellaneous silverware, one pool table, barroom chairs, card tables. This had formerly been a saloon, hence the back bar and the glasses.

For a sixteen-year-old boy with no previous knowledge

of a business in a metropolis like Silver Lake, I did two smart things:

1. I hired Billy Burton, a man who knew how to run a pool hall, and gave him complete charge.
2. I stopped bootlegging that had been going on and stopped gambling for real money.

Some original thinker had named the place THE PAS-TIME.

Prohibition was in effect. We had all of those glasses and a bar, so I had a painter put up a nice sign:

"We sell near beer here because there's no beer near here"

The business flourished.

Later Archie financed me some more and we bought the pool hall and the land, in our names, jointly. We made money. But money by staying in one place didn't appeal to Archie, so I paid him back all he had put into the partnership.

I kept this operation for nearly ten years, then decided to sell out. When I went to turn over the deed, I discovered that the law was a lot more particular than Archie, for legally he still owned half of my property.

The buyer said, "We'd better call this off, he'll never agree to sign over his half now, since it's worth a lot more." I found Archie out on the desert and he signed over his half interest to me without even any discussion. He had sold it and he wasn't concerned with its present value.

In those days most people on the desert had a code of ethics. Many big deals were made in land, sheep, horses, cattle, hay, and services, with never a word on paper. In my own case, I soon found the way to get along—drive a hard bargain, then make a liberal settlement. This always left the other man willing to do business again.

Remember, I went into these business deals at the ripe old age of sixteen. I still liked to have fun. I liked it lots better than Billy Burton did.

Tom Nelson came to town on a wild mule. I jumped

on behind him and we rode into the pool hall. We thought this was all right, for it was his mule and my pool hall.

Billy Burton was furious—humiliated. He shouted, "A Rube by name and a rube by nature. I've been farther under the barn hunting eggs than you've ever been away from home. I quit!"

I got on my horse and went into the desert for a week. He couldn't find me and I knew he had too much sense of responsibility to walk off while I was away. When I came back, he was in good humor again.

One year a man bought up a lot of hay around Silver Lake and brought in a herd of cattle to feed. Such things gave us a chance to get a little money occasionally. He hired five of us to stay out there and see that the cattle got plenty of hay and that the water supply didn't freeze up. In such cases, the boys play poker for small stakes, go to town to find something to drink, or to get into a fight just for fun. So the winter passes.

But this bunch didn't care about cards, drinking, or fighting. They were all bent on reading, so once every ten days one of us would go in and get an armload of books. There was one old chap with a thick moustache that strained his syllables into a peculiar sound, as though talking through his hat. Our conduct was incomprehensible to him. He tried to organize pitch or poker games, or to interest us in some bootleg whiskey ideas. No luck. At last, in self-defense, he started to read a book, reading slowly and following each line with his finger. He cut off the end of his buckskin bootlace for a bookmark. When he had gotten over to page 100, the cook slipped his bookmark back ten or twenty pages, and kept on doing that at intervals, so the reader was making no progress in his book. He had to read as hard as he could to stay even.

One of the men said, "Bill, how do you like your book?"

Bill said, through his moustache, in his deep voice, "It's the god damndest book I ever see in all my born days. It just keeps sayin' the same thing over and over."

THIS WAS RYE HAY LAND ON THE OREGON DESERT

The owner, Reub Long, is seeding to grass-alfalfa. He uses about five thousand acres of seedings. They are of all stages of excellence, depending partly upon the weather the following year. Grass seedings on the desert need a little luck to succeed.

Dude Wrangling

Fish Creek Valley is a nice place, about a mile long and half a quarter wide, grassy, mossy in the cool places, high in the mountains, rimmed with tall trees. The creek runs into the North Umpqua. In my dude herding days, it was my favorite camping spot. It is remote, cool, pleasant, and, with plenty of feed, the horses would stay there without constant watching. I had plenty of bells. Some horses didn't need bells, because they had a horse pal they would always stay with.

I was camped there with six dudes, Fish Mountain on one side, Rattlesnake Mountain on the other. I was just sitting in the grass along the creek, listening to the bells and full of content. Each bell had a different tone. As a horse moved, a quarter of a mile away, I'd think dreamily, "That's Old Bess." Her bell would echo prettily back and forth between the mountains. The day was balmy, I had plenty of wood, and everything was peaceful and beautiful.

I said to one dude, as a bell echoed sweetly, "Listen to that heavenly music." The dude listened, straining his ears, and frowning. He said, "I can't hear a thing for those ———— bells."

You have trouble keeping a dude on a horse when the going is tough—they always want to get off. I told them repeatedly that the safest place on a steep mountainside was on the horse, because a horse has four feet and a man just has two.

Occasionally, on the start of a trip, one would come to me apologetically and explain that he had never ridden a horse. I always reassured him by saying, "Oh, that's all right. I've got a horse that's never been ridden, so you can have *him* and both of you can start together."

A bear is normally mighty fast on the getaway. He wants no truck with the two-legged breed. Around the campfires I always liked to have a few stories to entertain these people. They especially liked bear stories. I told one about

REUB LONG AND HIS WIFE ELEANOR
In the background is the extinct volcano called Fort Rock, on land recently deeded by the Longs to the state of Oregon for a park.

Photo by Shorty Gustafson, Bend, Ore.

REUB'S PACK STRING, DUDE WRANG

HE CASCADES, FORDING A STREAM

a group of Portland people who came out to hunt lava bears. They hunted from dawn to dark, and by the end of the week their legs were worn right down to their hocks. On Sunday they sat around the breakfast fire, ready to pack up and leave.

The cook was a local man with a cleft palate, hence a pronounced lisp, or difficulty in speaking. He had worked steadily all week, but now, his work finished, he said to the campfire group, "By Jethus, I'll jutht walk out here and find me a nithe bear." A short way from camp he really did find a bear, a tiny one you could hold in one hand. He picked up the little animal, that promptly sent out a call of danger. The mother came running, blood in her eye, and the cook departed for camp, leaving the little bear right up in the air. He was only a short distance away, and when in sight yelled, "Thoot her! Thoot her!" The entire group were so dumbfounded they just sat there, open-mouthed. He ran through them and around the tent, yelling frantically, "Thoot her! Thoot her!" with the bear only a step and a half behind. The men sat paralyzed. On the next trip around he yelled, "Thay! If one of you ——— don't thoot her, I'll take her back to the woodth where I got her!"

Hathaway Jones, down on Rogue River, was a man much like the cook in that he had the same disability in talking. He made a living by trapping, renting his boat, and acting as guide for hunting and fishing parties. He lived all alone most of his life far down the river beyond roads. He would tell wonderful stories, but if you laughed, or professed disbelief, he wouldn't tell you any more. If you said, "I'm awful glad to hear about that, Mr. Jones, and I can see how it might happen to anybody," he'd tell you more.

Mr. Chinnock, of Grants Pass, was returning with him to his cabin when Hathaway put out a restraining arm. "Thee that long thand bar running out in the river? Onth I wath walking down thith very path, and right here thide of thith very tree, I theed the biggetht bar there I ever

theed in my life. He had jutht fithed a thalmon out of
the river and he wath jutht thtanding thar thort of gloatin'
over it, I gueth you might thay. Up on the mountainthide
come a terrible ruthin' and roarin' thound and another big
bar ath big ath the firtht bar come rathin' down, breakin'
the little treeth ath it came, and run out on the bar and
tried to take the thalmon away from the firtht bar.

"The firtht bar didn't want hith thalmon took away
and jumped on top of the thecond bar. Then the thecond
bar jumped on top of him and ——" Here Hathaway
illustrated by rapidly shifting hands to put each alternately
on top and raising them in the air with each change. "I
watthed them until they wath jutht a little thpeck in the
thky. Then the thpeck dithappeared, but I knowed they
wath thill a-fightin', becauth now and then a—ha'r—come
—a-driftin'—down." At the end his animated voice became
slow, barely audible, signifying "end of story."

My experience with bears is that unless wounded or pro-
tecting cubs, they are as harmless as deer. A problem arises
when you meet one. You may say, with every sign of pleasure, "Oh! Good morning, Bear. We've been talking of
you. Do you have cubs and are you wounded?" If he
growls disagreeably and charges, your problem is more acute,
even though that gives you the answer.

Most of the dudes liked to go into unfrequented spots.
There were many nice places not even on maps, and with
no trails to them. I'd climb a mountain peak and from
there, with help from a contour map, made out by town-
ships, I'd locate hidden lakes or nice little valleys, and I'd
try to trace out a way to get where I wanted to go—someplace where I'd never been before. Many of the routes I
picked out were later made into trails by the Forest Service.

In picking camp spots, I tried to find good horse feed.
I always camped between the place where the horses pastured and the direction I'd come from, so, if the horses
decided to leave, they'd have to pass me and I could head
them off. A horse in a country strange to him will rarely

try to leave some other way—he will follow his own trail out.

Other things to look for in a camp were good clear drinking water and firewood. Nights are cold in the high mountains but days may be hot. I tried to get a level spot with morning sun, but afternoon shade.

Professional and business people made up most of the parties, including women and children. They liked to fish, but the main idea was to get clear beyond modern things— to pretend, at least, that they were out fighting nature, roughing it. They were, of course, because we had insects; wild animals were, or could be, around; we cooked over the fire; and a person can get tired riding in the mountains all day, taking rain or shine as it came.

One of my best customers was Lynn Mowat, in charge of the Community Chest in Los Angeles. He and his wife Bess came back for years. They were fine campers and fine to be with. They now have a summer place at Marial in Curry County.

We went to lots of lakes. We took a string of ten or twelve horses and struck out, not knowing where we would end up. That is rough country, full of deep canyons. There is a constant element of adventure going into rough, unknown places.

I furnished all of the horses, both riding and pack, but I soon learned to let the campers buy the food. They would get what they wanted; they couldn't blame me for buying too much or too little; and as soon as they had bought the supplies, I knew how many packhorses to take. I have taken as many as twenty-five.

The horses liked some camps, but disliked others and were uneasy there all the time. The dislike might be due to cougars. They didn't seem to mind bears, but if there was a cougar around, they knew it—probably by smell. They wouldn't eat quietly, and they would try to leave. If we camped at some beautiful little lake and had an experience with a cougar, the horses remembered it. Years later, if I tried to camp there, the horses distrusted the place.

In many camps I just turned the horses loose, unhobbled. If the horses ever left the meadow where they pastured and came to camp, I never chased them back. I gave them a handful of grain, and led them back to the grass. I rewarded them for coming to see me. I always checked them at night and at daylight in the morning. If horses are going to go AWOL, they will normally try it about daybreak.

I carried enough grain for such rewards—not as a source of feed. In those days we could find plenty of natural feed.

Once we were camped near the head of the Middle Fork of the Willamette at the Edeleo Lakes, named for three men—Ed, Dee, and Leo, who discovered them.

A cougar screamed at night and the horses stole away. They can follow a trail at night, or most of them can. I don't know whether they can see well, or whether it is something inside that tells them where to turn. They can normally follow their trail in, even if there is no sign of a trail. If they go over a mountainside once—right through brush and down timber, they can go back that same identical way, making hundreds of turns that no man could remember. If someone knows for sure how they do this, let me know.

Indians used to say, long before horses came, that Indians and coyotes never get lost. I'd add horses to the list. A man who has lived much out of doors has some of this instinct. Probably all men have it to start with, but gas engines, newspapers, electric stoves, and telephones have so much friction they rub off natural built-in gadgets we are born with. This instinct can be developed by use.

I heard the bells coming in the middle of the night and by the time I was dressed, two of the string had gotten by; a little gray pack mare, Bessie, and a stocking-legged sorrel bald-faced horse named Sourdough. I headed off the rest of the string, caught and tied them. Then, bareback, I got on a horse called Dollar, let him take his head and go in the dark. I overtook the two wanderers on a little meadow two and a half miles on the back trail.

Dollar had an exceptionally good trail instinct, tested and proved many times in both dark and daylight in all kinds of terrain. When I overtook the two, I led Bessie, let Sourdough follow. I started with utmost confidence that Dollar would take me back to camp on a nonexistent trail.

After a quarter of an hour, Dollar stopped and I couldn't make him go a foot farther. The night was black and tall trees were all around, making the dark almost total. I got out my flashlight and we were on the brink of a precipice—a sheer drop—a place I'd never seen before. I turned the horses and started back. Dollar took me right back to where we had caught the horses. I deliberately started toward camp and he took me back to the cliff again. We turned around and again returned to where we overtook the horses. Dollar was just telling me that he didn't care a whoop for our camp.

So then I put Sourdough in the lead and Bessie, Dollar, and I followed him closely. We landed in camp.

A few horses completely lack sense of direction, or don't give a damn. I was near Tiller, in Douglas County, packing supplies for fire fighters, the Forest Service in charge. I took a notion to go to Fish Creek on a big dapple gray named Stranger. I left Tiller in the afternoon and rode up the South Umpqua. When I reached the divide between the North and South Umpqua, it was dark. I was on a good, well-traveled trail.

Stranger just simply wouldn't follow that trail in the dark. Finally I had to get off, sit down with my back to a tree, and wait for morning light.

The times, though, that they *did* follow a trail, night or day, were many, so the two failures I've mentioned were exceptions. If lost, and riding a horse, don't try to outguess him. It may be humiliating, but he knows more than you do. He'll take you out if he has ever been there.

I started dude wrangling as the only way I could figure out to make a little money while off from the desert. I had hay fever so badly on the desert in the summer that

I had to leave. I stayed with that occupation for twenty years—from 1926 to 1946. In that time I met some of the finest persons I have known. When a man or woman who had never been on such a trip before would ask a question that seemed right out of the silly box, I was often tempted to make a smart remark, but I was stopped by the realization that if I were suddenly thrown into the business of that person, I would have been equally green. So I always tried to answer every question as carefully and completely as I could.

Even now, some of them come back to visit me. One such family was Mr. and Mrs. Harry Dace and their daughter Cathy. Her married name is Flynn. They were from the San Fernando Valley. I could name many others.

Packing

The most awkward thing I ever had to pack was a Forest Service lookout house, with windows, floor, siding, fourteen-foot sills, and a sheet metal flue ten feet long. A fourteen-foot timber on a horse can get you into trouble. The horse isn't accustomed to reckoning on things that stick way out, front and back. He may bump the horse ahead, who will kick. So, with hooves in his face, he stops abruptly, ramming the long timbers into the face of the horse behind.

I had several of these houses to pack in and usually uncrated the flue and put it on top. It worked better that way, but was strictly against regulations.

A lookout house on level ground wouldn't be much account, so they were always located on the exact top of the highest, steepest, rockiest point to be found for twenty-five miles around. Taking a 14 x 14 house up a 50 per cent slope has problems. The long timbers ram into the mountainside in front. Of course, a horse had to have two of them, one on each side. Now shut your eyes and think of this: because of steepness, huge rocks, precipices, down logs, and thickets, you have to make a switchback or hair-pin turn. You'll make dozens of them on the way up.

But when you turn your string sharply, the back ends of the long timbers gouge into the rock, or hit trees, or sweep the next horse off the trail.

Lumber of any kind is trouble. It isn't made for pack-ing, and the pack isn't made for it. It slips in the hitches; it galls the horses if you aren't extremely careful in using lots of packing; and timbers, straight, long, and unyielding, just aren't good pack material.

In any job there are a multitude of little details you can't see by watching. The successful packer won't get his horses skinned up; won't get into trouble on the trail; won't get anything broken. But what he does to avoid catastrophies can be learned only by packing.

The first thing is balance, composed of two things: weight and bulk. If two packages weigh the same, but one is big and the other small, the big one will overbalance the small because it is out, away from the horse, which gives it a different leverage—we'd say, "There is more shook to it." It swings and tosses around, so will work the ropes loose.

Get the heavy stuff as far down on the side of the horse as possible, with the light or bulky things on top.

The diamond hitch is most popular, but I rarely used it. It's good, of course, and is regulation in most pack outfits, such as Forest Service and mapping or surveying parties. I used a cross between the Lang hitch and the squaw hitch —an invention of my own. It was faster, would hold as well, and was built upon the saddle rather than the horse, so was not so likely to gall him.

If a squaw hitch works loose a little, it keeps getting looser. Mine, built on the saddle, didn't do that. The squaw hitch was designed by the Indians, who used it originally with no packsaddle at all. It was designed for wrapping a pack right around the horse, fastening at the top with a half hitch drawn tight, then running the loose ends around the horse and tying them again, giving two chances to pull the rope tight. Early fur traders used it and it was ideal for furs, because they could be made to follow the contours of the horse. Lots of cowboys, hunters, and miners use it. Advantages: fast, adaptable to large or small packs, can be used without a packsaddle. The latter is a real advantage at times, in case a packsaddle is broken, burned, or lost, or, in the case of trappers, material to be packed increases in amount each day.

The Lang hitch will hold a pack well. One man can put it on, but it works better with two. So it takes two men, and a special saddle cinch is needed. It is more likely to hurt a horse, because it is lashed directly to the horse and can cause cinch sores. The special cinch has two extra rings, one on each side, fastened to the cinch below the cinch rings.

Photo by Jones Studio, Lakeview, Ore.

JACK DAVIDSON, GOOD AND DEPENDABLE PACKER, THROWING THE REUB LONG HITCH

Its advantages, compared to the well-known diamond, are: greater speed, it is easier on the horse, and it holds fully as well.

The rope used to fasten the pack has no cinch on it at all—you use the two rings on the saddle cinch as holding points, run the rope through them, draw it very tight, so the pack will stay on as long as the rigging holds. If tight to start with, and properly put on, the load is held tight all day and drawn down against the side of the horse. Advantages: no special pack rope is needed; it will stay tight. Disadvantages: two men are needed, you need a special pack saddle cinch, and it *can* cause sores on the horse.

My own hitch: start with a lash cinch as with a diamond, but with a longer rope than you need for either a diamond or a squaw hitch. The start is the same as with a diamond —you work from the left side, throw a loop clear around the horse and pack and pull tight, using the hook on the end of the lash cinch. Pull the rope right back over the horse and throw a hitch similar to the Lang, except that you do not use a special cinch. Tighten by pulling down from the top, then up from the bottom, which lifts the pack away from the horse. Then repeat with the left side. So far as I know, I invented it, though I have shown it to dozens of packers who adopted it at once. Advantages: very fast, less likely to cause sores; one man can do it alone; it stays tight; the hitch swings with the pack, so that a horse that walks with a rocking motion doesn't work the hitch loose.

I realize that you can't take this written description and follow it as you do a blueprint. Like the Irishman's new boots that he couldn't get on 'til after he'd worn them a time or two, you can't fasten a pack with this hitch 'til you do it a few times.

There are other hitches, such as the "box" and the "barrel." The barrel hitch was used in the early mining days. All sorts of things came in barrels then. A partial list would be: whiskey, flour, beer, crackers, salt pork, pickles. Small barrels could be packed with a barrel on each side, but a large barrel had to go on top, and, due to its shape, had to be held on with a special hitch.

In making a pack you must know your horses and pack according to their nature and habits. Just as each human walks differently, the horses' gaits differ. Some walk with a twisting rack; others walk so evenly you could set a pan of milk on top of the pack; some know how to dodge trees and overhanging rocks; some don't give a damn about you or your pack.

Never tie a string together by tying to the rigging or the saddle of the horse in front. It tears up rigging; it may injure the horse in front; and you can buy yourself an all-day job of gathering pieces, if, for example, the pack string stirs up an army of yellow jackets who live in an old log by the trail or in a hole in the ground near enough to feel the jar of the horses' hooves. Yellow jackets complicate a pack string something awful.

I usually tied to the tail of the front horse if he had a full tail, being sure to tie below the tail bone so any pull would be on the hair.

Put the free leading horses at the back end of the string, for a balky or cranky horse in the rear can disrupt the whole thing. Some horses will follow without being led or fastened to anything, but they must be trained to stay back. If a free horse is wandering around, then suddenly decides to get into the middle of the string on a narrow trail, you are in trouble.

Another thing I learned early was to be careful how I packed eggs, whiskey, syrup, kerosene, catsup, and sheep-dip. It's astounding what you can do to a sack of flour or sugar with a few drops of sheep-dip or kerosene. The biscuits and pancakes never live it down.

The folks who want to go on pack trips are mainly wonderful persons. Once in a great while a man or woman slightly below that classification will sit in his warm city apartment and read a book about the character improvement the great out-of-doors can build. He knows nothing about dust, horseflies, and mosquitos. So he signs up and is a pain in the neck to the packer and to all others on the trip.

Jack Horton, of the United States Forest Service, told of a feisty little doctor from Philadelphia who went with one of the Trail Rider guided tours arranged by that capable organization, USFS. Jack was in charge. Right from the first the doctor made trouble. He demanded a different horse, then a different saddle. He didn't think much of his assigned place in the long string of riders—too much dust. He didn't care at all for the cold noon lunch.

That night Jack chose a good grassy place and dealt out the sleeping bags. The doctor put his down and tried it by lying on top. The place was too sloping. The next place was too rough, the third place too close to a man he disliked on sight. The little man eventually took his bag out of sight of the others.

The next morning Jack was making hot cakes and amusing the riders by flipping the cakes in the air. The doctor appeared with bloodshot eyes. Jack said pleasantly, "Good morning, Doctor, how did you sleep?"

Doctor: "Hardly at all."

Jack: "What was the matter?"

Doctor: "I guess it was that sleeping bag. I almost smothered to death and my feet froze."

CHAPTER SEVENTEEN

EVERY DAY IS AN ADVENTURE

R. A. LONG

I FREIGHTED WHEN I WAS YOUNG, BECAUSE THERE WAS LOTS of freighting to do. Homesteaders kept coming and what they owned had to be hauled to their places: bed and mattress; a cookstove and a heater of some sort, some farming tools, pots and pans; and most of them had enough boards to throw a shack together. I hauled for them for money, a cow, an old horse, or a promise. A few years later I hauled out some of the same families I had hauled in. They had less to haul out than when they came, and had less money to pay me.

Legitimate stockmen around had cattle or sheep in one place and hay in another, or there was no water where the hay was. In this case it was cheaper to haul the hay to them than to haul water. It's simple arithmetic—a cow will drink one hundred pounds of water a day, but can only eat twenty pounds of hay—or less if the hay isn't very good. So you have only a fifth as much hauling if you leave stock at the water and bring hay to them.

Road builders needed things hauled. They built roads with horses in those days and horses ate hay and grain and drank water. All three had to be hauled.

Wool and hides moved to town by wagons. For a long time The Dalles, far to the north, was the destination for Lake County wool. When the railroad reached Shaniko in southern Wasco County in 1901, the large wool market changed to Shaniko. The wagons hauled wool to both places, clear from Lake County, and later hauled eastward to Vale. In my time wool still moved by wagon, but trucks appeared soon.

So I freighted. I had a mania for stringing out six- or eight-horse teams. I didn't have any money, but that didn't stop me. Boys now rob junk piles, trade with friends, work a little for a wrecking yard, and accumulate a car. It may look funny, because it has parts from a dozen different kinds of vehicles, plus a few old boards, some rope and wire. That's the way I accumulated freight outfits. Wrecked wagons on mountainsides, junk behind blacksmith shops, discarded pieces around ranches furnished parts for my outfits. With wagons built this way, patched-up harness and half-broken horses, modern roads unknown, adventure lurked around every turn. I became a lurk specialist. I expected trouble and it never failed me.

Occasionally I'd latch onto a job where I needed a helper. Then I had to do some scurrying around to put together two outfits. I took a contract to haul cement from Lakeview to Summer Lake where irrigationists were building the Ana River dam. I had one eight-horse outfit hauling 14,000 pounds, and a six-horse team that hauled 12,000 pounds. I

DOUG LINEBAUGH ARRIVING TO WORK FOR THE ZX RANCH ABOUT 1906
The lantern was always on the outside, easy to reach, and with no danger of getting kerosene on the groceries.

found a youngster in Silver Lake who needed a job, and I needed a helper who would work for very little money, which happened to be what I had. He was six feet four and flourished under the name of Shorty—Shorty Hawkins. Fellows that tall weren't too plentiful then, and he attracted attention. I found out later he came from the mountains of Tennessee and just had to grow to see out. Anyhow, Shorty and I hauled cement.

In November it rained for days on end and the road along Crooked Creek north of Lakeview became a loblolly; no surface, just a grade.

My wagon had a California bed that features a high seat on a built-up place on the front. Ahead I saw an old high-wheeled car chugging painfully through the mud. I pulled over as far as I could on the slippery grade. The car had room to pass, but barely. The driver made no attempt to pull out, just drove his car up against my leaders and stopped. In the car were four big huskies who would hardly qualify as gentlemen. One asked loudly why I didn't give them half the road. I reasoned with them—said there was plenty of room to pass, that if I went off the grade with seven tons of cement in the rain and mud, they couldn't help me one bit, but if they slipped off, I would pull them back. This seemed a good statement, but it didn't impress those folks.

Shorty drove up behind me, set his brake, tied his lines

Courtesy Ed Lundy, Paisley, Ore.

FREIGHTING SUPPLIES IN 1907 FOR A RAILROAD SURVEY CREW
No railroad ever came. Stanley Martin and Frank Wyman were the freighters

to the brake handle, got down and hurried up. When he hurried he didn't walk faster, just took longer steps. His long arms swung as he walked, making him look determined and aggressive. The four men watched him come and before he could even say a word, they climbed in hastily and drove by.

I had found Shorty in town, broke, friendless, green. I took him home and he became a good man. He was only seventeen and wonderfully good-natured. A more loyal man never lived.

This was during prohibition. One day the sheriff and a helper came to the place. I was gone. They sized up Shorty as a green, ignorant boy. Here was the conversation, as the sheriff told it afterward:

Sheriff: How long since you've had a drink?

Shorty: Oh, my, mister, a long time! I ain't had a drink for—let's see—well, since yesterday anyhow.

Sheriff: Is there any law enforcement around here?

Shorty: I ain't seed anything that I could scarcely describe as enforcement, I guess.

Sheriff: What's the talk around here about the sheriff?

Shorty: You see, I'm a stranger and I don't know him a-tall, but from what I hear, he's a real sure nuf ———.

Sheriff: We're strangers, too. Where can we buy a drink around here?

Courtesy Ed Lundy, Paisley, Ore.
LES DUNCAN'S OUTFIT HAULING WOOL OFF THE DESERT, 1914
The wagons were bound for Shaniko, Oregon, about 170 miles away

Shorty: Down to the neighbors right over there.
He pointed out the ranch of the only sure-fire prohibition-
ist in that end of Lake County. His Tennessee training
probably taught him what to say.

Once Shorty and I were camped in a cabin near Sink
of Peters Creek. We found a human skeleton in a dune
where the sand had blown away, exposing it. The bones
were scattered. Shorty and I gathered up what we could
find and were busy assembling them on the cabin floor,
out of the wind. Shorty called the stranger "Sandy"
and gave him character traits. We stepped out to look
after the horses and a cowboy came by. We forgot all
about the skeleton and told him to go on in, get warm, and
get himself something to eat. When we came back, no one
was there. Shorty said, "That's funny. Sandy likes most
people."

Later that winter I was hauling hay from Silver Lake to
Sink—forty-five miles. I had six horses and two wagons,
and it was real cold. I was feeding a dozen cattle and fifty
horses. The best I could do, over the winter road, was to
take two days going, lay over a day, then take two days
getting back for more hay. In the five days I'd feed to
my work horses nearly half the hay I could haul. I doled

Courtesy Ed Lundy, Paisley, Ore.
ZX COOK WAGON AND THE FAMOUS OLD-TIME CHUCK-WAGON COOK,
ED LUNDY
He supplied this picture with the suggested caption, "All seven of us"

out just enough to keep the stock alive—I think they call it a "bare maintenance ration." They made it through alive, though they ate the poles of the corral halfway in two.

The freighters liked to tell of the bad roads, steep grades, impossible mudholes that occurred on *their* routes. My dad told of such a conversation with a freighter from Alturas to Lakeview. This man claimed that the Fandango grade north of Alturas really took the cake. Father asked him if he had to put his long string of horses around any sharp turns. The freighter said, "On this very trip a feller at Alturas asked me to deliver a dog to a man here. I tied him behind the trail wagon. After coming up the Fandango grade, I stopped to let the team blow. I tied the lines and walked back behind the trail wagon to see how the dog was coming. He was gone, and I couldn't see him anywhere. So I walked back down the grade, and there he was, cramped on a turn."

I mostly drove horses, but have had some experience with mules—just enough to pick up some rules: If you have anything to say to a mule, say it to his face; if you are in a hurry, don't let the mule know a thing about it.

My father was a jerk-line driver. He said a horse would go where you asked him to go, but a mule just went where it was safe. In spite of the highly advertised "Twenty Mule Team" of the Pacific Coast Borax Company, a horse makes a better jerk-line animal than a mule. A mule does a first-class job of looking after himself. In case of a sharp turn when you have to put the leaders clear off a grade down the side of a mountain, the mule looks at that and says plain as can be, "Not me, mister. If you want somebody to go down there, you go, but I ain't a-goin' with you."

The "long line skinner," driver of the jerk-line teams, has never had his just share in Western drama. He was hundreds of times more useful than the short-lived pony express. He was even more important than the celebrated stagecoach drivers, because they delivered a few passengers each, while he kept entire communities supplied with goods. He hauled supplies to the stage stations, or they couldn't have operated.

The jerk-line teams usually ran from ten to twenty horses. The driver rode the "near" or left wheel horse, with a long, small, hard-twist rope running along the entire team and ending in the bit ring of the left leader. A steady pull on this rope meant a left turn, a few sharp jerks, a right turn—hence, the name jerk line. The rope passed through "keepers" on the harness of all the near horses except the wheelers and the team in front, usually called the swing team.

In cases of turns, the leaders might have to go off the road, but in spite of this, the pull would be diagonal, tending to pull the wagons into a mountainside or over the outside. To combat this, the swing horse on the inside of the turn had to jump the long draw chain so he and his partner could both pull at an angle so as to keep the wagon on the road. Then, the danger past, he had to jump back. This, together with training of the leaders, took plenty of patient work, and when trucks finally put the teamsters out of business, the world lost a group of persons who did a hard job wonderfully well. You weren't "almost" able to operate a jerk-line team. There wasn't any degree of expertness. If you couldn't do it, you'd lose the whole outfit on the first trip. These folks were perfectionists, through necessity.

The first big jerk-line team that I remember that stopped at our place had a full load of pulled wool, taken from dead sheep killed in a sheepman-cattleman range dispute near Benjamin Lake. I was a small boy, but this was such an unusual load that I remember it. This was a mule team owned by Creed Conn and driven by Ed Henderson. Creed was the uncle of Ted Conn, of Lakeview, well known in Oregon.

In freighting, a tire off a wagon was far more serious than a flat tire on a truck today. It marooned you and a string of horses halfway to nowhere, maybe with water two or three looks away.

Trapping

Most men my age who lived in the Western country, trapped some as boys. About fifty years ago furs were in some demand, in many cases higher than now, and a boy could go and trap without saying a thing to anyone. A dollar then was worth a lot more than now. Winters were a time of slack work, and furs were prime then. If a man had no regular work, he could go into the open country and make a dollar or two a day trapping. It was a far healthier pastime than sitting in an office waiting for unemployment checks, unknown then. So I trapped.

Later, after my school days were over, I trapped early each fall for ten years. My trapping was of two kinds. When going to school I had a line of traps that I looked at on the way to school and on the way home, so the time wouldn't be wasted. I had another line up on the mountainside near the rimrocks. These were for bobcats and I looked at these on weekends. On one of these trips, when I was ten years old, a trap I'd set under a rimrock was gone. Snow had melted off quickly and tracking was hard. I had left my horse and was making my way slowly, following the bobcat by looking for bent sagebrush twigs, small rocks dislodged, and other dim signs. Melting snow had erased all real tracks. After half an hour of this slow, uncertain tracking below the rim, I heard a faint jingle of the trap chain, looked up, and the bobcat was on the rim, right at my eye level and only a few feet away. One who has never looked a mad bobcat in the eye at close range has no idea what the word "malice" means.

Trappers had long lines of traps, even when traveling horseback, and when Model T's came in, a man could cover still more country. I tended five hundred traps over a course of fifty miles. Some of the professionals would have one thousand or more. These men lived on their trap lines, carrying all their supplies, including bed, grub, and water, and stopping where night found them.

I would start early in the fall, before furs were quite prime. The roads were good then; you could cover lots more territory than later on; coyote pups were inexperienced; both young and old congregated around the few water holes. Later on, when snow came, coyotes could scatter everywhere. With early trapping it was easier to keep the traps in working order—they didn't freeze down, could be hidden by sifting sand over them, and the coyotes would spring them by sinking into the dry sand. On frozen ground it was harder to conceal them, and a little frozen sand under the pan would make them hard to spring.

Trappers got into ruckuses over the good places to set the traps—such as water holes. An occasional trapper wasn't above stealing furs from another man, especially if he figured the other man was poaching on his territory.

A humane passerby would occasionally shoot the trapped coyote. If the weather was warm, the animal would spoil and make the skin worthless; if cold, he'd freeze solid and be hard to skin.

Most trappers fastened their traps to toggle, rather than to something firm, because, if solid, the trapped animal would often twist loose. If he could move the trap, he'd concentrate upon getting away.

Trappers all used scent instead of bait for these reasons:

1. With bait, birds and small animals would keep the traps sprung.
2. With bait it was necessary to carry it along on every trip, and with a long line of traps, this was almost impossible. With scent, a bottle of it would be enough to last for days.

Each trapper had his own brand of scent and guarded it

as his professional secret. Many old trappers went to their graves without revealing the ingredients.

The places for setting traps would include:

1. Near carcasses of animals.
2. Where trails crossed.
3. On high ground in the open. Coyotes fight shy of close quarters. They like to be able to see in all directions.
4. The best sets of all were those places where the coyotes regularly left their calling cards, just as domestic dogs visit certain lampposts. The coyote's world is a world of smells.

You can't outsmart an old coyote. He just gets caught when he gets careless. He knows the location of every one of your traps and often shows his disdain by fouling your trap. He couldn't show contempt more plainly.

You learn how to be a real good trapper in just one way —trap a lot, observe closely, and remember what you see. A coyote can teach a man many things.

I have known some expert old-time trappers, such as Al Andrews and Walt Lowe. Following is part of a letter Raymond Morris, of Plush, sent to me recently:

Letter from Raymond Morris

I started trapping the spring of 1937 under the U.S. Biological Survey. I went to the desert around Big and Little Juniper. Sheepmen were losing twenty percent of their lambs from predators.

The first coyote den I found was in a rimrock. I crawled back in the hole and was trying to get the pups with a forked stick when the old coyote started out. I backed out fast.

I found a den two miles east of Big Juniper and next morning went back with my boss, Fred Sankey. We were digging the pups out just after sun-up, looked toward Big Juniper and saw the two old coyotes coming. They had killed some lambs that morning way over beyond, and there were four herds of ewes and lambs within a quarter mile of their den. They hadn't bothered these at all.

Trappers like me got $100 a month and furnished everything but the traps. That fall I moved to Plush where I stayed trapping until the fall of 1960. I was retired on disability pay. Most of my work was on the high desert, 23 years of it.

We didn't make much headway on the coyotes until we started using Humane Coyote Getters, started dropping bait from planes, and then began to use 1080.

The first time I went out with Harold Dobyns in his plane, he scared the daylights out of me, dropping off the rims into steep deep canyons. But we'd get up to 13 coyotes from one of these stations.

Bobcats are not usually bad killers, unless one happens to kill a bunch of lambs and then it's too much fun for him so he never quits. They are easier to get than the coyotes.

Some cattlemen didn't like to see us killing coyotes, but now, since sheep are about gone, coyotes have turned to calves for easy meat.

I have seen deer and antelope kills made by both coyotes and bobcats. I have seen lots of pieces of sage hens, ducks, and pheasants lying around the dens. One bad winter at the Con Taylor ranch on upper Honey Creek, I found eight deer kills. Hardly any of the deer were eaten—just torn to pieces, apparently for fun.

While I was working for the government, I turned in scalps and skins of 5,009 coyotes and 1,108 bobcats. But if you will look around over the country I worked in, you'll see plenty of signs any time.

RAYMOND MORRIS

Tracks

A man can only be in one place for a few minutes, but all sorts of things will be happening there when he isn't around. So tracks are important. They help the observant to know what goes on in his absence.

If tracking horses, you soon learn the tracks of each. You can tell whether a horse is loose or ridden. It's important to know how old the tracks are, and lots of things help you determine.

If tracking on the desert and there is mouse evidence in the tracks, you know that a night has passed, for most of the desert creatures travel at night. But in the timber they travel also in the daytime, and some only in the daytime.

If evidence of wind, remember back to when the wind

blew. Remember whether there was a sharp frost. In some soils tracks hold well—in others they disappear quickly. Hot afternoon sun will dull tracks faster than morning shade.

The habits of animals and their line of travel are often influenced by insects, and you need to know what insects are abundant and at what time of day they feed.

Some types of plants stay bent longer than others, and this helps you fix the time. What you learn tracking wild animals helps you in case you need to track a domestic animal, or even a man. Good trackers are disappearing fast.

Making Movies

I have left-handed acquaintance with movies in that I supplied horses, wagons, horse equipment and know-how in handling horses to two movies: *Canyon Passage* and *Indian Fighter.* I was in some of the scenes, as driver of one of the four-horse wagon outfits that tore through stumps, rocks, and across rivers when Indians attacked.

Neighbors and friends all wanted to know what the movie folks were like. I became well acquainted with some of

BRIAN DONLEVY AND SUSAN HAYWARD
Working for the movies near Diamond Lake, Oregon

the famous ones and they were pleasant, easy to know, and likable.

You often hear that most of the scenes in Westerns are fake or trick photography. There are tricks in picture taking, but in these two pictures at least, the scenes that depicted dangerous experiences really were dangerous.

In *Indian Fighter* ten covered wagons were making a run for the fort at Benham Falls on the Deschutes. They usually kept the area wet down to avoid dust hazard, but on this morning the dust was bad. With the teams running toward the fort, one of the four-horse wagons directly ahead of my team straddled a stump that was high enough to catch the front axle. The lead team took the stretchers off the wagon tongue and the wheel team went right out through their harness. The driver, Mr. Pollard, a professional teamster with the company, sailed through the air and lit beyond the end of the tongue. He was shaken up, but not permanently injured.

I was following with my horses on a hard run. I saw the trouble through the dust fog just in time to swing out.

Some of the best hands with horses I have seen lately

DANA ANDREWS
The horse belongs to Dean Hollinshead, of Bend

were drivers and riders with the picture companies. This applies to driving, packing, and riding. They are good men. They *have* to be good. If they aren't, they may find themselves quite permanently dead. They get along well with horses, cattle, and stock, and they are experts at getting along with people. They have to be friendly with all the extras, hired locally; they must please exacting directors; they must have the confidence of actors and actresses.

Some I knew were: Gordon Jones; Jimmie Locks; the Dave Richardsons, father and son; Rusty McDonald; and Buddy Sherwood. These fine people were called "wranglers."

A few of the name folks I got to know included: Dana Andrews, Susan Hayward, Andy Devine, Ward Bond, Brian Donlevy, Lloyd Bridges, and Kirk Douglas.

My wife Eleanor, Dean and Lilly Hollinshead, Lester Weisenberger, and half a dozen other friends worked as extras. My pay and that for the extras was good, but it was all so much fun that even if they had cut off my pay, I'd have stayed right on the job.

In *Canyon Passage* I started with twelve head of horses and my own ranch crew of three. I worked seven weeks

ANDY DEVINE AND HIS TWO BOYS

DAD WORTHINGTON, BUCKAROO BOSS OF THE ZX RANCH,
PAISLEY, OREGON (see page 23)

and by the time it was over, I was supplying thirty-six horses and mules and seven men, besides lots of equipment.

I liked the work and the movie people seemed to like me.

The moral of this chapter is that you can usually get along if you aren't a specialist. Nowadays men list their jobs as "freight car wheel inspectors" or "bottle fillers," and if those particular jobs aren't available, the men are eligible for unemployment checks. My only way to check unemployment was to go to work—it beats hunger quite a bit even if the work is out of one's line. So I cooked, trapped, freighted, wrangled dudes, trained horses, lambed sheep—just anything there was to do. I learned to do lots of things, but some of the things aren't of much use to me now—for example, how to put a six- or eight-horse team around a sharp bend. But some are real useful. What you learn from horses helps in dealing with humans. A horse is good for a boy or a man. It helps something inside of him. A man trained by a horse for many years is never quite the same afterward, and is better.

Some horses and some men can't be trained. Outside

SUSAN HAYWARD AS A PIONEER GIRL

Photo by Schmink Museum, Lakeview, Ore.

SHIPMENT OF BUGGIES, 1897, TO BERNARD & SON, LAKEVIEW, OREGON
The kind of buggy in those days was a status symbol, just as the kind of auto is now

ideas can't seep in. A man like that can harm you, even if he is your friend. A horse like that is an awful waste of time. Avoid both.

ELEANOR LONG WORKING AS AN EXTRA

ELEANOR AND REUB LONG READY TO WORK IN THE MOVING PICTURE,
CANYON PASSAGE
With them is Dave Richardson, wrangler for the moving picture company

Courtesy Ted Conn, Lakeview, Ore.

CREED CONN FREIGHT TEAM, ABOUT 1900

Teamster, Ed Henderson. Line mule, Nellie. This team hauled supplies from Shaniko to Silver Lake, about 170 miles

CHAPTER EIGHTEEN

THE DESERT-WISE PLANTS

E. R. JACKMAN

THE BOOKS CALL IT ECOLOGY—THE AMAZING ABILITY OF plants to get along with what they have. Some have only a few hours of filtered sunlight in a forest, others the blazing, pitiless, endless sun of the Southwestern desert; some must emerge from the ice on a mountaintop in July, bloom and bear seeds within thirty days, before the August freezes kill them; hardy specimens must endure continual cropping to the ground by animals; a fraction of an inch of soil on a windswept rock is the home of others.

Some things that determine size, form, seeding habits, kind of leaf, age, and habit of growth of desert plants include the obvious: rainfall, elevation, length of growing season, kind and depth of soil, competition, wind, trampling.

But less noticeable characters lurk behind the scenery, enter the drama, and shape the plot. Some are villains, some heros. Acidity, alkalinity, subsoil moisture at time of snowmelt, deer, ants, elk, gophers, root competition, degree of slope, heaving of surface soil by frost, depth of snow, frequency of summer frosts, seed-eating or leaf-eating insects—these and hundreds more are Nature's landscape gardeners who wrangle incessantly among themselves over the location of this tree or that flower. Such things are the foot soldiers of General Ecology.

It would be bad enough if the landscape would stay put. But the strangest things have happened to it in Oregon. At one time eastern Oregon was semitropical. Rainfall was

NATIVE BUNCHGRASS ON THE RANGE OF ELEANOR LONG, FORT ROCK

Grass such as this is still found on well-used ranges. On others, hurt by wildlife, rodents, insects, wild horses, domestic animals, or drought, sagebrush and other plants have invaded.

heavy, growth was lush, and lakes and swamps made fine homes for the rambling rhinoceros types and the queer elephantlike beasts that can live only where vegetation runs riot.

Then lava began to flow from fissures and cones all around. Dozens of flows occurred—over forty have been counted. After two or three thousand feet of lava had covered the country from Canada to Mexico, the internal fires still burned, gases formed, and this huge lava coverlet began to toss like a bed quilt over a restless sleeper. The vast underground forces raised the entire surface into long waves, mostly running north and south. These waves were forced up and up until the tension became unbearable, and they broke, often near the top. One side would then fall, prop-

Photo by Sylvesta Munnerlyn, Fort Rock, Ore.

AN ODD-SHAPED JUNIPER

Junipers are found with every shape imaginable. They are a range menace in some places, but they are also handy for wood, posts, shelter, watershed protection, and, lately, for doodads for tourists.

DIFFERENT FORMS OF JUNIPERS IN REDMOND CITY PARK

ping the other side up into the air, forming a cliff perhaps
three thousand feet high.

The Cascade Mountains formed and cast all of eastern
Oregon into a drought shadow three hundred miles wide.
The moist air still flowed in from the sea, but the snow-
capped peaks caught it and wrung out the precious moisture
as giant hands would wring a mop.

At that point the vegetation had to change. Ferns, red-
woods, and other moisture lovers abruptly left. The country-
side slowly filled with the plants we have now.

The desert has been changed by man the least of any
part of Oregon. Our forests have been cut and burned; our
lands have been plowed and seeded to every plant, wild or
tame, that grows in this zone; our prairies have been close-
cropped until scarcely a native plant remains in place—
but our desert still has the same plant citizens that white
man found here when the canvas-topped wagons rolled to
Oregon.

In the Willamette Valley most of the common wild flowers
are natives of some other place; the weeds that grow in
our fields are mainly weeds from the East, Midwest, or the
Old World. But our desert-wise shrubs of central Oregon
came when Mount Mazama, Mount Multnomah, Mount
Hood and the others blew their millions of tons of volcanic tuff and dust into the air. The heat sucked in winds
from the west, the Cascade slopes formed vast chimneys
through which the winds roared and carried the dust over
eastern Oregon.

With the rains cut off by the mountains, the big lakes
dried, the glaciers retreated and disappeared, rivers became
rills, and spectacular dry gulches marked the location of
former streams. Now the only sign of our bygone wealth
of vegetation lies in the imprints in the rocks—the fossils.

Then the new vegetation came. We can only guess now
at the painful failures made by Nature. Here she would
try a tree. It would thrive for maybe a century, only to
shrivel and die in a drought cycle. Then she would hope-

fully transplant a grass from the Midwest, watch it cover a wide prairie, only to disappear, seared and killed by a hot summer.

But finally, from the errors of a thousand failures, some rules were worked out. Each plant that wanted to homestead from Bend to Ontario, or from Burns to Lakeview, had to subscribe to these rules or die. Here are some of them. Not every plant has agreed to all. If an individual were superbly endowed in some one respect, it was sometimes allowed to ignore the other rules.

Rules for Life in the Oregon Desert

1. The color must be predominantly gray. It can be gray-green, or gray-blue. Sagebrush is mostly dusty gray-green, junipers are gray-blue. One kind of rabbit brush is bright gray-green, the other kind has so little green that it is called gray rabbit brush.

2. The plant must be unattractive to animals, including buffalo, elk, antelope, deer, and rabbits. That rule was worked out maybe 500,000 years before there were any cattle, sheep, or horses in Oregon. But, unfortunately, leaves that are spit out disgustedly by buffalo, elk, antelope, deer, and rabbits, are heartily disliked by cattle, sheep, and horses—even mules. It doesn't matter why the leaves are unattractive. Different plants have worked this out to suit themselves. Some are astringent, or puckery; some bitter; others are poisonous; cacti, of course, have thorns; mullein has woolly leaves that do not absorb saliva readily; wild phlox has dry and leathery leaves; juniper has a resin that is sticky as glue—and so on.

Some of the human denizens of the desert take on these plant characteristics, too—some tend to get bitter, thorny, dry, and leathery.

3. Plants must have some moisture-saving device. The leaves of Idaho fescue roll inward and appear much like pine needles; the small desert succulents hold the water

instead of passing it off into the air; rabbit brush in dry years goes dormant, making no new growth at all; junipers have modified scales instead of leaves; the annuals bear seed quickly in the spring and die; larkspur has its showy flowers in May, the top dies, and the deeply buried crown sends up a new top next year; perennials, as sagebrush, must have small leaves, not divided much, with smooth or nearly smooth margins, and the plant must have a large proportion of wood to leaf.

When alfalfa is dry, it will commonly have about 50 per cent leaves, 50 per cent stems. But the desert shrubs will run at least 80 per cent stem, only 20 per cent leaves. And alfalfa will come closer to living in the desert than any other cultivated perennial. There are desert forms in old Persia and in the drylands of North Africa. Our scientists, obsessed by the "yield" fetish, have ignored them. They would be a godsend to our desert lands, even though the yield might be low.

Desert plants are ingenious in working out water-saving schemes. Root, stem, and leaf all work together on the project. Even the seeds get into the act. In a true desert you don't find many seeds surrounded by a watery pulp, as with the peach. Seeds are small, dry, and hard. "Stone seed" is the name of a common Oregon desert plant and the name truly describes the seed.

Has anyone commented upon the lack of parasites on the desert plants? In jungles, in the midst of excess food of all kinds, plant parasites are plentiful. They live on leaves, stems, and roots. A multitude, vegetative buzzards, live upon the decaying remains of the dead plants. No parasitic desert plants come to mind. As a plant moved into the desert, dwarfed its size, reduced its leaf surface, shortened its growth period, the parasites dropped away as dependents may leave, one by one, when a rich man loses his fortune.

A few years ago the Society of Range Management held its summer tour on the edge of the desert lands, and a learned man discussed plant improvement. He said, in substance, "When we wish plant breeding material to improve forage for drylands, one might imagine that we would go to even drier places, but that is not true. In the centuries it took to develop the desert plants, their cells dropped the genes that enable a plant to yield well, so by crossing two desert plants, there are no genes present to give us anything better than we started with."

Reub was asked to speak afterward and he said, "I am not qualified to speak upon this subject, because I do not even know the terms. But I listened carefully and judged that when our grasses lose their genes, we ranchers lose our shirts."

Food from the Land around Them

Before white man, and particularly before horses, each Indian tribe was fairly well tied to its own domain. The necessary chores of their civilization—maintenance work—took most of their time. A typical desert Indian group of perhaps forty persons had a different home for each season of the year, but the homes weren't too far apart. If, for example, the group had four homes, they might be located something like this:

Winter—near a hot spring or a creek so swift it didn't freeze.

Spring—near a camas meadow, with rocky ridges nearby where couses and wild onions grew.

Summer—hills with berries, haws, and rose hips.

Fall—good deer hunting.

Oregon Coast Indians had a completely different system, with salmon, clams, and crabs governing locations. The Middle West Indians had a buffalo economy. Salmon ruled the movement of tribes along the Columbia.

We are concerned here with the desert Indians, the Paiutes. Their groups were small because the desert gives food sparingly, and often each family lived apart from other tribal members most of the year. The women did much of the work of food gathering—except for meat. These Indians kept few horses, because a desert vegetation didn't supply enough feed. Horses didn't arrive here much before white men anyhow.

We often think of Indians as meat eaters or fish eaters. Neither classification is true. All tribes had variety with plenty of vitamins and minerals. They had over twenty salad dishes; a tremendous variety of starchy foods to correspond to potatoes and bread; protein dishes by the dozens; seasonings; fruits and berries. They had plant tonics and medicines, at least one medical treatment for each human ill—inside or out. This complicated diet was accomplished by using the plants and animals around them. Their supermarket basket was the squaw's basket woven from reed, grass, and root. They were pretty healthy until white man civilized them with his viruses and spirochetes.

We speak of the "underprivileged" peoples of the world —the "backward nations." They are mostly backward only because they spend all of their time getting food, just as the Indian did. When a nation's farmers can produce enough so that most of the populace can take to gadget making, we call that a "high standard of living." Judged that way, the Indians were uncivilized because it took all of their time to maintain themselves.

The Indians couldn't make a good living from the desert alone. They lived around the edges; they haunted the lakes for wildfowls, eggs, tules, cattails, and yellow water lilies. They moved to the hillsides for berries and wild plums. The few streams yielded fish. The marshes spread a fine table with bulbs, seeds, salads, and wildfowl.

Here are a few of the plants the Paiutes used:

Food from Seeds

Grasses—giant wild rye, Indian mountain rice, native bent,

manna grass, wild forms of wheat and barley grasses, various marsh grasses.

Weeds—dock, tarweed, mustard, lamb's-quarter.

Water plants—yellow pond lily, rushes, sedges, tules.

Hillside plants—balsamroot, mules-ears.

Trees—sugar pine.

Food from Leaves and Young Shoots

Dock, camas, sedge, cattail, reed, mint, wild parsnip, false dandelion, mushrooms, pigweed, watercress, shepherd's purse, lamb's-quarter, dandelion, mustard, fireweed, wild lettuce, peppergrass, mallow, wood sorrel, plantain, Solomon's seal, purslane, bracken fern, bulrush, sow thistle, chickweed, pennycress, nettle, wild violet. All of these furnished salads.

Food from Roots and Tubers

Wild onion, mariposa lily, camas, bitterroot, cous, Ipo (squawroot), cattail, Brodiaea, yellow bell, primrose, water parsley, balsamroot (Oregon sunflower), wocus (water lily). These roots corresponded in use to our potatoes, or, as with the onion, furnished flavoring.

Food from Fruits

Huckleberry, serviceberry, chokecherry, plum, currant, gooseberry, strawberry, raspberry, blackberry, manzanita, rose hips, Oregon grape, kinnikinnick (bearberry), haw, cactus (prickly pear), elderberry, juniper berries, false Solomon's seal, twinberry. These fruits were eaten fresh; were made into soft drinks; but above all, were dried and pounded into dried meat for flavoring.

Food from Trees

Lodgepole pine—this was only a famine food, but was

considered far superior to starving to death. Julia Rogers[1] reports that the trees were cut down, the thin layer of inner bark (cambium) stripped out, worked into a pulp and molded into cakes. Stones were heated in a hole in the ground, the cakes packed in with leaves, a fire built on top. The cakes were smoked for a week. They were hard and were prepared for eating by boiling. They would keep indefinitely.

We have no pine in Oregon to compare with the piñon pine of the Southwest as a food source.

Young yellow pines,[2] though, were often used. In spring the Indians stripped off a broad piece of bark, exposing a mucilaginous layer of cambium. This was eaten as is.

The Indians watched what animals ate, and figured that elk or deer feed wouldn't hurt humans. Deer in winter eat the black moss that hangs from trees, especially on the north slopes, and Indians ate that if real hungry. They would gnaw on younger shoots of willows if food were scarce.

Other Uses

Numerous plants furnished tea or spicy drinks. The list is too long and includes many plants already listed. For example, berries.

Plants served for other uses. Some were: baskets; poultices and medicines of all kinds, for both inner troubles and outer bruises; dyes for ornament, dress, war paint, picture making; leather tanning; footwear; bows and arrow shafts and war clubs; sticks for digging camas and other roots; papoose carriers; canoes; fuel; tepee frames; snares, traps, and pits for catching game; after horses came, saddle material.

Indian tribes in Oregon did not farm, and they existed

---

[1] Quoted in Oliver Perry Medsger, *Edible Wild Plants* (New York: The Macmillan Company, 1939).

[2] Quoted from Leslie Spier, *Klamath Ethnography* (Berkeley, Calif.: University of California Press, 1930).

by finding some use for everything that grew, whether plant, animal, bird, or fish. They were practical conservationists, and developed rules for taking of fish, game, and plant food so there would be some for next year.

Of all the plant foods listed, very few grew in the desert. Cous (biscuitroot), balsamroot, Ipo (squawroot), grass seeds (especially giant wild rye, beardless wild rye, and Indian mountain rice), juniper berries, serviceberries, pigweed, mustard—these grew with ten inches of rain. The desert-dwelling Paiutes lived along some stream near the desert, which they frequented to get obsidian for arrowheads; to hunt deer in the winter; to hunt waterfowl on the shallow lakes; or to dig for roots on the ridge tops.

They lived from the land. There are innumerable cases of starvation among whites in favorite food-gathering spots for Indians—where cous grows along a dry ridge, for example, or the similar food, Ipo.

A few elderly Indians still follow the old tribal food habits. In case of a nuclear war, with supermarkets out of business and no one to deliver the seven thousand items they sell, it might come in handy to know the edible plants all around us. Every native plant has some value—root, stem, leaf, flower, or seed. Man could live by browsing if he had enough sense.

Random Notes on Plants

Camas. The common Indian name was Quamash and whites gradually shook it down to camas. Indians ground the bulbs, dried them, and pressed them into large indestructible cakes. These were the first K rations. One could break off a chunk, moisten it, and serve a good meal in jig time. If a wandering individual had meat, he'd boil the meat and put in a chunk of camas root for seasoning, thus neatly mixing carbohydrates with his protein. The bloody and costly Bannock War of 1878 was indirectly caused by camas. Bannocks, after some fairly dirty work at the crossroads, consented to live like good boys provided the whites ceded to them Kamas Prairie, their ancestral grounds. This was done, with much ceremony. But a government clerk, noting other misspelled words, decided the writer must have meant Kansas Prairie, and wrote the treaty that way. When homesteaders settled on Camas Prairie, the Indians thought they'd been had, and war began.

Sego lily, or mariposa lily. One of our finest desert flowers. When Brigham Young's followers were in bad straights because the big crickets had destroyed their grain, the Indians showed them where the beautiful sego lilies grew. The white colony collected the bulbs, ground them, and thereby made it through the winter. Praying helped, but digging roots supplemented the prayers mightily. It is the Utah state flower.

Tule roots. Indians claimed the roots had a peculiar thirst-quenching effect, so when making a long trip across a waterless stretch, they munched on tules. Probably it was "for those who think young," or "the pause that refreshes."

Juniper berries. Indians watched coyotes closely. In the fall the coyote would find a tree loaded with misty blue berries and would return day after day to gorge on them. They are bitter, but he didn't mind. Indians began to eat them, too, experimenting with various recipes, such as boiling, crushing, baking, and eating raw. They weren't a preferred food, but were available—a strong argument.

Serviceberries. These were an Indian staple. They were crushed and dried in big loaves weighing ten to fifteen pounds. A piece of a loaf helped in building a stew, no matter what was in the stew before, and wise visitors did not ask.

Yarrow was steeped—the whole plant, and tea was used by the Paiutes as a spring tonic. In my childhood we did the same thing. We had to drink quarts of it to purify the blood. I guess it did, because our blood never spoiled after that.

Indians had many beverage plants—to drink after a hard

day, to take one for the road, or to drink for tired blood. They steeped Douglas fir needles and sumac berries. They crushed manzanita berries, strained water through them.

Death camas was well known to the Indians and dreaded. A Klamath medicine man developed a neat trick. He mixed death camas with tobacco and when an Indian with some wealth took it and became violently ill, the medicine man charged a fancy fee for making him well. This wasn't exactly in accord with the Hippocratic oath, but maybe the medicine man misspelled it.

The Indians used the fibrous nettle, after retting it as we do flax, for fish nets, ropes for packs, strings for garments, for hanging food high to keep away from animals, and for all things for which we use twine or rope. The Germans, during the war, short of flax, revived the use and put a guaranteed price on nettles. I don't know whether they accumulated a surplus and had to put an export subsidy on it or not. The Indians also used wild hemp and milkweed as fibers.

GRASS GROWS BY INCHES — IT IS DESTROYED BY FEET

E. R. JACKMAN

LARGE BOOKS HAVE BEEN WRITTEN ABOUT RANGE MANAGEment; colleges have four-year courses about it; a national society is devoted to it. When any common or everyday thing, such as a headache, a cold, a frost, or a dust storm gathers around it enough observations, it becomes a science. Doctorates are conferred upon those who give it prolonged study. A vocabulary is built up, understandable only to specialists in that subject.

This opens new vistas, new corridors of knowledge. But there is a tendency, at that point, for the students of the subject to become so immersed in it that they have little to tell the folks out there who are suffering from a cold, headache, dust storm, or untimely frost.

I think that Reub stated it better when he said, "A technician is a man who comes out to your ranch and tells you things you knew before, in terms you can't understand."

The management of a desert range doesn't *have* to be smothered in verbiage. There are a few elemental facts.

In any desert the vegetation that has survived did so only through thousands of years of intense struggle. During the combat, nature tried hundreds of species and found most of them unsuitable. If, for example, ten species remain, it is likely that a thousand have been discarded. The ten have some special device that lets them live where others failed.

But the ten are still fighting a constant battle royal with

Courtesy Soil Conservation Service, U.S. Dept. of Agriculture

UNLESS GRASS IS SEEDED, RABBIT BRUSH MAY COME IN WHEN SAGE IS DESTROYED

In this Fort Rock area of Lake County, the rabbit brush moved in following a fire that killed the sage

each other. You can find places on the desert where each of the ten has some slight advantage and it predominates at that point. The advantage may come from soil temperature, soil depth, runoff moisture, fire, shade, deer concentration, ant damage, trampling, gopher work, rabbit numbers—absolutely anything that goes on will affect and determine the vegetation. By looking at the species around you, wherever you stand, you can often tell what has happened. Here, fifteen years ago, a fire swept over a half section; there, fifty years ago, a quarter section was plowed; this south slope has been grazed closely by deer—and so on. Any change whatever will change the kinds and amounts of vegetation.

This is true because, with scanty moisture at best, the kinds that can live are pressed to their very limits of endurance—with conditions just a little worse, some are going to die and others will then increase.

Let's say that we have a section exactly as it was when white men first came—largely a grass community, but with suppressed sagebrush, larkspur, rabbit brush, and annual grasses. The suppressed plants anxiously wait for a sign of weakness on the part of the perennial grass. Then something happens: fire, grasshoppers, wildlife increase, root disease, overpopulation of gophers—anything.

The vegetation changes slowly. Gradually the grasses leave; more of the weedy types move in. With some of the grass leaves destroyed, the plants are weakened, and that gives the others a better chance. They crowd in.

Here is the point of all this. *Any grazing at all of native vegetation is overgrazing.* When deer become thick, as compared to the historic numbers, the vegetation will change. When gophers or mice get thick, it will change, and it will surely change if cattle, sheep, or horses appear in an area where they have never been before.

This introduces some bad results when we try to "manage" a desert range. Let's take an example. Say this range originally carried two hundred AUMs of cattle (animal unit

A BIG RANGE FIRE BETWEEN ARLINGTON AND HERMISTON, OREGON, SWEPT OVER MANY THOUSANDS OF ACRES OF CHEATGRASS RANGE IN 1939

The fire took fences, shrubs, buildings, and grass. But it stopped at this field of crested wheat grass. Seedings such as this save more soil, provide more food for game and livestock, and stop more fires than all other measures combined.

months) for five months of summer use—or forty head of mature cattle. But gradually the vegetation changes; perennial grasses are slowly displaced by annuals; sagebrush gets bigger and there is more of it. After careful analysis, it is determined that it can now carry only twenty head. The reduction is made, but the twenty head feed upon the remnants of the perennial grasses, weakening them still more. The cattle largely ignore the sagebrush and rabbit brush, so it increases. In ten or twenty years it is necessary to reduce numbers again—down to ten head. With reduced vigor and greatly reduced numbers of perennials, the range still goes downhill, and progressive reductions will be necessary down to almost zero.

This failure to recognize that *any grazing is over-grazing* has led to most of the arguments over range use. Then what can we do? Shall we just give up and remove all domestic stock from desert grazing lands? This would be a silly and defeatist thing to do. This land will swing its weight in taxes for roads, schools, and county government if we let it. Our failure to recognize this rule in grazing has led to costly mistakes, but we don't need to keep on making them.

The sensible way out of this chain of reduction piled upon reduction until we get down to zero livestock, is to remind ourselves that we don't need to start from here. If we accept true range improvement as our goal, we can't get there from here. If the largely useless types have driven out the valuable vegetation until the land is 90 per cent useless, we can't improve that situation by reducing livestock and it is senseless to try. At Squaw Butte, where trial ranges have been fenced, with no use for twenty-seven years, there has been practically no improvement. But they started in 1935 with 90 per cent of the ground in useless plants.

Suppose we kill all of that 90 per cent, replace with useful varieties, then start fresh with 100 per cent of useful plants. It took over fifty years of grazing for weedy species

A FAIRLY FREQUENT SCENE

Photo by Ernie Kirsch, Condon, Ore.

This picture was taken in the Columbia Basin. One rancher cared for his grass, the other did not

to replace the native perennial grasses. If we start new, don't graze so thoroughly, alternate the use from year to year, I think we have enough demonstrations to prove that we won't lose the good kinds for fifty years at least. We can seed better grasses than our own native kinds. It wouldn't be too bad a deal to kill the nearly useless invaders and start over again every fifty years. The land would turn off more wealth that way than it is doing now, surely.

Not every acre has its door open to this positive approach. Alkali, rocks, thin soil, steep slopes, may make improvement impossible.

Rocky land can be improved, but it is too expensive with cattle at present prices. When calves sell in the fall for fifty cents a pound, range improvement can spread onto all land that will grow grass. The alkaline flats can be forgotten unless some wonder grass should come along. At present prices for cattle, it pays very well indeed to improve the good ranges. It's far cheaper than it is to buy more land.

A vegetation community is exactly like a committee. Suppose we have a committee of ten working on a problem. Take one man out of that group and you have a completely different committee. His absence will change the actions of the other nine. Some will be more aggressive, some more timid. Some will be more definite in their ideas, some less. Scientists dedicated to human reactions, call that "group dynamics." If you remove one member of a vegetation community, the others all act differently. Plants respond to group dynamics, too. The presence of that one was favorable to some, unfavorable to others, due to its root habits, and the way it used moisture. It may have led some insects, rodents, or game to use that spot, and these had an influence upon the vigor of the other plants, their seed-bearing ability, or their tendency to spread.

We can erase all of these complicated reactions by eliminating the other plants and replacing them by one or two varieties adapted to the area. We can then adapt our use to the needs and habits of that one variety.

From that standpoint it is better to seed only one grass variety than to seed a mixture. With a mixture you immediately get into trouble again, for the use will be more favorable to one of the varieties than to the others, and you are likely to kill out all but one. Therefore, if you need more than one variety in order to spread out the grazing, seed two or more fields, each with a different grass.

Next point in range management is to keep things simple. In the books you will find fancy arrangements, labeled Pastures A, B, and C. They show how to move cattle two or three times each season, in a complicated rotation system, differing each year. This works well on an irrigated pasture where each field gets all the water it needs all summer. But on the desert, it has been my observation that if you get scientific enough to follow such a system, you are likely to go broke, and you will probably ruin your range along with your bank account.

Just make *alternate* use your rotation. Use this half of the range one year—the other half next year. Some who do that carry more stock on half the acreage each year than others do on all the acreage. Therefore, their income per acre is higher than their neighbors'. But to make this work, you've got to have something to improve. Neither a sagebrush range nor a cheatgrass range will be improved much by any kind of rotation.

The next point is that in judging the capacity of a range, the yield of beef per acre is worth fully as much as painstaking counting and weighing of the forage. When a man's cows come in year after year with four-hundred-pound calves, they are getting something to eat, no matter how the experts value the palatability of the species. I've seen Texas ranges that seemed to have nothing on them except species that no self-respecting cow would come within ten feet of, yet they have been producing beef for a hundred years. If you don't have cake you'll eat bread, and it may be better for you. Studies of palatability are fine for high-yielding dairy cows on irrigated pastures. They aren't worth much when it's a case of root, hog, or die. Permanence of a grass on the desert is worth ten times as much as palatability.

The single biggest headache in figuring carrying capacity on the desert is the very simple fact that the yield some years is ten times as high as in others—or, if you are a pessimist, in some years it's only a tenth of that the previous year. So, no matter where you put carrying capacity, you are wrong every year. In managing their own ranges, many ranchers do just as they do with hay—try to carry some over for the poor years.

It is a right good scheme to have a section or two that hasn't been grazed at all, for maybe several years. The grass grows up and falls down, is a bad fire hazard, and the cattle do not relish eating all the dead stuff to get the other. They'll avoid it if they can get any other feed. But in years when it forgets to rain for eight or ten months at a time, they will eat all of this dead grass right down to the ground. A little alfalfa will help, or protein cubes. It's best to have a crested wheat field for this purpose, just because one section is worth half a dozen sagebrush sections, and you've got to have it fenced to save it. It takes less fence for one section than for six. A rye field works pretty well, too. Turn cattle into it in the late summer instead of cutting for hay.

There isn't too much of the desert that will grow grazing alfalfas, but there is some—up next to timber. Wherever it will grow at all, a person should get some of it. Below ten inches of rain, it should be seeded alone—not with grass. I have seen it growing on some real dry land in Nevada in Humboldt County. Reub had some on his place that made a lot of feed in spite of antelope, deer, squirrels, porcupines, and mice, until one year when the mice were a scourge. They camped all winter on the scattered alfalfa crowns and by spring the crowns were pretty well destroyed. Even

GRASS ON R. A. LONG INDIVIDUAL ALLOTMENT, BUREAU OF LAND MANAGEMENT

This shows good grass cover, partly due to the fact that it is an individual grazing allotment, is far from water, and is in rough, rocky terrain so, some plants of the Nomad variety lived by generating new crowns.

The extra protein in alfalfa serves as a magnet for nearly all four-footed wild animals. A person shouldn't seed a little bit. He'd better seed a lot—at least 80 acres, and preferably 160 or more. If you have 10 acres of alfalfa, and get it to grow, you can count in it all of the deer there are for several miles around. It calls, "Come here!" to them in a loud, clear voice, and they all obey.

One big advantage of alfalfa is that it has extra protein, even when it is ripe. Grass starts at about 24 per cent protein, but, as it heads out and ripens, it gets down to about two per cent, or in poor years when most plants don't head out, it still runs down to 5 per cent.

The priceless ingredient of protein is nitrogen. This element is in great supply and we humans need it desperately, but we can't get at it. The air above us is four fifths nitrogen. Tons and tons float lazily over every acre on earth, land, or sea. Most reducing diets run heavily to lean meat, eggs, skim milk, cheese, and foods made from them, because these are protein foods. Babies need protein to grow and develop into strong, healthy adults.

Alfalfa and other legumes know how to do something that the smartest man can't do—in its daily living, it draws nitrogen from the air and fixes it in the soil for future plant use.

Grass needs nitrogen and desert soils are low in it. When we get a good year, the grass yield isn't so high as it could be, because there isn't enough nitrogen to let the grass reach its potential. There are only two ways out of this: grow a legume such as alfalfa, or use "store-bought" nitrogen. When beef gets high enough to justify commercial nitrogen, everyone will be using it. It pays right now, provided the land is covered with grass. But if the cover is mostly stuff that cattle don't use, it is poor business to spend five dollars an acre to make the brush grow better.

Alfalfa has another benefit: it puts the precious nitro-

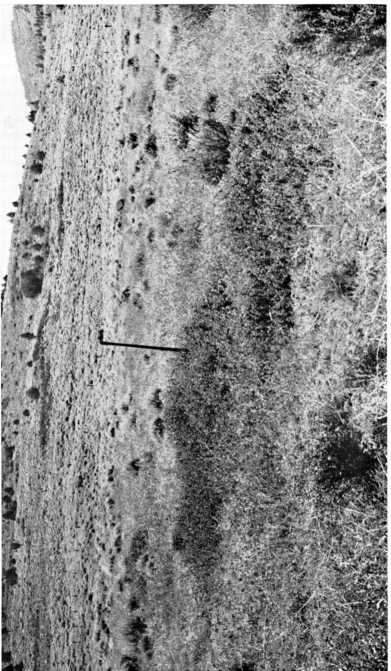

THIS IS A CLUMP OF NOMAD ALFALFA IN A LOW RAINFALL RANGE AREA

Heavy grazing killed most of the perennial grasses and even damaged juniper trees, but the alfalfa still lives. It spreads by short, underground runners and in time forms matted clumps. It resists damage from grazing. These clumps are forty or more years old.

gen into the ground as well as into the feed. So grass, growing with alfalfa, or growing where it has been, will out-
yield grass on land where no alfalfa has ever grown. If a
man is going to seed grass, it is good sense to include a pound
of grazing alfalfa in all areas where it will grow. If he is
lucky, and gets a stand, it will help him for many years.
The Negro who said, "De chicken is de greatest animal, fo
you eats him befo he is bohn an after he's daid," said something partly applicable to alfalfa. It helps a man while it
is growing and perhaps even more after it dies.

Here is a place to find some fault with the majority of
scientists working with alfalfa. This fault is not so common in Oregon as in many other states. If we could get
alfalfa on part of our 700,000,000 acres of Western range,
it would be worth more to America than anything that
any American plant scientist has ever done, so far. We
have varieties that will grow on much of that land. They
are called Nomad, Rambler, Teton; and we have a few
others, such as Rhizoma, that will grow in the upper rainfall areas. Let's call them grazing types. But when ranchers,
who need such varieties desperately, write to their experiment stations and ask about them, the scientists say that
these varieties yield only 82 per cent, or some other figure,
of the yield of the standard variety. This is pitifully lacking in imagination. The standard varieties aren't growing
on the range and won't grow there, so why refer to them?
If the grazing types will persist and the others won't, why
compare them? If a North Dakota farmer wants a hardy
gooseberry, it doesn't show good sense to tell him that bananas
yield better.

Grazing varieties are different from hay types. The grazing alfalfas will live, even if grazed closely, but close grazing
kills the hay varieties. If the mere presence of the grazing
types will double or triple the yield of the range, why go
out of one's way to discourage their use? The grazing
types can exist if pastured because they have the ability to

send up new sprouts from any place along the roots, and because they can go dormant if they run out of water.

The research we need is to locate other varieties that have these traits to an even greater extent. For range use, yield is of little or no importance; *persistence* is vastly important. Preoccupation with yield has set back range development many, many years. It shows up in grass breeding work, too. As Reub says, "In our country, we don't measure a crop by tons or height—if it's alive, it's a success." The desert is cruel to the unfit. Desert plants must take abuse and live.

The striving for comparative yields has created the wrong viewpoint for work on range plants. Some European agronomists seed fields to different varieties, pasture them *hard* and see what are alive in ten years. I'll guarantee it won't be those that give the highest yields in a nonused experiment station plot—either grasses or legumes. All plants now growing on the desert got there by ability to survive. Can't we learn anything from nature? Test all strains, imported or developed, by the cruel law of survival. The plant breeder who is the first to forget yield and accept nature's terms for desert survival will become famous.

All ranges in Oregon are used by plenty of animals, aside from cattle, sheep, and horses: porcupines; squirrels; rodents of many kinds; antelope; deer. We don't have many societies worrying about preserving skunks, mice, and grasshoppers. But we have dozens of clubs whose members fly into rages about the criminal actions of the State Game Commission by allowing killing of does.

The deer migrate from spring range to summer range to fall range to winter range, exactly as cattle move to the feed. Numbers of cattle are rigidly controlled by the owner, but deer numbers are not, except as the game managers attempt it by special area hunts.

The same persons who rage at stockmen for overuse of a range are often the ones who would allow deer to multiply unduly. There is no doubt about it—when domestic livestock began to appear in numbers in eastern Oregon about 1870, that spelled an eventual drastic change downward in carrying capacity. But we should have learned something from that. A thousand pounds of deer eat the same number of pounds of forage as a thousand pounds of cattle. If a cowman should figure what a range will carry, then a game manager should do exactly the same thing.

All over eastern Oregon we can see where unrestricted numbers of deer have damaged ranges. Overgrazing by deer has the same effect as overgrazing by cattle—the range will carry less of these animals—perhaps forever. A range abused by cattle will carry less, but the owner will take them somewhere else. The deer do not work that way. They spend the winter and early spring in some little valley, which is home to them. If numbers increase so that feed is killed, they will still stay in their home valley and starve to death there, even if feed is plentiful somewhere else. The Game Commission is trying to keep this from happening by decreeing special hunts and all of us should give them a hand, not a spiteful kick in the pants. Since deer kills in Oregon have been the highest of any state in the Union in recent years, and since the special area doe hunts are *not* resulting in deer scarcity, it would appear that effort to manage deer herds in accord with food supply is working well.

Deer herds on the desert are increasing enormously because of range improvement. Every time a rancher develops some water, or increases the feed supply for his cattle, he increases deer and antelope herds. In recent years seeding of alfalfa in Bear Valley has built up a flourishing antelope herd. In Baker County deer are increasing in every area where range alfalfa has been seeded. Yet we have some prominent men in America declaiming against range improvement because it is spoiling wildlife habitat. Smart men can be blind and ignorant on subjects out of their fields. A learned lawyer can give you some mighty poor advice upon range management.

CHAPTER TWENTY

THE DESERT TOWNS

R. A. LONG and E. R. JACKMAN

WHEN THE HOMESTEADERS' BREAKING PLOWS DISTURBED
the quiet of the desert, our town situation changed fast.
Before that, town was roughly one hundred miles away. To
the south was Lakeview, to the northwest was Bend, and
Prineville was north. Burns was northeast, also about one
hundred miles.

Homesteaders had to walk or ride horseback, their children had to get to school and get back the same day, so
towns blossomed in the desert. Like the desert flowers, the
towns soon faded. It usually took five years for a man to
arrive, build a house, fence some land, break it, put in a
crop, wait in vain to harvest it, lose his money, get tired
of jackrabbit stew, and leave.

But in that five years, he had to go to town, a school
had to be built, and when he and his neighbors left, the
towns died of malnutrition. Some towns were stubborn,
or lived on hope for a long time.[1]

Without exception, it is hard to find where these places
were. You may find a broken dish, a few rocks from an
old foundation, but these towns, all started hopefully, are
mostly not dignified by even a headstone to record their
deaths.

The desert has other towns that still live. These are sup-

---

[1] In Appendix I is a list of twenty-five ghost towns with the dates of establishment of
their post offices and the year of their deaths.

ported by ranchers with irrigated land, such as Silver Lake, or they are kept alive because of their location, as with Valley Falls and Hampton.

Others still living include: Adel, Andrews, Blitzen, Brothers, Denio, Fields, Fort Rock, Millican, Paisley, Paulina, Plush, Post, Rockville, Rome, Sheaville, Riley, Silver Lake, Summer Lake, Wagontire.

Some of these do not have post offices anymore, but all of them have *something*. In most cases, those that survived were not started by the dryland homesteaders, so the towns were still there after the homesteaders left.

The dead, or ghost, towns, got post offices, on the average, in 1912 and lost them in 1920. These dates do not

TOWN OF DENIO

Shown is the Nevada side of the town. The part of the building housing the saloon was in Nevada, the half with the post office was in Oregon.

Photo by Jones Studio, Lakeview, Ore.

A MOUNTING BLOCK IS ALL THAT IS LEFT OF THE ONCE THRIVING TOWN
OF FREMONT AT THE EDGE OF THE R. A. LONG RANCH

The desert has dozens of such ghost towns. The block is a juniper stump, with steps sawed in it so that ladies with the long skirts of the day could step into buggies or mount their sidesaddles without exposing their ankles. Fremont was a busy town in 1910.

coincide exactly with homestead activities. It usually took
a year or two to get a name legally adopted by the ponder-
ous Post Office Department, and the towns often lived on
memories for a year.

These embryo cities started the wheels to roll in 1910, on
the average. The closing date, 1920, is a little late for use
in estimating the death of the place. The time between
1910 and 1919 marked the years of the greatest homestead
activity. There were some homesteaders long before 1910,
and a few after 1919.

The desert towns had a few things in common.

The Village Blacksmith[2]

Big ranches, such as the ZX, had their own blacksmith
and he was busy all year. In horse days, a big ranch with
fifty hay hands couldn't stop operations to drive a hundred miles to town to repair a mower. They would lose
close to a week's work. They had their own shop and it
was better equipped than most of the town shops. It still
is. But the homesteaders couldn't afford shop equipment,
so they had to take things to professionals. The blacksmith
in one of these blossoming towns usually had one qualifi-
cation—he was strong.

He didn't stand under any spreading chestnut tree in
our country, but he had brawny arms, just as Longfellow
mentioned. Usually he wasn't quite the saintly character
the poet painted. I knew one who picked up spare change
by betting fifty cents that he could let anyone hit him in
the stomach with the bare fist without doing any damage,
except maybe to the fist.

The blacksmith shop was a magnet for country boys.
Flying sparks, red-hot metal, mighty blows on the anvil,
the heady talk of the grown-ups—these were better than
anything else around.

---

[2] By R. A. Long.

A little group congregated there every day. No chairs graced the place, but there were kegs the horseshoes came in, old wagon wheels, wrecks of buggies, all the assorted farm machinery of the time, robbed of parts in order to make a usable machine out of two or three broken ones.

There wasn't a woman in the place. To get away from women and all their fussy ways, a man had his choice: livery stable, saloon, or blacksmith shop. Something was going on all the time. The village smith ran a place with all the advantages of an Elks' Club, a male sewing society, and the newsroom of a city paper. For that's where the community news was known first. Each piece of news was sifted for important facts, boiled down to its essence, and analyzed for total digestible nutrients. After that, it was safe to take home for domestic use.

SHOP ON A DESERT RANCH

The larger ranches had their own shops; the homesteaders had to go to blacksmiths in the towns, whose shops were social gathering places.

We don't have a village blacksmith shop now. You can't get much in a city by hanging around a garage, with their union shops, and their talk about things you don't know anything about. There isn't any personal relationship. You are directed to the head of the thing, he consults some office bookkeeper, he gives you an itemized bill totaling $37.50, and you can't do much about it.

At our blacksmith shop we could bring a mower to be fixed, see the neighbors, watch a rod or axle as it heated to a beautiful cherry red, see the pounding and the hiss and steam as the smith plunged it into water, and then discuss details with the grimy smith. He allowed you a dollar on the old parts and charged you seventy-five cents to boot. Besides, you found that Ole Larson had a runaway and broke his hayrake all to hell; that Ole himself had gone underneath and was rolled over and over halfway across a forty-acre field and wasn't feeling too good; that John Charnok had tried to clean a mouse nest out of his mower sickle, the team had started up and cut off his second finger —and, oh, just lots of things. I've never learned a thing in any modern garage.

Around Fort Rock the two best-known smiths were Lewis Penrose and George Peryl, the latter an Austrian, trained in the old country, and a fine workman. He never did like our Western wild horses, but any break he welded stayed fixed. At Silver Lake were Tom Welch and Oscar Perrin, a Belgian, trained abroad.

I have never known a mean blacksmith. There was something about their work that attracted strong and dependable men, physically and spiritually.

The Livery Stable[3]

Anyone who thinks that Hertz has a new and ingenious business couldn't be wetter. You get off a plane, go to the

---

[3] By R. A. Long.

nearest Hertz place, rent a car, transact your day's business, then go to bed in a Pullman and arrive at the next city refreshed and clear-eyed. Whereas, if you drive your own car, you have to work all day and drive all night, arriving moody, tired, and dejected. You lose all your best customers and get fired.

The livery stable furnished the same kind of service for a hundred years before there was any Hertz. You came in by stage, hired your livery rig, drove all over the desert, bought steers, or whatever. The local people rented livery teams, too, especially for weddings and funerals. Cowboys and ranchers from way off somewhere would arrive with a jaded horse or team, "put them up" at the livery stable, and—if in a hurry—could even leave their horses as security and take those of the livery stable to the next place, where they made another change.

This service, that "puts you in the driver's seat" is pretty old stuff.

The stable was off limits for the ladies sixty years ago. Traveling salesmen were often gay blades who brought the latest jokes to town; the workers at the stables were sometimes more noted for profanity than gentility; the slightly pleasant smell of horse manure was all over the place, and ladies just didn't go there.

The stable was also a sort of headquarters for horse traders, and some of the proprietors made as much money buying and selling horses as they did in renting horses and rigs or taking care of strangers' animals.

Your position in life was rated at the livery barn by the horses and rig you rented. A good stable manager had all kinds for all purses. The proprietor might not have the social standing of the leading lawyer, but he was far more necessary. As times changed, many became garage owners.

A good going livery stable was in a prominent place and the town grew to it. The stable came first, later a hotel was built close to it, then a saloon. If painted at all, it was a peculiar dark color called "barn red." The stable had an alley running down the center, wide enough to drive a team and wagon through. It had a board floor, something that scarcely any other barn had, and nothing scared a young desert horse more than to ride him onto the resounding planks.

Over the driveway was the mow; the hay was pitched in through a door at each end of the barn and pitched back so as to fill the mow. The mangers were on each side of the driveway facing the wall, so the hay could be pitched down to the mangers. At the end closest to the main door, there were no stalls. On one side was a tack room for saddles, halters, and tools for repairing gear. This also held grain, and was kept locked. On the other side was a sort of combination office and bedroom. Prominent on the walls were several lanterns. The stableboy always slept in this office. Usually the owner had a home of his own.

This stableboy was right at the heart of the town and knew things others didn't. He knew when everyone got in at night; how far each rig had been driven; who had been in town the night of some skullduggery; who had money enough to pay cash.

Behind the barn was a corral with a high tight board fence with a locked gate. Horses were turned out there for exercise, or to make room for extra or unexpected horses.

The hay was thrown down from the loft into the mangers along both sides of the barn, so in storing it, a space was always left along both sides of the mow to allow the hay to drop freely.

Unless a bad storm was on, manure was hauled out daily.

The big double doors at each end could be closed in case of storms. Hours for the stableboy were twenty-four per day. A drink of whiskey was usually available for a good customer, if he arrived late and cold. This whiskey wasn't normally for sale. It was solely a fringe benefit for those who traded regularly and paid cash. Short boards were nailed across two or three of the two by six studding. A bottom was nailed in between the studs and currycombs

LIVERY STABLE AT REDMOND, OREGON, ABOUT 1910

The livery barn was the center of activity in nearly all the desert towns up until autos and trucks dethroned the horse about 1920

and brushes were dropped down behind the boards. This made a good place to keep a pint bottle. Here it was out of sight and could be kept right side up.

The stableboys came and went. Their pay was low, considering their long hours. Their social position was poor, their clothes smelled of horse sweat and manure, and they often just stayed long enough to accumulate a little money to buy a horse and a bed and get a job on a cattle ranch. They did gather knowledge about horses: how to treat sores; how to fit harness, bridles, collars; how to feed and care for saddle and harness animals; how to repair gear. These unofficial veterinary services were free. The boys deserved far better than they got in cash, comfort, and public esteem. They were always called "boys," and usually were, but occasionally a seventy-year-old was the stableboy.

The stable always kept some horse blankets and the boy used them on horses that came in covered with sweat. The blankets fastened at the neck with a strap and buckle, and two straps went beneath the belly. Blankets were either buff or blue. If blue, they had red canvas straps for fastening. They were tough, warm, and lasted for twenty years. They had good stuff in them.

If a wayfarer came regrettably short of money, the stableboy let him sleep in a clean, empty stall, using as many horse blankets as necessary. He was supposed to help with the manure the next day, or at least throw down the hay. Many persons distrusted a cigarette smoker, and no man slept in the barn if he smoked cigarettes. A pipe was all right, for such a smoker could control himself, but cigarettes were rumored to contain morphine, or opium, produced a craving, and these cigarette fiends were not allowed around the stable at all.

Fire was the only real enemy of the barn, and a stableful of horses, with flames leaping and smoke suffocating was a sight that lingered in bad dreams. The horses became terrified and often could not be led out, regarding the barn

as a safe haven. They screamed in panic and some burned
to death. The scream of a horse is a bad thing to remember.

Up to the first World War in 1917, no town was much
until it had a livery barn. Traveling salesmen could scarcely
operate without it, and neither could cattle buyers, doctors,
or homestead locaters. It was a vital spot in town and often
made good money for the owner. A present-day garage is
short of everything the barn had, including fragrance.

The Auction Sale[4]

For heart-stopping drama in everyday life, the farm
auction beat the best that TV can offer. From the start,
clear through to the last boxful of hens, there were suspense,
anger, bitter disappointment, heartsickness, greed, wholesome
delight, comedy, and despair.

It usually started around the breakfast table, though the
wife may have uneasily noted some signs before. Sometimes
it started with a letter. The homesteader would clear his
throat and say, "Mother, I've just been thinkin'. We ain't
gettin' ahead here any. The longer we stay the worse off
we are. The bank won't loan us any money and the only
thing that's kept us right side up is the hayin' job for the
ZX at two dollars a day. What do you say we just sell
out and move?"

The wife would look at the matrimony vine she had
carried water for until it shaded the kitchen in the summer.
She'd look around at the walls she'd papered neatly. She'd
look out the window and see the chickens busily chasing
bugs and hoppers. She'd think of the other moves they'd
made, first from Pennsylvania to Missouri, thence to Wyoming, and from there to Oregon. Each had started about
the same, except that with each move they had less. But
she knew the symptoms and probably he was right anyhow,

---

[4] By E. R. Jackman.

so she'd say, "If you think best, Henry. How much can we expect to leave here with?"

Henry would busily figure what he could get for his half section, what the horses would bring, what the few cattle were worth, what it would take to pay off the mercantile company where the egg money fought an unequal battle with the family's needs.

Mother would break in anxiously, "Where can we go, Henry?" This set off another train of thought; the talk down at the blacksmith shop about good wages on the Coast; the letter from his brother, Joe, in the oil fields of Texas; the news about the Olsons, who moved last year and were reported to be doing well in the Willamette Valley.

It might take some doing to sell the place—maybe no one would buy it. Or maybe it was partly surrounded by a large stock ranch and the owner would buy it just to keep someone else from getting it—"It rounded out his holdings." Any stockman can figure how most any place will round out his holdings.

But whether the farm was sold or just abandoned, the day of the auction would come and it seemed necessary to sell most of the household furniture to get enough money to leave. When you don't have much, it is more heartbreaking to part with that little.

First they had to get an auctioneer and set the day of sale. The date should be before hot weather came, because heat discouraged the bidding. If held too early, the sale might run into a day too cold and windy. Weather was important. It never really "made" a sale, but it could sure spoil one. A good rain *didn't* spoil the auction, it helped. Everybody on the desert was optimistic when it rained and the bidding showed it. George Marvin was a local auctioneer who "worked" many sales. For small sales a swift-talking neighbor sometimes got the job, maybe taking a horse or a bureau for pay.

Things to be sold had to be listed for handbills, and for an ad in the paper. Often a neighbor would hear of the sale and would bring over a few horses, or a plow, so as to make the sale sound bigger. After the auctioneer was hired, he would help write the handbills. He knew the words that stirred the most interest, and he knew exactly where to tack up the sale notices.

Terms listed were always "Cash or bankable note." This latter was mostly courtesy because attending were few whose notes would command any notice whatever at a bank.

If the auction were large enough to warrant it, the bank cashier was induced to come and clerk. He was a help because he could decide instantly whether the buyer's note was bankable or not. Occasionally, if the bidding were spirited, someone would get carried away and bid in a bed or a bull at a price beyond him. The clerk had to decide what to do. In order not to make a fuss and humiliate the man in public, the clerk would usually quietly hunt up one of the other bidders and offer him the article at the price he last bid. But if he couldn't remember the last bidder, then the article had to be sold privately.

Each auctioneer had tricks of his own. Usually he sold several small articles on the first or second bid at only a fraction of their worth. Or he took a boxful of miscellaneous things, such as extra mower sickle sections and harrow teeth and knocked them down at perhaps 10 per cent of their worth. At that he would make a speech, saying in his thirty-five years of experience he had never seen anything like this. He was amazed and speechless. "By all the stars in heaven, how can you people stand here and see valuable things *given* away without even raising your voices to share in practically free merchandise? Now I have other things to do—I've got to be on my way to Klamath Falls. I can't spend all day selling one grindstone. So I'm going to sell fast and you've got to get in your bid fast if you want any of these bargains."

After this pep talk, bidding was noticeably more eager, and, although there were some bargains, it worked out that things sold at about their actual worth. Maybe two men

who disliked each other would start to bid on the same
horse, become stubborn, and finally one of them paid one
hundred dollars for a forty-dollar horse. Whereupon the
buyer would blame the other bitterly because "He saw I
wanted the horse and made me bid way up to get him."

Some bidders had only so much money to spend and no
auctioneer could be tricky enough to flatter or taunt them
into paying a nickle more. Some just went for the social
experience and the free lunch. Others were flighty and
bought things they didn't need. The shops on many ranches
are full of boxes of odds and ends bought at auctions and
never looked at. The farmer will kid his wife unmerci-
fully for buying a butter mold for one dollar when she
hasn't made butter for twenty years, now they eat oleo
anyhow. This goes on until she asks him why he bought
those two wagon wheels, each a different size, when he
doesn't own wagons any longer.

A lunch was served at noon. Formerly it was free, but
at auctions now it is usually furnished by some organization raising money for a worthy purpose. At those I've
attended lately, there was a sack lunch for seventy-five
cents, with free coffee. In the old days, a wise seller would
provide a keg mounted on a plank on two sawhorses out
behind the barn. If the weather was just right, or if just
the right crowd gathered, this keg arrangement would nearly
double the receipts. It produced healthy rivalry in bidding,
made an old wagon look wonderful, and took five years
off the age of a horse. Whether it's the higher prices for
keg contents now, or whether crowds are not so easy to
influence, I don't know, but auctions now are kegless.

The wife, in spite of herself, resented the impersonal way
buyers looked over her family table or chest of drawers.
Each article was tied to her by a hundred strings of memory
and was cherished beyond its value. She came close to hating
the final buyer who loaded it roughly into a wagon. The
hardest thing to sell might be the boy's pony and neither
father nor mother dared look at their son's face.

The auctioneer was skilled. He knew exactly how to jolly the crowd—what buyer to have fun with, which man to treat with respectful attention, and when to stop and tell a story. If a bid started too low, then each succeeding bid would be just a small advance, and he must not let this happen. He might refuse to hear a low bid, and, when he judged a bidder correctly, he was not above hearing a mythical bid from the other side of the crowd, thus making a man raise his own bid two or three times.

There were always some funny things. Now and then a husband and wife, separated in the crowd, would decide independently to buy some article as a gift to the other. The bidding then often settled into a spirited race between them.

Odds and ends were gathered into boxes, baskets or barrels, and sold as "jib-job lots." Once in twenty years something valuable turned up in these conglomerations of binder chains, rusty wrenches, off-size bolts, and broken brackets. If the basket came from the house, it had bits of ribbon, little balls of yarn, odd-shaped piece goods left over from cutting out a dress, woolen socks too worn to darn—all things of no conceivable value. Such as the carefully preserved bag of the New England lady containing "pieces of string too short to use."

At the auction's end, the house bare and the farmstead stripped, the family had the task of bidding good-bye to their surroundings. No matter how unrewarding the years, the place had been their home, and they left with sadness and often tears. Many such families left with two horses hitched to a covered wagon. If they prospered somewhere else, they'd come back twenty years later in a shiny automobile to view the homestead.

They would climb hills to find the exact spot where their little boy had fired his first shot at a coyote, or where their little girl had found a fine Indian spearhead. Their home and all other buildings were probably gone, but the well would still be there, and a corner post of the corral. They would spend a few hours reminiscing of the funny or tragic events of their desert days, pointing out landmarks, remembering friends they hadn't thought about for a long time, and would leave feeling close together. Time wiped out disappointments, failures, the wind, the hardships. They remembered the desert as a happy place.

The Traveling Merchants[5]

Modern living has nearly doomed the traveling merchants of 1900 to 1915. In those days the family, living perhaps one hundred miles from the railroad, had no contact with what the fanciful writers of the day called the "marts of trade." Children halfway through grade school had never seen a town. Her uncle took one little grl from the desert into Bend in 1918—her first trip to any city. He treated her to ice cream, which seemed to make a deep impression upon her. Next Monday her school friends gathered around and questioned her. "What was it like in that place where you had the ice cream?" She, striving to make her story meaningful, said, "It had an open place in the middle and on the sides there were some little stalls, kind of like the calf barn."

Of course, everyone had catalogs from Monkey Ward and Sears and Sawbuck. These were worn out by the time the next edition came, but even the best description is not up to the real article that you can feel, smell and touch, or even taste. So the traveling merchants filled a need and kept everyone informed. They came with two-horse light wagons, specially built for carrying samples or goods. Mostly they traveled in the summer when roads were passable. When one arrived, the whole family gathered to look at his stock and marvel.

Here are some of those apostles of civilization who came to Lake County:

---

[5] By E. R. Jackman.

1. The medicine man. He sold remedies for man and beast, as well as household helps, such as spot cleaners, soap, and soda. Even in those days, with low professional fees, it cost more to get a veterinarian than the afflicted horse or cow was worth, so everyone trustfully bought stuff in a bottle that was guaranteed to cure anything that livestock flesh was heir to, from fistulas to flesh wounds, from burns to bots.

For human ailments, too, there were liniments and pills of all sizes and colors. The Pure Food and Drug Act hadn't gotten going, so the only limit to the claims for salves, ointments, pills, gargles, and pain panaceas was the imagination of the seller.

There were medicine men in those days, too, at the county fair, where some had their own shows, replete with singing girls, juggling act, perhaps a few animals, but the real show was put on by the doctor who had obtained the secret of his powerful healing fluid from an old Indian. To prove it, he had the Indian along.

2. The peddlers. Often Jewish, these practical working psychologists had the most amazing collection of articles in their ingenious wagons. It didn't make much difference whether the lady of the house wanted a dress or a new kind of cookie cutter, the peddler had it. He had cinches, conchas, buckles, straps and halters. From the interior of his cart he'd bring sarsaparilla or spices from the South Seas. His piece goods were marvels of springtime beauty, or, if the season were fall, he had overshoes, warm mittens, and Pond's Extract to cure chilblains. He was amazing and he supplied a need. He usually stayed with some homesteader he liked and he left a gift for each one in the house—something accurately chosen for fitness and desires. No one would accept pay for such an overnight stop, so the peddler always brought gifts. These were usually not valuable, but the peddlers were shrewd judges of people and were kind and well liked. Their gifts were things the family wouldn't buy for themselves, but each member would treasure the

gift, maybe for years. A really fine hair ribbon for the daughter, or a newfangled jackknife for the son were things to be shown with pride.

We talked to Anna Linebaugh, formerly Anna Long, and she told us:

"I can remember how thrilled I was when the peddler came one year when I had some money of my own. Mother let me select and buy some white dress goods with red polka dots. I paid the peddler ten cents a yard. Mother made a real pretty dress of it and bought some red slippers to match. They came from Weinstock-Leuben, a wholesale house.

"I wore this fine outfit to Silver Lake and stayed overnight with the Cooper family. I went with them to a church program. I had the prettiest dress there and they let me sing on the stage with some other girls. We sang 'Jesus Loves Me.'"

3. Wool and hide buyers. These gentry weren't quite so far up the scale as some of the other traveling merchandisers. Maybe it was their business, because a load of farm-skinned hides had a pungency that reached well over into the next section. Almost every farm had a critter or two that died during the year. The hide was the only salvage, but there were not enough to ship or to justify a special trip to town, but they brought a few dollars from the hide buyers.

A few such buyers prospered and became proprietors of mercantile establishments. They weren't "general stores." If they were big, these were "mercantile companies," preceded by the name of the town, as "Prineville Mercantile Company."

4. Watkins and Raleigh men. These weren't common in the desert. They couldn't make enough to pay for a route except in thickly settled areas. These two companies hired men to cover certain specified routes, just as some companies do today with cosmetics. A man with such a franchise might keep it his entire "productive life," making

the same rounds year after year. People got to know exactly what days he would arrive and they'd save up their orders for him if they liked him.

5. There was another itinerant merchant, but mainly he stayed in more thickly settled, more prosperous places because he depended upon fewer, but larger sales. This was

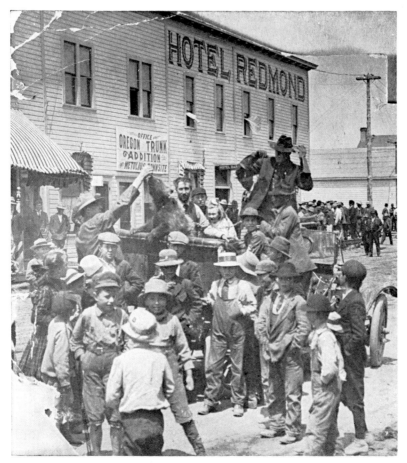

SELLING TOWN LOTS WAS A POPULAR PASTIME IN CENTRAL OREGON
FROM ABOUT 1900 TO 1910
The railroad was coming—hundreds of thousands of acres were to be irrigated—big mills were planned—the desert would bloom like a rose if plowed—the biggest cities in Oregon would be built! So promoters put on circuslike events and sold lots—many of them in towns that did not exist. Here is such a scene.

TOWN OF SILVER L
These ranchers gathered in the spring to, literally, "clean up the town." They scraped the streets, le
Lloyd Miner, Ross Karn, Einar Mack, Bill Lane, Tom W

N, ABOUT 1922
and hauled away the winter debris. Recognized persons are: Jack St. Clair, Leston Linebaugh,
Corum, Everett Long, Bobbie St. Clair, and Murel Long.

the representative of wholesale grocery companies or woolen factories that sold door to door. A San Francisco firm sold fancy and staple groceries to the big ranchers for years and a Utah woolen company sold blankets, mackinaws, and long, heavy, warm underwear. No nonsense about 40 per cent nylon then. All such places sold *only* virgin wool and were proud of it.

Desert Doctors[6]

DR. COE OF BEND

"I Will Go for the Benefit of the Sick"

This title is an abbreviated quotation from the Hippocratic oath. Few documents have had so much effect upon the human race as this two-thousand-year-old profession of faith. A few modern doctors look at it as partially outmoded, but all of them live up to it in part and the old general practitioner lived up to all of it. I do not know of any person so completely dedicated, anyone who followed his code so strictly, as the country doctor. He is rapidly disappearing, along with the buggy he rode in and his handy black bag. Armed with that odd-shaped bag he could bring a baby into the world, extract a bullet, or cure dyspepsias of obscure origins—perhaps all on the same trip.

For an inkling of what a country doctor did, *Frontier Doctor*,[7] by Urling C. Coe, M.D., is one of the best sources. It is inspiring and authentic, a combination hard to find. Dr. Coe came to Bend, then called Farewell Bend, in 1905 when he was twenty-three years old. His field of practice was past the summit of the Cascades, 120 miles west; to the end of the railroad 100 miles north; 92 miles south, and far out into the desert east. The nearest hospital was 160 miles away.

---

[6] By E. R. Jackman.

[7] Urling C. Coe, *Frontier Doctor* (New York: The Macmillan Company, 1939).

His patients were homesteaders, buckaroos, sheepherders, timber cruisers, freighters, gamblers, prostitutes, construction workers, outlaws. These folks had two things in common: they were more or less transient, and they had little or no money. The few well-established ranchers had money, and they were the financial backbone of his practice.

Dr. Coe commented frequently in his book upon the lack of infections following operations or dressing of wounds. He worked in such antiseptic places as horse barns, back porches, tents in construction camps, and right on the ground. Dust was often blowing and it churned up and over the patient with every movement. Yet, infections were

Photo by Merritt Parks, Fort Rock, Ore.

REUB LONG WELL AT FREMONT, WHICH WAS ONCE A FLOURISHING TOWN
The bull in the picture belongs to Long; so does the windmill. Such windmills supply water for livestock and wildlife. Note Reub's open AL brand, used for close to one hundred years on the desert.

almost unknown. He credited their scarcity to the high, pure, mountain air, and the 320 days of sunshine a year.

He delivered hundreds of babies with not even one case of infection of the mother. Deliveries were on the ground, on piles of hay, on the kitchen table—everywhere except in a hospital, for there was no such thing. In those days, women rarely called a doctor until labor pains started. Still, there were no infections.

Perhaps the high desert is the ideal place in America for a major hospital. The writers of this book have received hundreds, probably thousands, of cuts and bruises of all kinds, have rarely used disinfectants, and never had infection. I once jumped from a horse and lit on a nail sticking straight up through a board buried under some straw in a shed. Manure and dust were everywhere. The nail went clear through my foot. I had to stand on the board with my other foot and pull hard to get my foot free from the old rusty nail. I treated it by tying bacon rind to the sole of the wounded foot. No doctor ever saw it, but my comings and goings were restricted some for a couple of weeks.

Doctor Daly of Lakeview[8]

Dr. Bernard Daly, of Lakeview, will be remembered long after the other desert doctors are forgotten—not because of his medical ability or his character—but because of what he did with his plentiful supply of money. A bachelor, he left his fortune so that interest on it would forever be used to give Lake County boys and girls a college education. It has been used freely and a higher percentage of Lake County high-school graduates attend college than is the case in most counties.

He was born in Ireland, obtained his medical diploma in 1887 in this country, and came to Lakeview at once.

---

[8] By R. A. Long.

Unlike most doctors of the day, for country calls he charged mileage—one dollar a mile. Many trips totaled up to $100 and even $200, plus the house-call fee.

He saved his money, studied law, and was admitted to the bar. He and another man owned a large general merchandise store. He owned a drugstore, was county judge for one term, and was on the Board of Regents for the State Agricultural College. He was president of the Bank of Lakeview for many years. He was also president of the Lake County Land and Livestock Company, which he organized. He was in the legislature.

He could deliver a male baby, clothe him as he grew; sell him groceries, clothes, and medicines; lend him money to buy a ranch, or give him a job in one of many enterprises; defend him in court if he got into trouble; all for a fee, of course.

His most notable adventure was probably his night drive in a buggy in sub-zero weather to Silver Lake—100 miles. The story is told in more detail in Chapter 8. Unlike many doctors, he had a hard, tough, business sense, and was a soft touch for no one. This, plus his ability to get a profit from nearly every person in the county, made him a somewhat controversial character. In a county where generosity is the custom, he was close to the point of stinginess; in an area where personal friendship is valued higher than treasures upon earth, he chose the treasures. But no one questioned his ability. He was our (Long family) doctor and we admired and trusted him.

The disposition of his money made him a famous man in Oregon—after his death. He thereby made his money work for the good of his county as long as the U.S.A. lasts.

DOCTOR THOM OF SILVER LAKE[9]

A desert doctor couldn't be a specialist; he had to do

---

[9] By R. A. Long.

everything, including dental and veterinary work. It is amazing what a good job such doctors did, without benefit of modern drugs, sanitary surroundings, trained help, or modern techniques.

All country doctors I have known have been dedicated men. Hardship and difficulty went with them every step of the way, but these doctors went. Blizzard, cold, heat, dust, personal comfort—these were disregarded. They were part of the life they had chosen. They often knew when they set out on a hard trip, that they would get no pay. If they could relieve suffering or even give help to the spirit of a sufferer, that was considered pay enough.

I knew such a man intimately, Doctor Thom, for many years a resident of Silver Lake. He was short, slender, wirey, with capable and active hands. When he came into a sickroom, he brought something besides medicine. He brought strength, calmness, confidence, and a sense of well-being. These were often more powerful healing agents than any wonder drug.

He had many friends, and I never heard even one person speak of him except with respect. He had no enemies.

His understanding and sympathy were so genuine that no one could doubt them. I speak from experience because I went with him on many of his trips, and sometimes stood by the beds of patients beyond saving.

When Jewell Corum's first boy was born, and at the same time Lizzie Wright was having her first boy, they were twenty miles apart. One mother was at Fort Rock, one at Silver Lake. Doctor Thom delivered both babies, shuttling back and forth at full speed.

Contrary to Doctor Coe, at Bend, Doctor Thom owned his own driving horses, and a saddle horse or two for use when driving was impossible.

Once, after automobiles came, I rode forty-five miles to get Doctor Thom, then rode back on the same horse, and beat him and his car. This isn't a tribute to me. It's a tribute to my horse and a comment on the roads of the time.

In cases of epidemics, such as flu, Doctor Thom went night and day—often he was in his clothes for days at a time. I sometimes drove for him, giving him a chance to sleep on the way, if repose on a rutty, rocky road could be called sleep. I had two qualifications—I knew horses and I knew the roads. Others in the neighborhood helped him in the same way.

The biggest trouble a doctor had in those days was that the majority of people wouldn't call him in time. The desert itself will heal most ordinary bruises, cuts and the like, so, even in extreme trouble, the average desert patient would assume that he was going to get well without a doctor. Lack of money egged on his belief.

I could never see any difference between the care he gave an impoverished homesteader from whom he expected and asked nothing, and from the care he gave a well-to-do member of the community. He gave each all he had of knowledge and comfort, with many repeat visits, if necessary.

It's hard to keep from drawing a moral here. I won't do it except to say that maybe a few months of interne work with such a doctor might be far better training than a year or two in a well-equipped hospital. I think a young man might learn more. At the very least he'd learn to appreciate the hospital. But he might pick up some attitudes that would increase his stature in the community, or even in his own eyes. And irate patients would not be out plugging for government medicare.

CHAPTER TWENTY-ONE

WATER ON THE DESERT

R. A. LONG

WE HAVE MENTIONED THAT WATER IS WHAT A DESERT HAS the least of—a lack of it is what makes a desert. As soon as the heavenly sprinkling can delivers less than ten inches a year, desert conditions begin to take over the land—creeks dry up; lakes vanish or recede; valuable forest trees die, replaced by juniper; sagebrush, always waiting around, steals in and laps up the extra; and plants begin to appear that are harsh, thorny, dry, or in other ways unpalatable to livestock.

The scarcity of any product determines the price—if there are any buyers. Old paintings sell for two hundred thousand dollars at the same sale where a modern painter feels lucky to get a hundred; the one man who can belt out sixty home runs sells his services for more than the dozens who can deliver thirty; the horse that can trot a mile in 1:55 brings more money than the dozens that can do it in two minutes. In our country, when hay is scarce, it brings forty dollars a ton, but when there is more than can be eaten, it has gone clear down to six dollars, the cost of putting it up. This is the same hay, but the degree of scarcity makes the price, not the inner value. Forty-dollar hay doesn't put any more fat on the ribs than six-dollar hay.

As this is written, 1962, the desert is beginning to have a value because of its lack of things. On the positive side, it has the same things it always had, but California people are buying it up because:

It lacks smog.
It has no contaminated air.
There aren't any freeways.
It doesn't have crowds of people.
It isn't full of nerve-jangling noise.
It isn't man-made, or artificial.
It doesn't have cyclones.
There aren't many cloudy days.
Humidity isn't there to blame the heat on.

The lack of water isn't too much of an asset. I was out
with a professional soil conservation man one day. He was
telling of the criminal waste of soil in the Columbia Basin
and I told him that all of my neighbors for a hundred miles
around farmed so well that not one grain of sand from our
country was ever washed down to the sea. The statement
was true. For in this big desert area of Oregon, in most of
Nevada, and in parts of Idaho, Utah, and California, we
have a vast inland basin where no water *ever* reaches the
sea. We have some pretty respectable rivers, such as the
Chewaucan and the Donner und Blitzen, but the farther
they flow the smaller they get, until they peter out or flow
into shallow lakes with no outlet.

On my own place and the government land, where I
pay for pasturing, amounting to maybe fifty thousand acres,
there is not one stream, no lakes, no water on the surface
at all. Every drop of water my cattle and horses drink and
every drop my wife Eleanor and I drink, is pumped by
windmill or power. We measure humidity by the amount
of sand in the air. When it rains, we keep our hired man
in—we want all the water on the land.

Water is often the subject of conversation in our country. It is the basis for neighborhood quarrels and lawsuits.
The owner of a water hole is in a different situation than
the man without one. In well-watered counties, peacemakers
try to settle heated arguments by saying, "There's no reason
to get bothered by this matter—it's all water gone under

the bridge." Our peacemakers say, "It's sand over the dune."

Once a stranger stopped to ask about the country. His interest was stirred by the utter absence of anything in sight to show it had rained around Fort Rock. He said, "Has it *ever* rained here?"

I told him, "Yes, once. Do you remember how Noah, the first long-range weather forecaster, built the ark and floated it during forty days and nights of rain?" He said he had knowledge of that. I told him, "That time we got a quarter of an inch."

Our weather is responsible for things both good and bad. For example, the soil conservationists talk about the "valuable topsoil"—how it takes a thousand years to make an inch of topsoil that can be washed away in a big storm. But we haven't any topsoil. A man bent on making our desert blossom with pump irrigation sent away a sample. The topsoil averaged the same as the bottom soil. Neither had enough humus to measure. Topsoil in other places is different because plants have been growing and dying there for thousands of years, thus building some organic matter into the ground. But our soil doesn't grow enough organic matter to make any difference. If we irrigate, we can build it up by growing alfalfa and clover, but we don't have it naturally.

The kind of storm we pray for is a couple of feet of wet snow, a foot of manure on top, then a boiling hot rain. We haven't had it yet. We don't have much snow as a rule. When snow comes, it is often followed by a Chinook that takes it all off. I've been out in the snow lots of days when the cold south wind made me get off my horse to keep warm, and as the day went on, have seen the wind melt and carry away three or four inches of snow. The wind is dry, and even if it is below freezing, it draws the snow into it and carries it off to Wyoming or some place. The sagebrush hurries this along. If the field has a good stand of rabbit brush or sagebrush, that keeps the snow from ever getting to the ground, and then it is held up in the air where the wind can get on all four sides of it. As a blotter soaks up ink, the snow disappears into the wind. We have a rule: "When a snowstorm comes, it will lie on the ground a week for every day it lies on the brush."

Stories have grown up about the wind and snow. There is one to the effect that a homesteader came into Silver Lake for supplies in the wintertime. There was a foot of new snow, so he came with a bobsled. He lived forty miles north of Silver Lake. He put his team in the livery barn and started to shop. He had had experience with the way the wind could take the snow off and knew that if he got caught in Silver Lake with a bobsled and no snow, his plight was serious.

So when the south wind came suddenly, hitting his cheek with the force of a barn door slamming, he realized the danger. He went to the barn on a dead run, got the pilot in the livery barn to help hitch, then by whipping his team into a keen run, he was able to keep his front bobs on the snow. You have to remember the wind was from the south and he lived straight north.

At our elevation snow *can* come in any month, though it seldom does. We had a foot, though, on the Fourth of July one year, back in the late nineties. Lakeview then was full of ambition and big plans, so it had fireworks, horse races, foot races, games for all ages, to be followed at night by a big dance. All the cowboys, sheepherders, and dry-landers for a hundred miles around looked forward to it all year. Many came in the day before, just to train and get prepared properly. One Irish sheepman overtrained. Some friends got him into a room in the Lakeview Hotel, pushed him over on the bed, and left. The next morning he got up, felt in his pockets, found he had money, looked out at the snow that had fallen overnight, and said, "Be Jaysus, here I've been in town all summer and I still have money in me pocket!"

We were riding out at Saddle Butte one day, near Last

Chance, and an Irishman was there with a band of yearling ewes. We moved on down and he began shouting before we could hear what he was saying. When we could hear, we distinguished urgency and near panic in his tone. "If ye see me boss, tell him five hundred head of ZX cattle come in and drank up all me little lake."

This was serious. In northern Lake County is Venator Canyon. Jezreal Venator came to the county in 1870 from the Willamette Valley, as many of the early settlers did. In August, 1881, he started, horseback, on a trip to Harney County. His horse jerked away from him near the canyon bearing his name, and he died of thirst. My father was in the party that found him. It isn't the only case of the kind on record. So when cattle drank up "me little lake," both the Irishman and his sheep were in peril.

A man can live a long time without food. His tissues will shrink and he may look like a scarecrow, but he lives day after day. But without water in hot weather he is soon a goner. His skin can pass off, in evaporation, a quart an hour. That's why cowboys cover up their skin. You don't see a cowboy on a hot day with a short-sleeved sport shirt above and Bermuda shorts below.

Another weather characteristic of the desert is the mirage. You see amazing likenesses of a lake, reflections of the shore-line, mountains clear and plain. I have seen Iron Mountain from Christmas Lake, a distance of sixty-five miles, with high country between. Two strangers had been fooled by so many mirages they were getting a little wary. They were lost and attempted to hail down an Indian to ask directions. He didn't even look their way as he passed. One of them said, reflectively, "You know, he may have been farther away than he looked!"

Another is the remark of one cowboy to another, "There goes the ten-thirty mirage, right on time."

We measure space on the desert differently; we say, "His ranch is two looks from here." Dallas Lore Sharp, who

traveled in Oregon in 1912 and wrote a book about it,[1] said,
". . . this death of sound here on the desert, where the taut
silence seemed drawn like shrunken skin over the bones of
sand and sage." He speaks also of the way "time and space
take on a different concept . . . you are right on the distant
edge of time and space . . . they are independent things.
You can whittle them down and shovel them. They are
sagebrush and sand. . . ." Those are poetical thoughts, but
Mr. Sharp was a sensitive man, and all of us might be more
keenly aware of what's about us if we had more poetry
in us. Even if we can't say it, maybe we feel it.

This need for water has resulted in several schemes, all
partly successful, partly not. Harry A. Parks, head of the
School of Mines in what is now Oregon State University,
and later head of the Oregon Bureau of Mines and Geology,
became interested in what had gone on around Fort Rock
a million years ago. He reasoned that it once was flat, was
covered by a frosting of lava about two thousand feet thick.
It went along that way for a millenium or two, then vio-
lent things began to happen without the aid of any human
ignorance. Vast forces under the lava began to bestir themselves. First they shoved up the Cascade Mountains, then
broke at the summit and here and there the gases and lava
poured out to create the volcanoes that are now resting and
form our snow-capped peaks. Pumice, sand, lava, and such,
shot into the air and settled all over eastern Oregon.

In the meantime, Parks figured, the same forces shoved
up the big rims to the east of Fort Rock, more mountains
developed to the north and south, leaving our part of the
desert an immense cup with no ready outlet, and filled
almost to the brim with one thousand feet or more of volcanic debris, perhaps running heavily to pumice boulders
at the bottom. Volcanic tuff, he called it. On the Cascade
side of this cup, part of the plentiful rain and melted snow
should follow along the deeply buried side of the cup and

[1] Dallas Lore Sharp, *Where Rolls the Oregon* (Boston: Houghton Mifflin Company,
1913).

eventually come to rest at the bottom as a huge underground lake, possibly artesian, if anyone should bore into it.

He talked the legislature of 1921 into appropriating $40,000 to dig four wells to tap this theoretical water supply. The four wells are on land owned now by Merritt Parks, Britt Webster, Roy Morehouse estate, and Reub Long. They aren't artesian, but they had plenty of water—just as Parks figured. To show that he had faith in the project, he bought one of the wells, and came out to the desert to live in 1928. He raised his two children here, but he was ahead of his time.

Thirty years later, some speculative interests again tried the same idea. They were going to develop a large tract of land with irrigation, divide it into convenient farm sizes, and sell. The attempt was still premature. It took too long to sell, took too much money, the various promoters couldn't see eye to eye, and most important of all, the folks really interested couldn't see why they should pay a developer for land when they could get it more cheaply by homesteading, or by buying from an owner who didn't think it was worth much.

Anyhow, the desert land I had bought for such inflated prices as one dollar an acre, suddenly blossomed out as really worth something. It took a long time, but now I am vindicated. Originally there were only two classes of persons who stayed on the desert: those with not enough money to leave, and those without enough sense to leave. I qualified in both categories.

Some of the other folks who pioneered irrigation on the Fort Rock desert included the Cramptons, John Ernst, the Eskelins, Pitcher, Collins, and Miles. Even earlier, two men had the same idea, but failed—Ekimeyer at Fort Rock and Gooch at Christmas Lake.

The California promoters developing rural homes as a way to get away from distractions of cities, are dividing their land into small tracts. These are not large enough to make a living on by farming, but they are plenty large enough to move onto to get closer to nature. Statistically, a person should be able to get as much fresh air on twenty acres as on two thousand. He couldn't use it all up anyhow.

There were two other irrigation developments on or near the Fort Rock desert: the organized irrigation districts of Silver Lake and Summer Lake. As noted, these were only partly successful, but water reached some land, and still does. They were ahead of their time, money was hard to raise, a dry cycle had just started, and, in the case of Summer Lake, there were engineering troubles.

The aboveground water is all filed on and has been for a long time. There are some old and fine ranches in this part of Oregon, such as the Lane ranch, now owned by Mabel Shumacher, the places owned by the three Withers brothers and the big ZX Ranch at Paisley. There is the big GI Ranch at the head of Crooked River, Cameron Cliff at Silver Lake, and Warner Snyder and the Brattains at Paisley. These are founded upon water from dependable streams that rise in the mountains.

The Geological Survey men say that by pumping from the underground supply, thirty thousand acres in the Fort Rock basin can be irrigated. The thing that will determine it eventually is whether it will have an effect upon Ana River near Summer Lake, or on the streams to the south that feed into Klamath Lake. Our underground supply presumably spills out of the cup through an underground crack either to the west or south. If it didn't we'd have water closer to the surface and would just have an alkali valley.

Harry Parks was the first real believer in our underground supply. He was a highly intelligent man and, by his own reasoning, arrived at the thirty-thousand-acre figure. Parks's early work was hampered by the fact that the underground water table seemed almost flat. The water did not seem to be going anywhere. The four original test wells of 1921 had almost negligible drawdown when pumped—only three to five feet.

Modern geologists have had the chance to observe over a hundred wells with year by year water table fluctuations, as measured from bench marks at about fifty wells. From this they know that the movement of water is to the westward, not to the east as Mr. Parks had reasoned. But so far, they have all agreed to the Parks early-day figure of enough water for thirty thousand acres.

Mr. Parks was a cultured gentleman, whether addressing a group of fellow geologists, or some dryland ranchers and buckaroos. There have been no others like him in the Fort Rock basin. His dream was to develop the country with water and he might have achieved it in his day, except that the dismal and great depression started the same year he gave up his mining consultant work and settled permanently on a quarter section with a good well. He struggled with desperate bankers, starved-out homesteaders, large cattle owners, and, in the end, reached a measure of success on the desert by sheer force of character.

His son, Merritt, who provided some of the pictures for this book, has the ranch now. He has much of his father's steady, uncompromising manner of weighing the facts, whether they are favorable to his position or not.

A well costs more now than in Mr. Parks's time, but it is handier to operate after you get it. The water stands at less than one hundred feet down, some only twenty feet, but you have to drill farther than that to get a good supply. The cost of drilling and equipment such as pump, motor, and pipe for irrigating eighty acres, will amount to maybe $7,500, but it *can* cost more. If I were buying land here, I'd try to buy a place with a proven well on it. Electricity now does the pumping, as compared to makeshift gas or diesel engines in the day of Mr. Parks.

Whether the water comes from a stream or a pump, it is the single, most-important thing on the desert. I haven't seen a rancher succeed for long if he had to haul water for his own use. I have seen them succeed with bad physical handicaps, with no financial backing, with incredible runs of luck against them—but if they had to haul water for the home ranch, they didn't last long. This does not apply to all water hauling. For years and years many stockmen have hauled stock water for cattle or sheep, grazing in the pumice ranges south of Bend. Bradetich Brothers, of Bend, have hauled water into the Pine Mountain area and have been successful. There are many others.

Professor Warren, of Cornell University, defined a submarginal farm as one where the roof had fallen in. As long as there is a roof on the farm home, someone will live there and farm. In the high desert this could be changed to: a submarginal ranch is one where the well has failed.

In the years when I was riding nearly every day on the desert, the lakes would begin to dry up. The remaining water, sometimes only a small pool, would be muddy, foul-smelling, full of wigglers and little pink bugs. Most riders dipped this up in their hats and drank it. Better trained in sanitation, I always drank it through my handkerchief. I was glad to get it. Kipling knew what he was talking about when he wrote:

> . . . it was crawlin' and it stunk,
> But of all the drinks I've drunk,
> I'm gratefullest to one from Gunga Din.

THINGS TO SEE ON THE DESERT

R. A. LONG and E. R. JACKMAN

MANY SAY, "WE WANT TO SPEND A FEW DAYS IN THE DESERT country. What can we see?" At that we are a little baffled. How can we tell them to look at the stars and see the thin clear air? The desert defies description. It must be felt, and most of the inquirers can't feel it, because they don't understand it.

There are some things to see, though. Specific things in the Oregon high desert country would include:

1. Giant escarpments or "rims."
2. Hole-in-the-ground.
3. Blowouts and miniature volcanoes.
4. Recent lava flows.
5. Ice caves.
6. Lakes, alive and dead.
7. The Lost Forest of 9,000 acres in the middle of the desert.
8. The state's largest cattle ranches.
9. Indian artifacts.
10. Juniper trees. See how many different shapes you can photograph. Nearby is the largest juniper in Oregon.
11. Abandoned homestead shacks.
12. Hart Mountain Antelope Refuge.
13. Malheur Wildlife Refuge.
14. Fort Rock and other extinct volcanoes, large and small.
15. Devils Garden.
16. Active geysers.

17. Steens Mountain, with its wonderful glacier-cut gorges.
18. Wild animals.
19. Plants, including wild flowers.
20. Fossil Lake.
21. Wild birds around the infrequent water holes. You can probably see more different kinds of birds in one place than you can see in any other spot.

Geology[1]

A geologist should be a humble person immune to headline scareheads. As, in his imagination, he watches the millenniums march by, it should seem vastly unimportant that a spoiled brat in Hollywood had a new husband.

Perhaps it isn't too important whether a person knows his geology or not. What has geology ever done for him? But the subject itself is important. Without the high jinks of geology, there wouldn't be any scenery, and unless you know a little about geology, you don't know what you are looking at. Erosion is part of it and we are taught to abhor it, but without it we'd have no usable land.

Geology is a real slow kind of history. It may require a century just to make a grain of sand. But geology tosses the earth's surface about in the most disturbing fashion. As mountains form; as glaciers grow and recede; as this piece of continent aspires skyward and that piece sinks in despair, the climate follows the geological election returns quite closely.

In eastern Oregon we have had wet spells of maybe thirty million years at a time, when the land was warm and so saturated by rain that huge beasts could flounder around on the lake shores and live in luxury on lush vegetation.

With no game commission at the time to set seasons and establish game limits, the mastodons, rhinoceroses, oreodonts,

---

[1] By E. R. Jackman.

and strange camels, pigs, and giant dogs all disappeared. Without giving it a thought, they all became extinct.

Later, only yesterday, geologically speaking, came the pleistocene period. This was a million years ago, give or take a few months. Ice crept down from Canada and dammed the Columbia River. High inland points, such as Steens Mountain, sported their own personal glaciers. When these melted, great lakes formed. Summer and Abert lakes were one big body of water. The old shorelines built terraces that are still easy to see along the dry hillsides.

The Cascade Mountains formed about this time, and shut off the rain. If we ever have another CCC or WPA, the Bend Chamber of Commerce might consider a project to resettle the Three Sisters, giving them a home farther east, so the ocean air will flow over the high desert, and we'll have water again.

The center of the earth seems to be a fluid, boiling mass, and this is responsible for much of the desert's geology. Rocks will melt at about 1000° F and this temperature exists forty miles down. The continents are floating uneasily upon this hot sea.

The earth's surface is something akin to a thick crust of ice on a frozen lake. The lake is still there, but you can walk on it. As the ice gets thicker, it expands, causing pressure on the water below. When the pressure becomes great enough, the ice cracks, forming huge, floating blocks. The pressure will often tilt these blocks, one side rising and the other falling. The water below rises over the blocks in places, advancing on the ice until it cools and freezes.

This process, in an exaggerated form, went on all over eastern Oregon. First it was covered by two thousand feet of lava that spread out from cracks in the earth's crust. The lava cooled, but in the process it broke into huge blocks, and the pressures below, operating unevenly, tossed these blocks about, as ice blocks are tossed when the ice breaks up on a frozen river. Where one side was pushed up, adjacent

BUY
Oregon Salt

Our great vats at Summer and Abert Lakes will produce this season 200,000 tons of Soda, Potash and Salt. We are now ready to make contracts for September delivery of stock salt at prices lower than were ever known before in Lake County.

C. M. Sain,
Superintendent,
American Soda & Potash Co.

Courtesy Schmink Museum, Lakeview, Ore.

THE OLD LAKE BEDS IN THE DESERT HAVE HUNDREDS OF THOUSANDS OF TONS OF SALT IN THEM

One such deposit was worked at one time, witness the advertisement from an old copy of the newspaper at Paisley. The coming of the railroad to Lakeview killed the enterprise.

to an edge that remained stationary, or fell, we have the enormous scarps or faults.

In Lake County there are four main scarps, as the upthrust edges of blocks are called, but there are hundreds, maybe thousands, of small ones. All of them tend to run north and south, determined, perhaps, by magnetic forces that have warped the world into a sphere not quite true, whirling in space upon a north-south axis. The main Lake County scarps include:

1. Winter Ridge, named by Fremont, as he stood in the snow there and looked down upon the green borders of Summer Lake. The abrupt eastern face has been cut by a few minor erosion gullies, but most of the unevenness has been caused by a different kind of erosion—huge chunks have fallen off from what must have been a perpendicular face at one time. The top of the ridge is three thousand feet above the lake below. These landslides, or fallen blocks, have left numerous little depressions behind them, some with shallow lakes in them.

2. A smaller, more irregular scarp line starts near the south end of Abert Lake and runs northward along the Chewaucan Marsh and peters out in rough, broken terrain to the north. The extreme height, opposite Paisley, is about 1,300 feet.

3. The most famous of all is the scarp line that starts southeast of Lakeview and runs northward, past Goose, Abert, and Alkali lakes. It flattens out as it approaches Wagontire Mountain. The face of this scarp, above Abert Lake, is three thousand feet high and there are many sheer cliffs where a careless step might be six hundred feet long. Toward the south end, a few creeks come falling off the top, making small canyons, but they haven't had enough time yet to plan any big major mountain-forming jobs. Most of the disruptions of this scarp have been due to landslides or falls of blocks, thus making some jumbled hills at the base here and there, such as those opposite Valley

Falls. The apparent purpose of these is to furnish some fine deer hunting.

4. Warner Valley is a depression between a whopper of a scarp to the east, three thousand feet high, and a smaller scarp line to the west. In this long depression is a string of lakes that were one fine big trout pond in the past. Honey Creek, Deep Creek, and Twelvemile Creek flow into this big valley floor. In wet years, the lakes fill from the south, spilling into the next one north until, from the top of Hart Mountain, the lakes again look like one long lake with irregular shorelines. From the south, these lakes are: Pelican, Crump, Hart, Anderson, Swamp, Mugwump, Flagstaff, Campbell, Lower Campbell, Stone Corral, Bluejoint.

These scarps furnish another phenomenon in Lake County, and in most of the other western counties where they occur. If one will bore down through the two thousand feet of lava, he is closer to the hot interior of the earth. At the

Photo by Merritt Parks, Fort Rock, Ore.

THE TOP OF AN EXTINCT VOLCANO

Called by Reub Long the "Pasture Rock." The crater at the top has filled with lava dust and the grass growing there has never been pastured by domestic animals due to the fact that the cliffsides are too steep for them to climb.

uneven jagged edge of the scarp there may be a winding
channel down to the former face of the earth. If this
channel happens to be located near an old spring, the water
may be hot. So there are hot springs here and there below
the huge rims. Occasionally one can drill for water and
tap a perpetual supply of it, boiling hot.

Such a thing happened at Hunter's Hot Springs, just
north of Lakeview. The lodge there is heated by the water,
but when the owner wished to drill for cold water, he
became the owner of what is described as "the largest continuous geyser in the world."

There are other hot springs below the rim north of Paisley,
and another man-made geyser in Warner Valley, at the
Charlie Crump place. There is a fine small hot spring on
Hart Mountain on the wildlife refuge. Houses in the eastern
part of Klamath Falls are heated by this subterranean perpetual heating system. Below the huge fault called Steens
Mountain, in Harney County, are springs that carry borax
in the water, and the Rose Valley Borax Company hauled
borax 130 miles by jerk line mule power to Winnemucca
to get it to a railroad. Deposits were found closer to the
rails and the mine shut down. This borax mine was operated
from 1898 to 1912.

Farther to the east, near Vale, are hot springs that were
highly useful in the Oregon Trail days. When the wagons
arrived there, the immigrants were worn out physically,
and disorganized spiritually. The worst single thing was
the dust—day after day the dust sifted through food and
clothing until living was reduced to a numb, choking night-
mare. The road stretched ahead interminably and dust rolled
up in clouds, killing curiosity, ambition, and spirit. But
at Vale was a wonderful hot spring in a valley full of giant
wild ryegrass. To the gaunt oxen the grass was manna from
heaven.

Nearly every train stopped at the springs for days, while
the livestock rested and learned the meaning of fat again,

THE CRUMP GEYSER, WARNER VALLEY, LAKE COUNTY
The county has another such geyser north of Lakeview. Hot springs are common along the base of the three-thousand-foot-high faults of Lake and Harney counties.

and the immigrants could get clean. They forged on with reawakened spirit.

The Lost Forest[2]

This is a nine-thousand-acre full-fledged ponderosa pine forest growing at the east end of Christmas Lake basin with a rainfall too low to support such a forest. It is generally thought that fourteen inches of rain is necessary for yellow pine. Occasionally one or two will be found at lower rainfall, due to concentration of rain in a watercourse or a seep, but this is a forest. Tree ring studies of pines show that for six hundred years the weather has been about the way it is now, except that the long drought of 1920 to 1936 was more severe than any other similar drought since 1600.

The Lost Forest[3] trees are the same as ponderosa pines from other places, except for one thing. The seeds germinate more quickly. A student, Dick Berry, concluded that this forest is a relict of previous forests that covered the high desert ten thousand years ago when the huge lakes filled the basins. Forests grew all over the land not covered by water. This particular hilly area was covered by drifting sand that spread over a layer of compacted volcanic dust somewhat impervious to water. The sand acted as a mulch, allowing the scanty rain easy entrance, but holding it on top of the hard layer below, thus giving the trees more moisture than is usual with a rainfall of ten inches.

For anyone interested in vegetation in relation to its surroundings, this Lost Forest is a good place to go. As this is written, there are no tourist facilities there—no faucets— no motels—so take your own water.

Except for the vocabulary, any observant person can be an ecologist. Just look around you and see what you

---

[2] By E. R. Jackman.

[3] Part of this material comes from Dick Wallace Berry, graduate student at Oregon State University.

are looking at. If you see something you don't understand, ask the nearest cowboy. Most of them are practical, hard-working ecologists.

Hole-In-The-Ground—
Ice Caves—Blowouts[4]

Hole-in-the-ground is the descriptive title of a steep-sided three-hundred-foot hole about eight miles northwest of the town of Fort Rock. It was long thought to be the evidence of the landing of a huge meteorite, but we believe geologists consider it one of the "blowouts" abounding in northwestern Lake County. It is almost a mile across at the top and tapers downward at a slight angle, for all the world as though a meteorite had blasted it, coming from a direction a few degrees off from perpendicular. The sides

---

[4] By R. A. Long.

FORT ROCK—THE TOP OF AN EXTINCT VOLCANO
One side has eroded away and the base is covered by hundreds of feet of sand and volcanic tuff. A natural fortress-like structure, the rock is visible from many miles away. It was never used for any military purpose. The town of Fort Rock is nearby.

are raised, just as a hailstone in soft mud will make a depression by punching the sides upward to form a minute cup. It is similar to the well-known meteor crater near Winslow, Arizona, and compares well with it in size.

It does not look much like the numerous blowouts a few miles to the east. All of those are in more recent lava flows and the outpouring of molten lava, propelled by gas from below, is unmistakable. These are interesting, many are colorful, and nearby are numerous caves. The caves were apparently formed after a molten lava flow had cooled on the surface, but with great pressure building up below. The restless material below could find no outlet, such as it did to form the blowouts. Eventually an outlet was found far

Courtesy Jim Anderson, Oregon Museum of Science and Industry, Portland

HOLE-IN-THE-GROUND, NEAR FORT ROCK

The depression is three hundred feet deep, one mile across. It resembles a meteor crater, but geologists believe it is volcanic in origin, though it is unlike other "blowout" holes in the area.

Photo by Jim Anderson, Oregon Museum of Science and Industry, Portland

ICE STALAGMITE IN THE SOUTH ICE CAVE NORTHWEST OF FORT ROCK
Several of the long caves in the lava have everlasting ice, and one cave, in **Harney**
County, south of Burns, has a large lake.

368   THE OREGON DESERT

to one side, and the pressure was exerted in the direction of
the outlet. This formed a small river of lava flowing beneath the congealed surface, pushed along by a piston of
pressure, resulting in a cave, perhaps thirty feet wide, twenty
feet high, and half a mile or more long.

In places, a section of the roofs of these tunnels has
fallen in, exposing them. There are many of them, some
containing ice. Enthusiasts, called spelunkers, explore caves.
Such a group exists in Bend, and occasionally they find a
new tunnel. Photographers, rock hounds, mineralogists, en-
tomologists, and biologists all flock to the new cave together
with just plain adventure-minded folk. Now and then something new is found, such as a cave-dwelling insect, a new
rock formation, or a skeleton of an animal.

Hart Mountain Antelope Refuge[5]

This important antelope refuge contains an enormous
scarp or fault east of Warner Valley. From the top a person
can look nearly straight down to the long valley, sometimes
almost a continuous lake, at other times a vast meadow with
very little water visible.

There are 215,000 acres in the refuge. The highest point
is a little over eight thousand feet. The west side must have
been a sheer precipice of over three thousand feet at one
time. The land slopes away gently to the east, down to the
mile-high Catlow Valley in Harney County.

Numerous creeks run to the east and north. Four climatic zones exist in the refuge, arranged strictly by alti-
tude, Sonoran, Transition, Canadian, and Hudsonian. Each
has its appropriate plants and animals.

Timber is mostly juniper, with aspen at the high snowfall
areas. There is one ponderosa pine grove, the site of an
army post in 1867.

Visitors are numerous, including many scientists, photog-

---

[5] By E. R. Jackman.

BIG JUNIPER
OREGON'S LARGEST
WESTERN JUNIPER
HEIGHT 64 FT.
DIAMETER 5½ FT.

Photo by Merritt Parks, Fort Rock, Ore.

OREGON'S LARGEST JUNIPER IS ABOUT TWENTY MILES FROM FORT ROCK
E. R. Jackman, *left;* R. A. Long, *right*

raphers, and writers. Oregon has a total herd of twelve thousand antelope, and Hart Mountain is their headquarters.

Fort Rock—the Old Volcano[6]

The rock gives the name to Fort Rock, the town. They are close together, but this is confusing. "Go to Fort Rock, then turn right and go . . . etc." You have to stop and say whether you mean the rock or the town. The rock has recently (1962) been made into a state park. Eleanor and I owned part of it and donated it to the state, along with some surrounding acreage.

[6] By R. A. Long.

Photo by Merritt Parks, Fort Rock, Ore.

INTERIOR OF DERRICK CAVE, NEAR FORT ROCK

These caves, some of them miles long, were formed by volcanic gas, below the surface, which, acting as an elemental piston, forced long tubes of lava to some distant outlet, perhaps in a canyon. The piston action is plain to see here in the nearly circular walls. E. R. Jackman in the picture.

LAVA FLOW FROM NEWBERRY CRATER, PAULINA MOUNTAIN, BETWEEN BEND AND FORT ROCK, OREGON

The white is from an early snow, which outlines the ripples in the congealed lava river

It is over a third of a mile across and the thin walls rise over three hundred feet above the sandy plain. Geologists say that it is only the top of a fairly impressive volcano— that if the plain around it were excavated down to the true floor of the valley, we would have a nice extinct volcano with steep sides and a crater in the center.

The rock shows unmistakable wave action, indicating that at one time water covered all of the Fort Rock basin to a depth of fifty feet or more. I have a plan for the Rock. It would be perfect for a football stadium. The sides would encircle the playing field in the center and it would be simple to arrange tier after tier of seats on three sides, leaving the open side for parking and easy exit. All other universities were going for a long time before they got around

Photo by Jones Studio, Lakeview, Ore.

A FEW OF THE HUNDREDS OF INDIAN ARTIFACTS FOUND IN THE DESERT
BY REUB LONG

to building a football stadium. I have this stadium all built and now I need a university to use it—sort of putting brawn before brain.

The Old Indian Caves[7]

There are several of these in the area. Archeologists found them of more than passing interest when, by clearing away the volcanic dust of recent eruptions, they began to unearth artifacts with an age of over nine thousand years.

Apparently small tribes of Indians used the caves when the great lakes were on the land and only the hills showed above water. The artifacts showed these Indians to have been

[7] By R. A. Long.

Photo by Jones Studio, Lakeview, Ore.

VARIOUS TYPES OF INDIAN STONE PIPES
Part of the Reub Long collection

rather advanced. They used throwing sticks for hunting or warfare. They used sandals not at all like the moccasins in later use. These were woven from sagebrush fiber and resembled the old Greek sandals, with a cap over the toes, and thongs to fasten around the ankle. One such cave is on my home place only half a mile from the house. In this cave were over seventy of the sandals, indicating that this particular family were professional sandal makers, showing maybe that there were specialists even in those days, and that commerce and trade went on long ago—in Lake County at least.

Maybe civilization in America started at Fort Rock, and, in case of nuclear war, it may end there. The Russians

Photo by Jim Anderson, Oregon Museum of Science and Industry, Portland

A HORNED OWL, MOST COMMON OF THE SEVERAL DESERT OWLS
This is a young owl ready to leave the nest and on the defensive, threatening the photographer.

Courtesy Lake County (Ore.) Chamber of Commerce

WILD GEESE, IN HUGE FLOCKS SUCH AS THIS ONE, ALIGHT FOR FEEDING IN THE GRAINFIELDS ON THE OLD LAKE BEDS OF THE AREA

won't waste a bomb on a metropolis such as Fort Rock and, as for fallout, it comes down in the rain. Our frogs and dryland ducks would welcome a little rain.

Photo by Jim Anderson, Oregon Museum of Science and Industry, Portland

FLEDGLING GOLDEN EAGLES HATCHED ON COUGAR MOUNTAIN
NEAR FORT ROCK
The birdlife is an important part of the desert scenery. Birds are especially numerous around the few desert water sources.

LADY MARY, TRAINED TO FALCONRY BY JIM ANDERSON

Correct name: ferruginous rough-legged hawk. This falcon took rabbits with ease for her handler.

Photo by Jim Anderson, Oregon Museum of Science and Industry, Portland

YOUNG MAGPIES

They, with the buzzards and coyotes, are the scavengers of the desert. Gabrielson, co-author with Jewett of a book on Oregon birds, calls the magpies "jovial freebooters."

Photo by Jim Anderson, Oregon Museum of Science and Industry, Portland

FERRUGINOUS ROUGH-LEGGED HAWK AS A NESTLING

A-HORSEBACK AND ALONE

R. A. LONG

Conservation in Politics

LATELY SOIL CONSERVATION HAS COME IN FOR ATTENTION. By a trick of words, politicians have come to lump all conservation together. There isn't much connection between conservation of deer, for example, and conservation of soil —if you conserve too many of the deer, they destroy the forage, leave a hillside bare, and soil erosion will be terribly destructive. But the politician has learned to get votes by shouting that *he* is for conservation, and, by implication, his opponent is against it.

Such persons grew up on a city street and gave not one thought to conservation until they discovered its vote-getting power. They are politically ambitious rather than conservation conscious.

Memory

The older I get, the better I used to be.

Changing Needs

As a man rises in the world, his luxuries of yesterday become today's necessities.

Research

It's truly amazing how many people know so little about so much. Their trouble isn't ignorance; it's the fact that about 90 per cent of what they know isn't so. The more scanty the knowledge, the greater the certainty.

That is the real value of research. It establishes facts, and in the end a fact conquers. Huxley said that the greatest tragedy of science is the cold-blooded slaying of a beautiful theory by an ugly fact.

Land

My father, when I was young, said, "Reuben, my boy, when you grow up, get land. God has quit making land, but He keeps right on making people."

Self-Esteem

The reason why I have so much better an opinion of myself than others have of me is that I judge myself by my best efforts; others judge me by my poorest.

Conduct yourself in such a manner that you are in good company when you are alone.

Statistics

If you get to be eighty years old, you don't need to worry because statistics show that a very low percentage of men die after eighty.

Hard Work Ain't Easy

Lazy people work the hardest.

Credit

Nothing gets a man into such hot water so quickly as good credit. A lot of my troubles have come upon me because my credit was too good. Be careful not to acquire too much of it. It has ruined more people than bad credit ever did.

Necessities

A homesteader came into the desert in the spring of 1912 and settled about fifty miles east of our place. He hired me with my four-horse team to haul him in with supplies to last until fall and enough lumber and other material to put up a shack. I helped him check up on his supplies which were down to a bare minimum. It may surprise some, but he made it through until fall—seven long months—just fine without any toothbrush.

Horses

A horse has an active conscience. He will rarely hurt a baby, and never on purpose.

Talk

Talking without thinking is as dangerous as running in the dark—and the end result is about the same.

Patience

If I don't get it when I want it, maybe I'll want it when I get it.

A successful man and a good horse must first learn patience.

Caution

Some politicians remind me of a man I saw sneaking down through the brush riding a clumsy old big-footed white mare with a bell on.

Cow Sense

If you take care of your cows, your cows will take care of you.

Luck

In business, whether it is running a factory, or running wild horses, success depends upon two things: know-how and luck. Of the two, luck is the more important. The fortunate man has both.

Prudence

It's lots better to get home with a light load than to be stuck out on the road with a heavy one.

Looking Ahead

Don't build a reputation when young that will be hard to keep when old.

Importance

Of all the persons I've known, personally, who *tried* to be great, the only time they were the most important persons present was at their own funerals.

Serenity

Secret of serenity—get along with the things you can't help.

Coffee

Most people camp too close to the creek to make good coffee.

Gracious Living

I've lived in a lot of shacks on the desert. All of them had that desirable lived-in look.

Proper Niche

Several have asked me to run for the legislature. I tell them I'd rather be a fairly good sagebrush rancher than a poor lawmaker.

How To Be Wrong

When a man messes with things he knows nothing about, mistakes come his way with ease.

Resignation

When you get so you can't remember things—just forget it.

Thinking

Conversation is cheap; ideas are dear. They are seldom found in the same place.

Laughter

It's good to make people laugh. While a normal man is laughing, meanness is draining out. Persons such as Hitler and Castro don't laugh much.

Baldness

Bald-headed men may take comfort, for the Good Book says the Lord notes the fall of every sparrow and even the hairs of our heads are numbered. So a bald man may have a better chance by cutting down on the heavenly bookkeeping.

Haste

If you have a long, hard ride, a trot is the best gait.

We Love the Familiar

If heaven hasn't any old rusty patched-up wire fences, I'll never feel at home there.

Worry

Not able to do much of it myself, I once hired a man, for one hundred dollars a month, to worry for me. In about three days I found him worrying about how he was to get his money—on my time, too.

Invent a non-worry pill that works and you'll be rich and famous.

Desert Forage

The reason I've been able to produce some fast horses is that, where I graze them, they have to feed at thirty miles an hour to get enough to eat.

Self-Pity

An odd quirk I've noticed all my life: those who have the most to complain about do the least of it.

If you *must* be sorry for yourself, make it short.

The Circle

A man was digging a ditch. A passerby asked him what he was digging it for. He said, thoughtfully, "So far as I know, it's to get money to buy food to give me strength to dig the ditch."

Heredity

When I hire a man to break a horse for me, I tell him, "Now, just teach this horse to walk; he's bred to run."

Living

All of my life I have stumbled through a maze of mistakes.

Your Money's Worth

Two things we can pay too much for and still get our money's worth are research and conservation—and often you have to have the first to get the second. Conservation without research can make an advocate about as silly as anyone I know of.

Fate

Circumstances can bail you out or snow you under.

Adversity can make or break a man—according to his strength.

Horses and I

I was never too good a horse trader because, if I had a nice horse, it was hard for me to find anyone who liked him better than I did.

Trouble

Nature is *never* kind to the individual. To the race, perhaps, or the nation; never to the individual.

When in doubt, do nothing—the situation may get worse.

Mother

If my reputation is good, it came from trying to keep my mother from finding out I wasn't the wonder she thought I was.

Small Annoyances

Learn to ignore small annoyances. The trick, though, is to tell for sure which are the small ones.

Space Fillers

It's not too much to a man's credit to say he does no harm. If he hasn't done any good, he has just filled up space.

Every Man Has a Gift

No matter how worthless a man may seem, maybe he can wiggle his ears, and you can't, to save your life.

There are lots of ways to judge a man. A few I've heard recommended are: play poker with him; go on a week's camping trip; get him drunk. But I'd say the surest way is to find out what he worries about. Little men have unimportant worries.

Getting Along

What a man doesn't have in his head, he has to make up for some other way.

Try

Try for the good will of everyone, even the dog.

Foresight

It's good to know when to stop. It's better to know when not to start.

The Good and the Bad

It's hard to make people believe a story that is good. They will readily believe anything bad—and can hardly wait to repeat it.

Self-Importance

If you need something to make you feel important, find another man wrong.

A scapegoat in an organization is good for the morale of the crew.

Fame

A wealth accumulator is soon remembered only by the way he used it. Knowledge is the same.

Excuse

There may or may not be a difference between a reason and an excuse. It often depends upon the viewpoint of a second person.

Age of Specialization

Many of my friends are specialists. They include range specialists, soil specialists, eye specialists and specialists on corporation law. I am a distance specialist and deserve more pay.

Philosophy

The early worm gets got.

Listen

Sometimes you get heard most when you talk least.

Whose Ox Was Gored?

Overheard at a water adjudication meeting in Burns: First litigant: "My, Judge McCammant's mind is as keen as a razor." Second litigant, sourly: "Yeah, and just as wide."

Advice

Even if you are well loaded with advice, give it only sparingly; it is seldom wanted and little used. Besides, you might run out, right when you need it most for yourself.

Time

I try to avoid saying, "I didn't have time." I have as much time as the richest man in the world, twenty-four hours. I can't always organize these hours just right.

New Projects

Turn your horse around before you get on.

You Can See on the Desert

I was in San Francisco once and a prominent citizen drove around and showed me the town in a dense fog. I couldn't see any of the things he showed me. At the end he asked how my town compared with his. I told him, "Well, sir, in my town, Fort Rock, we don't have any bridges or islands, or harbors at all. But, if we had 'em, we could see 'em."

Democracy

When there was only one man camped at the water hole, democracy was easy.

Adversity

It's a long tough pull up Hard Luck Hill.

Tolerance

A man with many faults is likely to be tolerant.

Intolerance is worse than a flock of little faults.

Good Resolutions

The nicest time in all the day is tomorrow morning about sunup.

Regrets

Have no regrets if you've done your best, even if you failed.

Judging the Other Fellow

A man should be judged by what he stands for—also by what he falls for.

Humor and Philosophy

Brevity is the essence of humor—also of philosophy.

Complaining

Don't give the imps that torment you the satisfaction of hearing you curse your luck.

Political Note

The pendulum swings from extreme to extreme. This is all right, for if it stops, so does the clock.

Winning Friends

If you would make a man your friend, let him do you a favor.

Defeat and Despair

A defeat is a defeat only if you remain defeated.

APPENDIX

A

Words of Spanish Origin Pertaining to Horses or Horse Gear

Spanish Name	Meaning
Alforjas	Saddlebag
Aparejo	Leather pad
Caviatta	Group of horses used on a job such as a drive or roundup
Latigo	Whip, literally, but used in U.S. as the strap fastening the cinch to the saddle
Concha	Shell, literally—now used to refer to round metal ornaments
Chaparreros	Literally, leg armor. Shortened to chaps in U.S. Cover for the legs of riders
Vaquero	Rider, our word buckaroo derived from it, because the Spanish V is much like our B
La riata	Rawhide rope, our word lariat derived from it
Mecate	Pronounced "McCarty" in U.S. A horsehair rope
Jaquima	Headstall, we call it hackamore, the Spanish pronunciation is approximately "hakeema"
Romal	A weighted end to joined reins
Lasso	Verb, to snare, incorrectly used in U.S. referring to lariat
Hondu	Eye of a needle, our word "honda" derived from it
Tapaderos	Literally "lid" or "cover," when attached to the stirrup it covers the toes of the riders' boots. Shortened to "taps" in U.S.
Parada	Group of horses or cattle

Rodeo	Public display of horsemanship. Originally a roundup.
Rodero	The entire roundup crew with horses
Rosedero	The leather that protects the rider's legs from being chafed by the stirrup straps

B

Horses in Oregon—U.S. Census Estimates

1867	49,000
70	56,000
75	90,000
80	134,000
85	187,000
90	220,000
95	269,000
1900	275,000
10	270,000
15	298,000
20	272,000
30	178,000
40	140,000
50	72,000
58	40,000
61	70,000

C

Boundaries of Area where Reub Long and Partner Caught Wild Horses

East—Little and Big Juniper (southeast of Wagontire)
North—Bear Creek, Hampton Buttes, Horse Ridge
South—Abert Lake
West—Klamath Indian Reservation

D

Horse Buyers' Jargon

A cold collar—balky
A hole in him—the horse has a bad defect rot apparent. "Watch out. he's got a hole in him"
There's reading on him—branded

Afraid of the floor—type of St. Vitus's dance

An angel—a greenhorn buyer at an auction, who can be depended upon to buy unsound horses

Sold to halter—no guarantee whatever

Family broken—just opposite of the above, a gentle family horse

Brush or interfere—the horse hits one leg at some point with the opposite foot

Burglar—the dishonest trader often has several of these. A horse will have a defect that isn't apparent. The seller will carefully keep from guaranteeing that particular point. When the buyer discovers his error, he'll usually bring the horse back and get what little salvage he can. The trader thus sells this horse time after time

Can't keep a secret—broken winded

Careless—such a horse stands with knees sprung

Cold footed—stringhalted

Cow-hocked—hocks together, toes out

Cross-firing—when pacing, such a horse will strike the forefoot with the opposite hind foot

Dizzy—a dummy, a horse corresponding to a human imbecile

Falls out of bed—pulls back on halter

Forging—striking the heel of the front shoe by the toe of the rear shoe when traveling

Goosey—nervous

Hand—four inches, for measuring from the ground to the high point of withers

Hitch—short stride of one hind foot

Hogback—opposite of swayback

Indian—a horse completely dangerous to handle

Jibber—a green, untrained horse

Light in the timber—lower legs with bones too light

Lunker—big, heavy-boned

Michigan age—quite old

Pilgrim—horse once good, now too old

Plug—a horse of little worth, maybe worn out, no spirit, or so poor in conformation that he never was much good

A nickel's worth of hair off—slight wire cut or blemish

One bum lamp—blind in one eye

Paddle—to wing out with forefeet

Ripper—a good big horse with endurance

Scalper—a horse dealer of poor reputation

Shadow jumper—nervous, easily frightened

Side-wheeler—pacer

Smokes his pipe—lip torn at point where the bit commonly rests

Smooth mouth—teeth worn smooth with age
Snake-bite—wire marks
Ten minutes short of work—balky
Too much daylight under—leggy
Weaver—a horse that constantly weaves or sways in the stall as many wild animals do in a cage
Weed—undersized or otherwise inferior

E

Some of the Brands Seen on Drive of 10,000 Cattle

From Silver Lake were Hayes Brothers, MP brand; Charlie Pitcher with his pitcher brand; and Lane Ranch, OK. The O was on one hip, the K on the other, an unusual way to brand.

The Huttons, Linc and Francis, of Wagontire, brand respectively, Quarter Circle L and FSH, the latter on the ribs.

Pat Cecil, Woody Best, and Streets came from off to the north on Silver Creek. The Cecil brand was 71 Bar to notify one and all that they started in 1871.

Logans, Bennetts, and Hacklemans came from Hampton Butte and Bear Creek. Hackleman's iron was well known, a big Q on the ribs.

There were always a few Brattain cattle from Paisley and some from Warner Valley, far to the southeast. I remember a few 7O and some 7T from there.

F

The Coyote Has Crept into Our Language

I. Used **alone**
  1. The prairie wolf—*Canis latrans,* the original meaning
  2. To apply to persons—squatters, half-breeds of any kind
  3. A nickname for Dakotans
  4. A horse the color of coyotes, a buckskin

II. Used in special combinations
  1. Coyote days—early days of the West when many homesteaders, trappers, and others lived in dugouts
  2. Coyote dog—a domestic dog that acts like a coyote
  3. Coyote gold—fine gold obtained near the surface in small mining operations
  4. Coyote house—a dugout
  5. Coyote melon—calabagilla, a wild plant of the southwest

6. Coyote thistle—species of Eryngium
7. Coyote tobacco—*Nicotiania trigonophylla,* smoked by Indians
8. Coyote well—a hidden water hole
9. Coyote holes—where they dig shallow holes to get water
10. Coyote berries—wild currants

III. Referring to mining
   1. Coyote diggins—rundown excavations
   2. Coyote hole—prospector's hole, referring more to holes that produced no gold
   3. Coyote placers—hillside placers
   4. Coyote shaft—hillside shafts
   5. Coyoting—sink a shaft, thereafter digging small shafts from the bottom in all directions

IV. To coyote, used as a verb
   1. To get out of there surreptitiously or hurriedly
   2. To drift from place to place
   3. To chase a wild horse until he can be handled

V. Coyotero—any one of several Apache bands of Indians

G

Primary Life Zones in Oregon

1. Upper Sonoran—including the sagebrush desert
2. Transition—yellow pine, mountain mahogany, bitterbrush
3. Canadian—spruce, fir, lodgepole
4. Hudsonian—just below timberline, dwarfed trees
5. Arctic Alpine—tops of highest Oregon peaks

H

Food of Bobcats

Vernon Bailey reports that government hunters examined the stomach contents of two hundred Oregon bobcats, some from most of the eastern Oregon counties. Their counts showed:

95 had rabbits of the four common kinds
27 had sheep or lamb meat
23 had dined on sage hens
13 had caught mice of various sorts—
   no preference noted
12 had ground squirrels

8 with pine squirrels
3 fancied venison
3 had smelled out wood rats
1 woodchuck
1 chipmunk
3 with quail
3 other small birds
2 pheasants
1 grouse

I

Twenty-Five Ghost Towns

Town	Rough Location	Year Post Office Established	Year Post Office Discontinued
Arrow	NE of Silver Lake	1910	1918
Berdugo	Catlow Valley	1915	1927
Burleson	16 mi. ENE Silver Lake	1914	1915
Buffalo	12 mi. E Christmas Lake	1913	1918
Butte	Near Wagontire	1911	1922
Cliff	N of Christmas Lake	1906	1920
Connley	SE of Fort Rock	1912	1920
Dry Lake	Crook County	1913	1937
Fleetwood	N part of Fort Rock Valley	1913	1928
Fremont	6 mi. W of Fort Rock	1909	1915
Gist	Deschutes County, SE of Sisters	1907	1920
Hat Rock	Near Powell Butte	1910	1911
Held	S of Maury Mts.	1909	1919
Hemstead	E of Paulina Mts.	1917	1918
Lake	Near Christmas Lake	1906	1920
Loma Vista	Fort Rock Valley	1913	1918
Mooreville	25 mi. SSE of Riverside	1912	1919
Oroville	Near Pueblo Mt.	1911	1915
Rivers	NE of Brothers	1913	1918
Saddlebutte	E side of Harney Basin	1916	1920
Sageview	West of Catlow Valley	1916	1918
Sink	Near Sink of Peters Creek	1911	1920

Thelake	Near Mann Lake	1914	1919
Viewpoint	S part of Christmas Lake Valley	1910	1918
Woodrow	10 mi. E of Fort Rock	1914	1916

INDEX

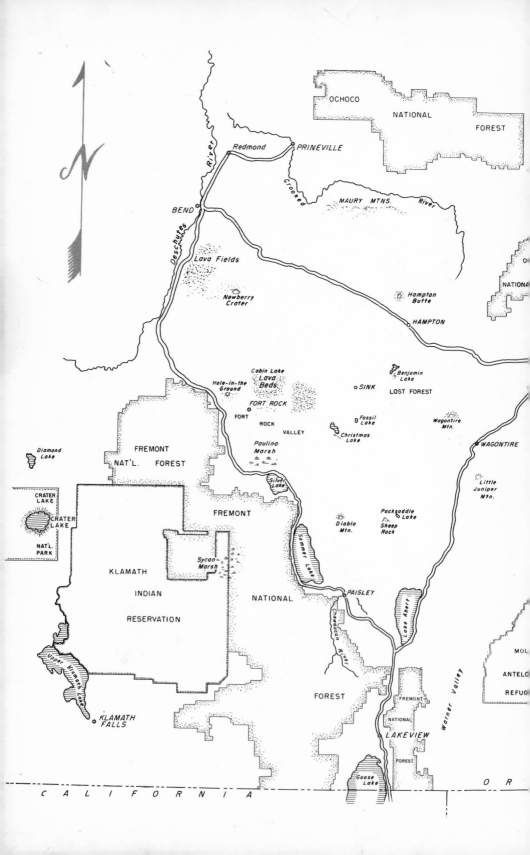